COMMANDER
STEVEN HAINES
ROYAL NAVY

SPEAK·TRUTH·TO·POWER

ROUGH
WATERS

New Perspectives on Maritime History and Nautical Archaeology
James C. Bradford and Gene A. Smith, editors

Rivers, seas, oceans, and lakes have provided food and transportation for man since the beginning of time. As avenues of communication they link the peoples of the world, continuing to the present to transport more commodities and trade goods than all other methods of conveyance combined. The New Perspectives on Maritime History and Nautical Archaeology series is devoted to exploring the significance of the earth's waterways while providing lively and important books that cover the spectrum of maritime history and nautical archaeology broadly defined. The series includes works that focus on the role of canals, rivers, lakes, and oceans in history; on the economic, military, and political use of those waters; on the exploration of waters and their secrets by seafarers, archeologists, oceanographers, and other scientists; and upon the people, communities, and industries that support maritime endeavors. Limited by neither geography nor time, volumes in the series contribute to the overall understanding of maritime history and can be read with profit by both general readers and specialists alike.

ROUGH WATERS

Sovereignty and the
American Merchant Flag

RODNEY P. CARLISLE

NAVAL INSTITUTE PRESS
ANNAPOLIS, MARYLAND

This book has been brought to publication with the generous assistance of
Marguerite and Gerry Lenfest.

NAVAL INSTITUTE PRESS
291 Wood Road
Annapolis, MD 21402

Library of Congress Cataloging-in-Publication Data

Names: Carlisle, Rodney P., author.
Title: Rough waters : sovereignty and the American merchant flag / Rodney P.
  Carlisle with Bradford Smith.
Description: Annapolis, Maryland : Naval Institute Press, [2017] | Series:
  New perspectives on maritime history and nautical archaeology | Includes
  bibliographical references and index.
Identifiers: LCCN 2016030922 (print) | LCCN 2016045418 (ebook) | ISBN
  9781682470091 (hardback) | ISBN 9781682470879 (ePDF) | ISBN
9781682470879 (ePub) | ISBN 9781682470879 (mobi)
Subjects: LCSH: Ships—Registration and transfer—United States—History. |
  Flags of convenience—United States—History. | Ship transfers to foreign
  registry—United States—History. | Merchant marine—United
  States—History. | BISAC: HISTORY / Military / Naval.
Classification: LCC HE589.U5 C37 2017 (print) | LCC HE589.U5 (ebook) | DDC
  387.50973—dc23
LC record available at https://lccn.loc.gov/2016030922

Book design and composition: Alcorn Publication Design

Contents

Tables

Acknowledgments

I wish to thank the following people for specific and general suggestions: Paul Adamthwaite, George Billy, Jim Bradford, Elizabeth De Sombre, Paul Fontenoy, John Hattendorf, Jamie Rife, Gene Allen Smith, and Josh Smith. Bruce Dennis provided professional help in locating documents in the British National Archives. Joseph Gibbs tracked Omani records in the library of the American University of Sharjah, United Arab Emirates. Thanks are also due to the anonymous peer reviewers at the journal of the North American Society of Oceanic History, *Northern Mariner*, for their many helpful suggestions and to the editor of the journal, Roger Sarty, for permission to reproduce the elements of chapters 2–8, 13, and 14 that previously appeared in the journal. Sarty's encouragement and fine critiques were invaluable. Discussions with participants at North American Society of Oceanic History conferences led to refinement of my thinking and many helpful leads. I am particularly grateful to my wife, Loretta Carlisle, for her patience and support.

Abbreviations

ACFN	American Committee of Flags of Necessity
ACN	amity, commerce, and navigation
AMEX	American Stock Exchange
ANAVE	Asociación de Navieros Españoles
AOTC	American Overseas Tanker Corporation
Bapico	Baltic-American Petroleum Import Company
CIA	Central Intelligence Agency
CMB	Compagnie Maritime Belge
DAPG	Deutsch-Amerikanische Petroleum Gesellschaft, Hamburg
DIS	Danish International Ship Register
EUSC	effective U.S. control
FACS	Federation of American-Controlled Shipping
FCN	friendship, commerce, and navigation
GIS	German International Shipping Register
ICJ	International Court of Justice
ILC	International Law Commission
IMCO	Intergovernmental Maritime Consultative Organization
IRI	International Registries Inc.
ITC	International Trust Company
ITF	International Transport Workers Federation
JCS	Joint Chiefs of Staff
LISCR	Liberian International Shipping Corporate Registry
MAR	Madeira Open Shipping Register
MarAd	Maritime Administration
MEBA	Marine Engineers Beneficial Association
MOU	memorandum of understanding
MSC	Military Sealift Command
NATO	North Atlantic Treaty Organization

NIS	Norwegian International Ship Registry
NLRB	National Labor Relations Board
OSG	Overseas Shipholding Group
OSS	Office of Strategic Services
ÖTV	Öffentliche Dienste, Transport und Verkehr
PCA	Permanent Court of Arbitration
ULCC	ultra large crude carrier
UNCTAD	UN Commission on Trade and Development
VLCC	very large crude carrier
WSA	War Shipping Administration

INTRODUCTION

The Flight from Flag to Flag

The flag of a nation is a powerful symbol, and protection of the flag is no mere ritual. When the flag is physically attacked, the people and the government naturally respond. Thus, the story of the merchant fleet's flag is a crucial and central part of the history of a nation's engagement abroad, in peace and war.

The United States has a rich history of engagement with the sea. The thirteen British colonies in North America that declared their independence in 1776 all had seaports on the Atlantic coast or on waterways that led to the Atlantic Ocean. Some of the grievances that led to the Declaration of Independence were maritime in nature—particularly the Sugar Act of 1764 and the Tea Act of 1773. With the exception of some of the Indian wars, all of America's wars engaged the American Navy, and indeed, many of the wars that the United States fought in the nineteenth and twentieth centuries were caused by incidents involving attacks on U.S. naval or merchant shipping or bombardment of a fortification in a harbor. In the twenty-first century, the U.S. Navy remains the strongest in the world, but its flagged merchant fleet is small, ranking at twenty-second in the world in registered tonnage.[1]

The United States' sensitivity to the reception of its merchant flag in foreign ports and on the high seas is deeply related to the nation's sense of its identity. In the eighteenth-century world in which the United States declared its sovereignty, acceptance of and respect for U.S.-flagged ships were both essential to national identity. If the flag were not respected, foreign trade by American merchants in U.S. ships would have been nearly impossible. Recognition of the merchant flag was a matter not only of practical business or legal national status but also—and perhaps most important—of national honor. The principle of freedom of the seas, which held that ships of all nations had equal rights to travel on the high seas (out of the territorial waters of any nation), had been articulated in 1609 by Hugo Grotius in *Mare Liberum*.

U.S. statesmen and journalists were well aware of this principle in the early years of the republic and understood that failure to recognize the right of ships under the U.S. flag to sail the open seas would be a failure to recognize the United States as a nation.[2]

Flags, of course, are highly emotional symbols, not only in the United States but around the world. Often the presence of a national flag on board a merchant ship is a source of pride, but if a ship is attacked, disrespected, or discriminated against, its flag can be a source of dismay.

When the United States entered into treaties of commerce and navigation and exchanged consuls, ministers, and ambassadors with other nations, recognition of the nation took legal, economic, and diplomatic form. But the symbol of that recognition was respect and honor shown to the flag itself, both on ships and at the diplomatic outposts of the nation abroad. Later in the nineteenth century, Americans developed their version of the cult of the flag, a phenomenon found in Europe and Asia in the same period. As the cult flourished in the United States, it was replete with ceremonial practices and a pledge of allegiance to the flag; the symbolism of the stars and stripes became even more deeply embedded in the American psyche.

From the earliest days of the American republic, the treatment of U.S.-flagged merchant ships abroad was considered a matter of honor. The code of honor among ships was similar to the code of honor among gentlemen that led to hundreds of duels in that era. Throughout the nineteenth century, ships flying the U.S. flag frequently, in the course of legitimate (and sometimes illegitimate) business, drew the nation into conflict with other nations—sometimes into war and more often into maritime "incidents" that only threatened to lead to larger armed conflict. While the honor code among gentlemen declined in the United States in the nineteenth century and nearly vanished after the Civil War, the rhetoric of national honor still shaped public discussion of the treatment of the national flag, whether it was flying on a naval ship, on a merchant ship, or at an embassy or consulate in a foreign city. The issue took on far greater significance in 1917, when German U-boats sank U.S. merchant ships that prominently displayed the flag, dragging the United States into World War I. Following that war, the public and Congress, disillusioned with Woodrow Wilson's lofty and largely unrealized war goals, were content to see the transfer of some U.S.-owned shipping to foreign flags, under which the ships could be operated at lower cost and without drawing the nation into another military conflict in defense of the flag's honor.

When war broke out in Europe again in September 1939, the United States was able to remain neutral for twenty-seven months precisely because much U.S.-owned shipping had rapidly shifted to foreign flags; when some of those foreign-flagged ships carrying petroleum and other cargo to the Allies were sunk, the American flag was not endangered, and national honor did not require U.S. involvement in the war. The handful of episodes directly involving U.S.-flagged merchant ships did not generate the crisis that had arisen in 1917. The nation entered the war only after Japan's direct attack on the U.S. naval base at Pearl Harbor, an attack characterized by President Franklin Roosevelt as "dastardly" and perceived by the public as a stab in the back. The flag and the nation had been struck, not on merchant ships but on Navy ships, a naval base, and U.S. airfields without warning, even as peace talks supposedly proceeded in Washington. During U.S. participation in World War II, official U.S. policy further endorsed the use of the Panamanian and other flags for some U.S.-owned or -controlled ships.

Aside from diplomatic and military considerations, the straightforward business and profit lessons U.S. ship-owning corporations learned in the period of neutrality (1939–1941) and during World War II led them in the 1950s and 1960s to greatly expand their flight from the flag, primarily to the flags of Panama and then Liberia. Operating a ship with a foreign crew under a foreign flag was simply cheaper. Despite the protests of American merchant mariners and their unions, the courts ruled that U.S. law did not apply to labor conditions on board American-owned, foreign-flagged ships; instead, the laws of the flag state applied. In these decisions, the courts reflected an obscure 1905 ruling of the Permanent Court of Arbitration at The Hague regarding the grant of the French flag to slave-trading dhows in the Indian Ocean operating out of the sultanate of Muscat. The flight from the flag and the flight from U.S. labor law have become firmly and legally established.

In the late twentieth century and early twenty-first century, the decline in the number of ships flying the U.S. flag remained a concern to American mariners who found employment opportunities greatly reduced; cruise ships, tankers, and freighters, owned by American corporations or American investors in foreign corporations, fly foreign flags and hire very few, if any, Americans. The dismay at the decline of the U.S.-flagged merchant fleet is shared by many Americans who take pride in the national maritime heritage, not from any personal economic motive but as part of their sense of national identity.

The attraction of operation under foreign flags in the late twentieth century produced a new generation of flags of convenience that drew shipowners from the major maritime nations of Europe as well as from the United States. Consequently, in the early twenty-first century, the face of the world's merchant shipping is entirely altered, with a large percentage of ships now registered under flags of microstates around the world.

From time to time in recent decades, one of the few merchant ships flying the U.S. flag has set off an international incident, requiring a short display of U.S. military force that echoes the honor code of the earliest days of the republic. However, since 1939 the United States has avoided becoming involved in war to defend freedom of the seas and the honor of the American flag because of the flight of American-owned shipping from flag to flag. This work unfolds that tale.

1

The Maritime *Code Duello*

N aval officers in the United States in the first two decades of the
nation's independence were drawn from the self-defined gentleman class. Speaking of gentlemen in southern folkways, David
Hackett Fischer noted that status "could be shattered by loss of honor."
An honorable gentleman never "lied, cheated, stole, or betrayed his
family or friends." However, when a gentleman was accused of such
behavior, he was obliged to defend his honor. The honor code was a
widespread phenomenon, influencing public discourse not only in the
South but also in the North. Among historians, Bertram Wyatt-Brown, in
A Warring Nation, described the honor code's national power in the early
republic. The language, rhetoric, and values of honor shaped national
discourse on matters of international relations and the personal conduct
of prominent figures.[1]

Among several recent studies of the honor code's influence is *Affairs
of Honor: National Politics in the New Republic* by Joanne Freeman. As Freeman points out, "Far more than directives for negotiating a duel, the code
of honor was a way of life." She continues, "The code of honor did more
than channel and monitor political conflict; it formed the very infrastruc-
ture of national politics, providing a governing logic and weapons of war."[2]

Paul A. Gilje, in *Free Trade and Sailors' Rights in the War of 1812*, sees
the British challenge to national honor and the way it evoked the principles of the *code duello* as forming the basis for the rhetoric of political
leaders in the era. He argues further that the fundamental causes of
the War of 1812 were British challenges to national honor, especially
affronts against American shipping and merchant sailors. Hence, Gilje
shows, the motto of the war, Free Trade and Sailors' Rights, perfectly
captured the central importance of defending national honor.[3]

In the early days of the republic, most naval and political leaders
lived by the underlying values of honor. Few New Englanders participated in duels, although one, Congressman Jonathan Cilley of Maine,

felt obliged to respond to a personal challenge in 1838. His death in that duel led to widespread efforts (largely unsuccessful) to suppress the practice of dueling in the years before the Civil War.[4] As Joanne Freeman points out, "Northerners were as well versed in the code as southerners; it was in their utilization of violence that they differed most noticeably. . . . In a sense northerners and southerners spoke different dialects of the language of honor, balancing the conflicting value systems of honor, religion, and the law in regionally distinct ways."[5]

Naval officers, southern or northern, were conscious of a gentleman's code that applied both in private life and in naval warfare.[6] Among naval officers, honorable behavior on board a ship or ashore was so well understood that its principles did not need to be articulated in a formal statement. Historians can glean the maritime application of the gentleman's code from contemporary and historical accounts of events of naval warfare, which suggest that naval officers were expected to behave at sea in accord with many of the same principles that governed their personal lives. By twenty-first-century standards, the values of the gentleman's code were not only redolent of class arrogance but also deeply rooted in sexist and racist attitudes. Because these values are so scorned in the modern era, it is difficult to recognize how natural and coherent they were at the time and how they shaped discourse between individuals as well as discussions of national politics, international commerce, foreign affairs, naval engagements, and military preparedness. The early status of the maritime flag for merchant ships was intimately connected to these broader systems of the honor code and the rhetoric of honor.

Honor was associated with the flag even though there was no specific design for either the national flag or the maritime flag flown from ships in the period before the 1820s. Several alternate designs of the flag were in common usage simultaneously, although all had either thirteen or fifteen red and white stripes and a blue field in the upper left corner (the canton) with varying numbers of white stars. However, even though different ships might have flown different versions of the flag in these decades, at a distance and viewed through a telescope of the era, the white-starred blue canton and the red and white stripes identified the naval or commercial ship as from the United States. Highly revered as a symbol of the nation's honor, the flags in use on board ships continued to vary even after Congress enacted a law in 1818 specifying the official design with twenty stars.[7]

Quite broadly, the issue of national honor was frequently invoked when people discussed the treatment of the nation and its flag abroad. On an international level, the mutually understood honor code was shared by officers in Britain, France, Spain, and, to a great extent, other navies of the period.[8]

Maritime *Code Duello* Standards and Expectations

The honor code applied to warships in very conscious and explicit ways, in effect regulating encounters between naval ships and the way naval battles were fought in the late eighteenth and early nineteenth centuries. The expectations and standards of the personal honor code extended to a wide variety of ship-handling and battle etiquette issues, not only for U.S. officers but also for the officers of naval ships of Britain, France, and Spain in the period.

The codes were not always explicitly stated. As in encounters between gentlemen, one ship might offer a challenge to another. This could result from an insult to the flag or to a ship. When at war, the master of a naval ship would sometimes directly issue a challenge to an equivalent enemy ship.[9] A duel between warships was explicitly characterized as two equally matched ships confronting each other—frigate to frigate, for example.[10] Sometimes, the British Admiralty forbade its officers from entering single ship-on-ship frigate battles on the grounds that some foreign "frigates" were more equivalent to a Royal Navy line-of-battle ship (in modern parlance, a battleship), and thus, to avoid a ship-on-ship duel was no reflection on honor.[11]

Not only were one-on-one ship engagements rhetorically dealt with as duels, but they were sometimes specifically set up in much the same fashion as gentleman-to-gentleman duels, with a location specified and rules of engagement agreed between combatants, often ensuring no third ship become involved that would make the battle unequal. At sea and on shore, it was understood that the weapons should be equivalent. Thus, there was great emphasis at the time and in later literature on the issue of equivalency of ship size, speed, manning, and weight of guns. Frequently, at-sea engagements were noted as occurring within "pistol shot" distance.

The victory of a lesser-armed ship against a better-equipped ship represented an unequal contest; such a victory demonstrated manly qualities: seamanship, bravery, and superior fortitude at the guns. Skills, character, bravery, and honor were expected. These qualities of the individual were also attributed racially to the seamen, and the vocabulary of honor was often employed when discussing military engagements. A reverse victory (of a stronger ship against a weaker) should not have been fought, but the weaker could simply have evaded the encounter or, if trapped, should have surrendered with honor; for a stronger ship to continue to fire on a weaker ship without providing a chance for honorable surrender was a violation of the code and was dastardly.

On the high seas, ships were due a set of ritualized courtesies, such as greetings and the showing of flags; outrages or affronts could come in the form of the inappropriate use of a naval or armed coastal patrol. Apologies could take the form of firing gun salutes. Gentlemen on board a ship (officers and midshipmen) were expected to demonstrate courage by standing up when being fired on. The lower orders (especially passengers who were nongentlemen or women and children) were expected to lie down, go below, or take cover. Someone claiming to be a gentleman would lose that status if he took cover; a midshipman (a youth) could be forgiven lying down because of his age. Officers and petty officers who took cover would be court-martialed.[12]

U.S. naval officers were particularly prone to engage in duels in the early decades of the nineteenth century. Naval historian Charles Oscar Paullin wrote, "During the first fifty years of the Old Navy, 1798–1848, the mortality of naval officers resulting from duels was two-thirds that resulting from naval wars."[13]

In addition to using the same language at sea as was used to talk about honor on land, seamen followed practices in maritime engagements that very directly reflected the personal code of honor: insults were avenged, challenges were issued, to refuse a challenge was dastardly, the stuff one was made of (e.g., whether one was red-blooded and courageous) was revealed in battle or in a duel, ceasing resistance after being wounded (overwhelmingly damaged in ship battle) was expected in order to preserve life.

An unarmed ship that was fired on was being treated as of lower social standing than the ship that fired; the firing on an unarmed U.S. merchant ship by a ship crewed or controlled by people perceived as racially or politically inferior was therefore an outrage. U.S. officers often regarded Spanish Americans as inferior; Spaniards themselves were sometimes so regarded. U.S. seamen and naval personnel did not perceive British, French, and other northern Europeans as ethnically inferior, but all people of color were seen as lower caste and, therefore, any action by them against a U.S. ship was an outrage. The notorious capture and retention as forced labor of U.S. crews by the corsairs of the Barbary States were perhaps the most famous such outrages of the era. Americans perceived the North Africans as "primitive, sordid, and cruel." The term "outrage" is often encountered in reference to episodes at sea in this and later periods.[14]

Historical treatments written later in the nineteenth century (and some written in the twentieth century) reflected many of the underlying values of the maritime honor code: naval officers were expected to be cool under fire, equivalence of ships was considered in evaluating the performance of officers, and officers and men desired a fair fight. Mines (known then as "torpedoes") were regarded as "infernal machines." Because they provided no opportunity for a fair fight, they were despised by naval officers.[15]

That naval officers, drawn from the gentleman class, would carry the values of the honor code to their conduct as officers on board ships is perfectly understandable. Their definitions of proper personal behavior, particularly in situations involving mortal risk, would naturally carry over to conduct in warfare or in situations in which well-armed potential adversaries met in the lawless reaches of the high seas. Exchanges of identification; careful determination of whether a strange ship was a friend, foe, or neutral; and determination of whether that ship should display deference were all regulated by the mutually understood rhetoric and rules of gentlemanly intercourse. Because these values were shared by officers of the English, French, Spanish, and other navies, most encounters between ships had a degree of predictability. Identification by flag and hailing within earshot were crucial parts of ship-on-ship behavior at sea.

For these reasons, the naval honor code had certain very practical functions, not only for the United States but for all the navies of the period. In the sailing ship era, when armed warships of different nations encountered each other at sea, the rituals and practices embodied in the honor code actually prevented unnecessary loss of life. The understanding that a lesser-armed ship (such as a frigate) could honorably surrender without an extended exchange of gunfire to a heavier and better-armed line-of-battle ship meant that the surrendering officers and men could live; later, they might be released under a prisoner exchange or cartel, or peace treaty, and live to fight another day. In strict terms of labor and warfighting capability, this aspect of the naval honor code had a humane, practical function. The practices spelled out in documents of the era were all quite suited to the demands of independently sailing naval and merchant ships in a time before rapid radio communication between ship and shore or ship and ship.

So, stripped of the emotional, symbolic, and rhetorical appeals to underlying psychological values of the era, the U.S. flag on board naval ships was recognized and respected internationally for practical economic and military reasons. Similar principles carried over to merchant shipping and the merchant flag, as did the need to prevent the violation of those standards on U.S. naval and merchant ships.

The Honor Code in Diplomacy and International Affairs

From the earliest days of the republic, the application of the honor code and its language to maritime and international affairs became embodied in treaties, public pronouncements, founding documents, political disputation, and presidential statements. When the United States obtained its independence, almost its only contact with the other nations of the world was by sea.[16] If U.S. merchant ships were recognized and treated at sea with the same respect as ships from other independent nations, that respect would represent the world's acceptance of the United States' equal status as a sovereign state. If U.S. merchant ships and seamen were not extended the rights and status on the high seas that went with sovereignty, that disrespect would represent both a failure to treat the United States as a sovereign nation and a failure to accord the U.S. ships the freedom of the seas. In territorial waters, diplomatic recognition and respect were not the only concerns; treatment of ships engaged in mundane practices—such as entering and leaving harbors, discharging and receiving cargoes, paying port and harbor charges, and being subject to quarantine in times of plague or contagion—was also important. Recognition of and respect for the U.S. merchant flag was both a matter of honor and a matter of practical importance.

These practical matters were regulated by amity, commerce, and navigation (ACN) treaties, which defined exactly how U.S. honor was to be protected and respected. Such treaties, later called friendship, commerce, and navigation (FCN) treaties, were signed by the United States and dozens of other countries.[17] One of the first of these treaties, which served at least as a partial model for later such treaties, was Jay's Treaty with Great Britain, signed in 1794. Jay's Treaty used vocabulary common in the honor code.

The ACN treaties of the era all reflect similar language, and all were intended to record other nations' obligation to treat U.S. merchant ships with the proper expected courtesies and procedures, under the principle of freedom of the seas propounded by Grotius. The use of terms such as "word of honor," "respect," "insult," and "outrages," and the courtesy that small boats be used when a crew approached another ship to avoid giving offense—all suggest the degree to which the code of honor carried over to the relations between states on the high seas and in ports. The language was not merely a colorful reminder of the internationally understood honor code or a common maritime rhetoric; it created a set of practical, functioning arrangements designed to facilitate commerce and to ensure that U.S. merchant ships were treated equally with those of other recognized nations.

The honor code and the maritime side of it, with its focus on the flag as the emblem of national identity, thus applied to the merchant flag. A series of clashes between the United States and foreign powers over the treatment of U.S. merchant ships abroad characterized the diplomatic issues of the first few decades of the nation's existence. The Quasi War with France of 1798–1799, the Barbary Wars of 1803–1808, and the War of 1812 all grew out (wholly or in part) of the failure of foreign nations to extend to U.S. merchant and naval ships the respect or deference consistent with the treatment by one gentleman of the prerogatives and status of another gentleman or the treatment of one recognized sovereign state by another.[18]

Notably, the rhetoric used in discussing the merchant marine and naval skirmishes that engendered these military clashes was used not only by the gentleman class of the South but also by journalists, politicians, and public assemblies found throughout the fledgling nation. In that era, gentlemen frequently made it clear that they did not regard any journalist as a gentleman; when insulted in an editorial, the proper response was to horsewhip or thrash the offender. Nevertheless, the rhetoric did not simply reflect the elite that dominated the Navy. Nor was it simply a carryover of that language from personal and naval circles to diplomacy. Rather, the rhetoric and the set of values it represented were part and parcel of all national discourse over international affairs.

Honor Code Rhetoric in International Affairs

The use of this language by people other than naval officers, including northern civilians and political leaders of various persuasions, was common throughout the period from the ratification of the Constitution to the War of 1812. Selections from the vast public literature and journalistic comment of the period concerned with maritime issues and foreign policy reflect this theme.

Guadeloupe Incident, 1786

In 1786, during the period of the Articles of Confederation, eighteen U.S. merchant ship masters signed a petition complaining of indignities suffered in Pointe-à-Pitre, Guadeloupe. The complaints indicated a rising demand for a more effective national identity embodied in a national constitution and a national government. In part, the ship masters said, "The little respect that is paid to the American flag and the repeated insults which subjects of the United States meet with in foreign ports, must convince the good people of this continent, that it is absolutely necessary we should invest Congress with a power to regulate our commerce and to support our dignity as free and independent states; without which, we must soon become a reproach and bye-word among the nations."[19]

Ratification of the Constitution

A review of the 1787–1788 debates over ratification of the U.S. Constitution reveals numerous discussions regarding the establishment of a navy. Antinavalists argued that a navy would impose a burden on an essentially agricultural and isolated people, that it would favor New England and other coastal regions engaged in maritime pursuits, and that it would be an unneeded expense. Navalists argued that a navy would be necessary to protect U.S. commerce in times of American neutrality and the nation itself in time of war.[20]

While this strategic thinking appears logical enough by modern standards of realpolitik, some of the vocabulary used was based on appeals to honor and respect. For example, at the Pennsylvania constitutional ratifying convention, James Wilson said, "With what propriety can we hope our flag will be respected, while we have not a single gun to fire in its defence?"[21] James Madison reflected a similar sentiment in his choice of words: "Weakness will invite insults."[22]

In the Federalist Papers, Alexander Hamilton logically spelled out the strategic-commercial reasons for having a navy. However, even in his dispassionate analysis, one sees the evocation of some emotional terms that echo the underlying code. Without a navy, Hamilton reasoned, "our commerce would be a prey to the wanton intermeddlings of all nations at war with each other; who, having nothing to fear from us, would with little scruple or remorse, supply their wants by depredations on our property as often as it fell in their way. The rights of neutrality will only be respected when they are defended by an adequate power. A nation, despicable by its weakness, forfeits even the privilege of being neutral."[23]

Hamilton was a passionate follower of the honor code in his personal life, although he had objections to killing someone, out of concern with both the law and religious principles. One study shows he engaged in eleven personal "affairs of honor," that is, duels, and of course, he famously died in the 1804 duel with Aaron Burr.[24]

John Jay warned that oversensitivity to foreign "insult" could lead to unjust wars, and he thought the moderating influence of a federal government would help temper such excitements.[25]

Algerine Pirates and Funding a Navy

Thomas Jefferson, who was generally not in favor of a strong navy, advocated the use of force to preserve national honor in the face of demands for ransom from the Algerine (Barbary) pirates in a letter to John Adams on July 11, 1786.[26]

George Washington, in his last address to Congress in December 1796, alluded to the problems of U.S. captives in Algiers who, despite Jefferson's arguments, had been ransomed. He went on to recommend that Congress see to the financing of a navy to protect the nation's ability to carry on foreign trade as a neutral during time of war between two major foreign belligerents. Washington echoed the themes of respect and insult:

> To an active external commerce, the protection of a naval force is indispensible. This is manifest with regard to wars in which a State is itself a party. But besides this, it is in our own experience, that the most sincere neutrality is not sufficient guard against the depredations of nations at war. To secure respect to a neutral flag requires a naval force, organized to vindicate it from insult or aggression. . . . It would seem as if our trade to

the Mediterranean, without a protecting force, will always be insecure, and our citizens exposed to the calamities from which numbers of them have but just been relieved.[27]

The debate over the funding of the Navy in 1798 was cast in terms of defense of national honor. Historian Martin Smelser argues convincingly that the XYZ affair of 1798 represented the turning point in U.S. support for a navy; he demonstrates how the public press at the time reacted to the demand from French officials for a bribe in order for U.S. delegates to meet with French authorities. The demand for a bribe was widely perceived as an insult to U.S. honor, a point also made by Paul Gilje in his recent study of the period.[28] Democratic Republican opponents of a strong navy were thrown into disrepute on the grounds that they willingly accepted such French insults.[29] Out of the refusal to pay the bribe to French officials in the XYZ affair came the famous line "Millions for defense, not a penny for tribute."[30]

Thomas Jefferson had expressed some ambiguity on the issue of naval forces, and by the time of his presidency, he generally opposed an expansion of the Navy. Like John Jay, he warned that maritime incidents could be blown out of proportion or wrongly and rashly misconstrued. Nevertheless, the language he used in his 1803 State of the Union address (in those days written, not delivered orally) reflected exactly the same underlying values that we have observed among more hawkish writers of the time:

> In the course of this conflict [between France and Britain], let it be our endeavor . . . to punish severely those persons, citizen or alien, who shall usurp the cover of our flag, for vessels not entitled to it, infecting thereby with suspicion those of real Americans, and committing us into controversies, for the redress of wrongs not our own; to exact from every nation the observance, toward our vessels and citizens, of those principles and practices which all civilized people acknowledge; to merit the character of a great nation and maintain that of an independent one, preferring every consequence to insult and habitual wrong.[31]

In his oblique fashion, Jefferson first warned that misuse of the flag by others could wrongly lead the United States into conflict. However, he also asserted that the United States should prefer "every consequence," that is, armed confrontation, to accepting "insult." Jefferson preferred economic sanction and diplomatic negotiation to war, but he, like his Federalist opponents, was sensitive to issues of national honor, and if it came to that, he preferred war to accepting an insult.

Official State Department correspondence of the era reflected the same language. Charles Pinckney (Thomas Jefferson's minister to Spain, 1801–1805), writing to the Spanish minister of state in 1804, provided a list of complaints regarding Spanish mistreatment of U.S. shipping, indicating that the United States had shown forbearance even when the "honor of our flag" had been violated: "Under all these accumulated injuries and sufferings of our citizens, under the breach of solemn treaties, of the laws of nations, and in many instances, violations of the honor of our flag, what has been the conduct of the United States?"[32]

During the Jeffersonian period, the development of a naval force was seen as designed to "protect the flag from insult." Although the principle could be expressed less symbolically by stating that the Navy would protect merchant shipping from abuse by foreign powers, the language used in a pronaval expansion editorial from 1805 was typical, reflecting the underlying honor code with terms such as "respect" and "insult": "We may venture to predict, that the time is not far distant when America shall be respected as one of the most powerful of nations, and when her flag shall sail on the ocean, without any daring to insult it."[33]

When reporting on specific episodes seen as insults to the flag, U.S. consular officials abroad used similar vocabulary. In 1805, when an American merchant sloop was attacked by a Spanish privateer schooner and personal goods were stolen from the crew, John Gavino, U.S. consul in Gibraltar, filed a report of the incident concluding with this phrasing: "The commander and crew of the said schooner privateer behaved in a most insulting and abusive manner and they seemed by their appearance, language, dress, and manners to have been Spaniards, wherefore [the officers of sloop *Ranger*] make this declaration and protest, not only the robbery committed, but also for the insult shown the flag under which they sailed."[34]

Chesapeake Affair, 1807

In the *Chesapeake* affair, an overzealous British naval officer arrested four British deserters from a U.S. warship. The event was seen then, and in numerous historical treatments, as a broader insult to U.S. honor, as well as a specific and clear insult to the honor of the U.S. naval commander of the *Chesapeake*, James Barron. In the public debates over the incident (and other seizures by British officers of seamen from U.S.-flagged merchant ships), those seeking to engage the United States in retaliatory naval engagements construed the episode in terms reflecting honor. A wide variety of individuals used the same rhetoric whether they were speaking from commercial interest, patriotic fervor, or political motives seeking to bring into disrepute either pro-French Jeffersonians or pro-English Federalists. That is, the appeals for action very often took the form of seeking satisfaction for an insult or affront to the merchant flag as well as to the U.S. flag on board naval ships, both of which were taken to symbolize the nation's honor. Those opposed to action, following John Jay's thinking, believed that some merchant shippers unnecessarily exposed the flag to insult. Opponents and proponents shared the same rhetoric and used similar language to express opposing viewpoints.

The notion that national honor, like personal honor, had to be redeemed by obtaining satisfaction ran throughout the written editorial commentary on the *Chesapeake* incident. A physical and manly response to an insult to national honor, similar to the proper response to a personal insult, was deemed appropriate in the press at the time.[35]

A public meeting in Culpepper County, Virginia, succinctly resolved "that an insult to the American flag is an insult to the nation, and that until the former is treated with respect, the sword of vengeance ought not to be sheathed by the latter."[36] An insult to the flag was seen as an insult to the nation, and an insult to the nation should be taken personally by every man; a challenge to the national honor should be felt as a challenge to the individual's honor. The sentiment was almost self-evident then. Similar sentiments were expressed in a wide variety of memorials and editorials.[37]

As an example of the rhetoric used in response to the *Chesapeake* incident, the *National Intelligencer and Washington Advertiser* reported "a respectable meeting of the inhabitants of Fairfax county, held at their court house, on the 11th of July, 1807, for the purpose of taking into consideration the late atrocious outrage committed on the U.S. frigate Chesapeake, by a British ship of war the Leopard."[38] The *Niles Register* and other periodicals of the era, both Federalist and Democratic

Republican, provide numerous further examples of honor code rhetoric used in reporting on the *Chesapeake* incident and other maritime affairs.

Insults from Low-Status Opponents, 1810

Writers for the public press were often more explicit in their evocation of honor and the related concept that insults from the "lower orders" should be met with direct punishment without the benefit of a challenge and an evenly matched duel. For example, "An American" writing from the ship *Aurora* in St. Bartholomew in the West Indies in 1810 reported on an "insult offered to the flag" entirely separate from the growing conflict with Britain:

> Being at this island on commercial pursuits, for a few days past, a circumstance has occurred, which excited my sensibility as an American, in the highest degree, and as I consider it the duty of every citizen to make notorious any insult offered to the flag of the United States, or any violence committed on the person of any of their fellow citizens in a foreign country. . . . [I seek to] make known to my fellow citizens the insult offered to the American flag and the unprecedented violence committed on the person of one of our fellow citizens by the government of this insignificant island.[39]

The insult consisted of a local official, accompanied by a "crew principally composed of negro slaves," forcing the chief mate, Mr. Johnson, of the ship *Mary Ann Eliza* off the ship after the local official's crew had beat him. Johnson was further beaten on order of the colony's governor. The affront, it seemed, was considered more egregious because of its racial component.

Honor Rhetoric and the War of 1812

The War of 1812 against Britain tended to be favored by westerners and southerners more than by representatives of New England seafaring communities. Many westerners and their congressional representatives believed that Canada could be readily conquered, and they also resented British support for hostile Native American tribes on the frontier. New England merchants had more to fear from British raids, blockade, and interference with seaborne commerce; maritime New England almost seceded from the Union over opposition to the war after it had begun. The Federalist leanings and the generally pro-British views of New Englanders also played a role in the lack of support there for the War of 1812. Furthermore, both then and later, southerners and westerners showed more concern with issues of honor than New Englanders; this perhaps reflects the different religious and cultural origins of the regions' settlers.[40]

When President James Madison finally asked Congress to support war measures against Britain, he explicitly did so in order to "maintain the honor of the flag."[41] While such a turn of phrase might seem so conventional as to go unnoticed, in fact it reflects the deeper and widespread honor code attached to the flag as the symbol of the nation.

By the War of 1812, the issue of respect shown to the U.S. maritime flag had become deeply entrenched in the U.S. psyche. Certainly, the rhetoric reflecting the honor code permeated all public discourse about the issue of U.S. shipping abroad and U.S. relations with Britain, France, and other nations. The honor code, as noted by several historians, became the basis for political rhetoric when dealing with maritime and international affairs.[42]

The vocabulary of honor surrounding maritime issues had several levels of meaning and usage: at one level, the language had practical functional value in regulating affairs at sea; at another level, it evoked deeply held emotional values reflecting the social usages of the era; at the political level, it represented a tool for enlisting broad support for economic and power goals. The American merchant flag had become an emblem of the nation, and its recognition by diplomats had been one of the first orders of business of the new nation. With the Quasi War, the Barbary Wars, and the War of 1812, the United States had gone to war three times in defense of that flag in the first three decades of the nation's existence. In domestic politics as well as international affairs, the merchant flag on board privately owned trading vessels had become, like the Stars and Stripes over Fort McHenry, a symbol of the nation.

2

Right of Search, 1812–58

At the diplomatic level, the central issues leading to the War of 1812 were in fact maritime. The blockades of Britain against France and France against Britain affected U.S. commerce and shipping. The U.S. effort to remain neutral collapsed, and the country was drawn into war against Britain. The impressment, right of search, and blockade issues were presented and conceived as matters of honor.[1]

For many prominent politicians, the issues that led to the War of 1812 were, simply put, matters of national honor. For example, Congressman George Bibb from Kentucky echoed the national view that the only honorable course in the face of British actions was "a most base and disgraceful submission" or war. John C. Calhoun used similar rhetoric: "God grant that the people may have spirit to maintain our interest and honor in this momentous period." Henry Clay argued, "Not a man in the nation could really doubt the sincerity with which those in power have sought, by all honorable pacific means, to protect the interests of the country." Quoting these men and others, historian Roger H. Brown argues in *The Republic in Peril*, "A concern for national honor also led Republicans toward war. Many anticipated that failure to resist would degrade and demoralize Americans. They could reason from their own sense of honor."[2]

Republicans had largely opposed the construction of a large navy, and most navalists were found in the Federalist camp, even though Republicans tended to support the war and Federalists opposed the war. Historian Craig Symonds has argued that "emotional navalism," seeking a greatly expanded navy based on appeals to national honor, had not won great support in the period; the practical view that the

Portions of this chapter appeared in conference presentations and in two articles by the author and are reused with permission: "The American Maritime *Code Duello*," *Northern Mariner* 21, no. 2 (April 2011): 159–69; and "The Right of Search Controversies, 1841–42 and 1857–58," *Northern Mariner* 22, no. 4 (October 2012): 409–20.

world's seas could be better patrolled by the British navy prevailed in the years following the War of 1812. What Symonds identifies as "emotional navalism" was not revived until the 1880s. As we will see, the more strident navalism that emerged in the post–Civil War era was intimately wrapped up in, and expressed in terms of, national honor.[3]

In the War of 1812, the U.S. Navy had a distinguished record of victories against the British, in striking contrast to the Army's failure to effectively fight land battles. Among notable U.S. naval victories were the following: The frigate *Essex* accepted the surrender of the HMS *Alert* on August 13, 1812, off the Azores. The *Constitution* captured the HMS *Guerrière* on August 19, 1812, about five hundred miles southeast of Newfoundland. The *Wasp* accepted the surrender of the HMS *Frolic* on October 18, 1812, about three hundred miles north of Bermuda. The *United States* defeated the HMS *Macedonian* on October 25, 1812, after a two-hour battle about five hundred miles west of the Canary Islands. The *Constitution* so damaged the HMS *Java* on December 29, 1812, off the coast of Brazil that her master ordered her scuttled. The two sloops the *Hornet* and the HMS *Peacock* met on February 24, 1813, off South America; the *Hornet* sank the *Peacock*, rescued most of the *Peacock* survivors, and took them to the United States as prisoners. Differences in size and rigging in several of these engagements were part of British complaints that the actions were not between equivalent ships.

In contemporary news accounts, these major naval battles, as well as others, provided a vindication of U.S. honor, with the reports couched in exactly that language. In later historical accounts, U.S. historians continued to portray these victories as properly fought duels in which the U.S. victory resulted from superior seamanship and valor. By contrast, several U.S. naval defeats were depicted as due to the superior armament or fighting condition of the British ship, the result of an "unfair" match. The body of historiography on these battles is as redolent of the maritime code of honor as contemporary accounts, from the nineteenth century into the twenty-first century.

For example, in repeated treatments of naval engagements, Edgar Stanton Maclay, in his *A History of the United States Navy from 1775 to 1898*, carefully enumerated the number and weight of cannon on board the opposing vessels in two-ship encounters, or duels, and recorded to the extent possible precise casualty figures in the U.S.-British naval encounters of the War of 1812. An undercurrent of such a presentation was the "manhood" displayed by U.S. sailors, especially when they emerged victorious from an encounter in which they operated at a disadvantage in armament or size and weight of ship. Maclay repeatedly described a success in such battles as "gallant."

The language of Maclay, writing in 1893–1898 about affairs eight decades earlier, might be thought to reflect the jingoistic sentiment of the 1890s, with all its sensitivities, values, ideas, concepts, and rhetoric. The full-blown "cult of the flag" had taken hold by the 1890s, and perhaps Maclay represented that era, not the earlier one, with his interpretation and focus. However, Maclay's concern with "indignities," "insults," and "outrages" suffered by the U.S. flag and their role in causing conflict was not simply an imposition of a later point of view on evidence from an earlier era. Although that historiographic perception is correct in that Maclay did reflect values of his own era, the same rhetoric had been applied in precisely the same fashion in the first decades of the 1800s and had taken root in that period. The primary documents that Maclay and other later historians cited, as well as Maclay's and other historians' own text, used language reflecting ship duels, gallant officers, and dozens of turns of phrase and descriptions of incidents that reflected the honor code values.

Maclay provided mind-numbing detail on the equality of armament of the *Frolic* and the *Wasp* and the *Wasp* victory. He went to great lengths to detail manpower, tonnage, armament, and casualty figures in each encounter, generally in order to demonstrate that U.S. sailors fought in equal encounters or in encounters in which they were outgunned with great success.[4]

Later historians have continued to describe the War of 1812 naval encounters in maritime honor code terms. *The War of 1812*, written by John K. Mahon and published in 1991, references the "gentleman's code of naval warfare" violated by the British in the eyes of Capt. David Porter off South America on March 28, 1814.[5] Roy Adkins and Lesley Adkins, in their *The War for All the Oceans*, repeat many of the classic analyses that evoked the maritime *code duello*, often through direct quotes from contemporary sources. For example, an officer on board the *President* wrote to the *New York Herald* demonstrating that he wanted an equal match in accord with the code: "We have made the complete preparation for battle. Every one wishes it. She is exactly our force, but we have the *Argus* [sloop] with us, which none of us are pleased with, as we wish a fair trial of courage and skill. . . . The commodore [John Rodgers] will demand the person impressed; the demand will doubtless be refused, and the battle will instantly commence."[6]

As another example, the following passage from *The War for All the Oceans* demonstrates the parallel between exposing oneself in a duel and gentlemen in a gun battle at sea: "[The master] in an encounter between *Amphion* and French *Flore*, ordered gun crews to lie down 'as by standing they were uselessly exposed, it being impossible to bring a gun to bear on the enemy at the moment. With the young gentlemen [midshipmen] or officers I left it optional to act as they pleased, and they remained erect with me, and I lament to say suffered in consequence of their gallantry, for Messrs. Barnard and Farewell, two promising young men, were immediately knocked down and taken to the cockpit, badly, though not mortally wounded.'"[7]

The sources cited in the Adkinses' study of the War of 1812 as well as many other works are replete with examples of terminology and rhetoric that consciously or unconsciously reflected the honor code.[8]

Honor, the Flag, and Policy

With the (perceived) victorious end of the War of 1812, there was a change in the tone of editorialists, politicians, and public assemblies regarding the issue of the flag and honor. The first generation of those who had fought in the Revolution had begun to die off. Having survived a second war with Britain, journalists, politicians, and probably most of the American public no longer seemed quite as sensitive to affronts to honor.[9]

Americans now had reason to believe that the republic would survive; recognition by foreign powers had increased, and it was clear that the U.S. Navy had proved itself a match for the world's strongest maritime power, Great Britain. With attention turning to issues such as the suppression of piracy, the removal of Indians from the Old Southwest and newly acquired Florida, the expansion of the cotton frontier, and the settlement of the trans-Mississippi West, the tone of insecurity and chip-on-the-shoulder defensiveness in editorials declined to an extent.

Nevertheless, the honor code persisted and shaped not only personal values but national attitudes and policies as well. Duels were still fought, scoundrels and poltroons were publicly thrashed by self-defined gentlemen, and the general informed public still expected that the United States and its honor would be respected abroad. As will be seen, the code of honor persisted to shape the logic of encounters at sea, while on land a code of behavior based on honor still not only shaped the conduct of personal affairs and polite discourse but also cropped up in public discussion of military action and international relations.

Joanne Freeman argues in *Affairs of Honor*, "The resulting style of politics—self-conscious, anxious, and inter-twined with the rites and rituals of the honor code—fell to the wayside with the acceptance of political parties."[10] The research and findings in the present work show that the honor code and its associated rhetoric continued to shape much of political discourse far longer, particularly when it came to the role of U.S. merchant shipping on the world's oceans.

Presidents, secretaries of state, members of Congress, and other public figures judged their own actions and those of domestic and foreign opponents by the standards of the unwritten, but understood, code of honor. Accordingly, when the maritime flag, as the symbol of the nation, was disrespected, affronted, or dishonored, the outrage became a cause for editorial outbursts from journalists, public dismay, and sometimes executive action leading to military engagement. This pattern was at work through the maritime disputes of the antebellum period, during the Civil War, into the late nineteenth century, and well into the twentieth century.

The Merchant Flag, 1815–60

In the four decades following the War of 1812, a variety of events and developments shaped the standing of the American merchant marine. The division between the interests of seaboard states and territories and those of interior states and territories became clear in congressional debates over tariffs and internal improvements. As new western states were admitted to the union, representatives in the coastal states had increased incentive to portray the maritime issue as one of national pride and status in order to enlist (or shame) representatives of the interior into supporting a navy and other policies beneficial to the seaport cities.

Steam propulsion of ships began with Robert Fulton's river steamers on the Hudson in 1807, and soon the extensive U.S. river system was busy with dozens, then hundreds, of paddlewheel-driven steamboats. The seemingly inexhaustible supply of firewood along the riverbanks allowed fueling. In seaports, steam tugs and local excursion boats and ferries soon clogged the harbors; some began using coal as fuel. However,

America's foreign trade was conducted across oceans, and steam propulsion was not practical for most transoceanic travel, simply because the tons of fuel required for such a trip left little space for cargo. Engines and propulsion improved rapidly, but even by the 1850s, U.S.-owned transoceanic cargo ships remained either sailing vessels or combined sail-and-steam vessels.

So, despite the development of a new technology that would revolutionize ocean travel and maritime warfare in later decades, the oceangoing trade of the United States before the Civil War was almost entirely conducted in wind-powered brigs, schooners, barks, and clipper ships, with some conducted on board the hybrid sail-and-steam ships. The clippers were particularly used in runs around Cape Horn to and from China and to California, following the gold rush of 1849, while sail-and-steam ships ran packet services between East and Gulf Coast cities, Havana, and Panama.

As steam railroads and river steamboats facilitated westward expansion, the dominating influence of the seaboard maritime states slowly diminished. Between 1791 and 1837, thirteen new states were admitted to the Union to join the original thirteen. Of the thirteen new states, only Maine, Louisiana, Mississippi, and Alabama had seacoasts. This basic geopolitical reality meant that by 1837 coastal states had a somewhat diminished power in the Senate. Whereas in 1789 all twenty-six senators were from coastal states, by 1837 the tally was thirty-four seacoast senators and eighteen inland senators. An ever slimmer majority in the House of Representatives represented seaport constituencies.[11] The balance between slave states and nonslave states was carefully maintained in the Senate, but the Senate had gone from 100 percent representation of seaboard states to 73 percent seaboard, and the number was declining.

Of course, there was no effort to maintain a balance of maritime states with interior states similar to the effort to maintain the slave-holding-nonslaveholding balance. The trend for the gradual increase of inland representation would continue. Although many inland states, particularly in the Ohio and Mississippi River basins, shipped products by river to New Orleans for transshipment by sea to overseas destinations, the country's ocean or maritime focus had begun to diminish somewhat by the 1850s. Nevertheless, the rhetoric of honor, with its focus on the flag at sea, still had considerable power to evoke political support and remained a staple of both journalistic and historical writing throughout the nineteenth century and beyond.

The Flag as a National Emblem

In the years between the War of 1812 and the Civil War, editorialists, politicians, and others made it clear that the flag itself had come to symbolize the nation and had become even more deeply revered. Arctic and Antarctic explorers proudly reported that they had "carried the flag" to these previously unexplored regions. U.S. ambassador to Mexico Joel Roberts Poinsett offered sanctuary to Spanish civilians when they were attacked by a mob; he claimed to have awed the mob into submission by waving the U.S. flag from the balcony of the embassy. In the Mexican War, the conquest of California was symbolized by the raising of the U.S. flag there; the victory in Mexico City was represented by raising the U.S. flag over the castle at Chapultepec. The advance of the Panama Railroad across the Isthmus of Panama was marked by the progress of the flag there. In each of these cases, the flag itself was prominently displayed and written about as the emblem of American enterprise, fortitude, and courage.[12] These and many other episodes in the period reflected the strong association between the flag and American national identity formed in the first decades and well embedded in discourse and national sentiments. The development was not unique to the United States, as the French Tricolor and the British Union Jack, among other imperial flags, were on display at coaling stations, embassies, consulates, and colonies all across the planet.

U.S. Navy Defense of the Merchant Ship Flag, 1831–60

The association between flag and national identity still extended clearly to the flag on board merchant ships at sea. When Sumatran pirates attacked the U.S. merchant ship *Friendship* at Kuala Batu in 1831, seizing the cargo and killing the crew, President Andrew Jackson ordered retaliation.[13] The *Potomac*, disguised as a merchant ship, conducted a raid on the pirate haven in 1832, destroying five forts and slaughtering more than a hundred villagers.[14] However, the chastisement seemed to have little effect. In August 1838 the U.S. merchant ship *Eclipse* was attacked in the same area, its master murdered, and the ship plundered of opium and some $18,000. Hearing of this second outrage, the commander of

U.S. frigate *Columbia* sailed from Ceylon, bombarded Kuala Batu again, and destroyed another nearby town, Muka, in retaliation.[15] The Kuala Batu raids of 1832 and 1838 illustrated that the merchant flag, like the flags of railroad entrepreneurs, explorers, ambassadors, and U.S. troops abroad, represented the United States and that the underlying honor code would continue to determine the appropriate response to affronts to the flag. Considering that the Sumatran pirates had no commerce that the United States could effectively interdict, no diplomatic channels through which protests could be made, and no regime from which restitution or reparations could be obtained, a direct reprisal with force was the only alternative.

U.S. merchant ships were often subject to blockades, harassment, and sometimes outright confiscation during the many rebellions, conflicting claims of jurisdiction, and civil conflicts in Latin America from 1831 to 1859, and the U.S. Navy responded to affronts to the merchant flag on just a few occasions in these years. Historian John H. Schroeder has detailed several such episodes. Among them was one that followed after Argentine officials seized the U.S. sealer *Harriet* in 1831 in the Falkland Islands for killing seals on the island shores. In retaliation, Capt. Silas Duncan, in command of the Navy's *Lexington*, ordered his ship to the islands, where he spiked the guns of the fort and posted a notice that interference with U.S. sealers was an act of piracy. The episode led to a break in diplomatic relations between the United States and Argentina that lasted until 1844.[16]

In 1841, in an episode in what is now the Ivory Coast (Côte d'Ivoire), the U.S. merchant schooner *Mary Carver* was captured and its crew murdered. Finally, more than a year later, Commo. Matthew C. Perry took his antislavery squadron of four naval ships and anchored off the offending village of Berebee on December 13, 1843. When an attempt to negotiate turned into a brawl, Perry's sailors killed the local king and burned the village.[17]

As noted by historian Brian Rouleau, as "representatives" of U.S. culture, early nineteenth-century merchant crew members far outnumbered officials and more polite citizens, like missionaries and government representatives such as consuls, ministerial staff, and naval officers. While Yankee tars perceived their trips to foreign ports as carrying the flag abroad, often their antics had adverse effects. Sometimes U.S. merchant seamen, sealers, and whalers in ports abroad created local incidents that had the making for international incidents. Minstrel shows by seamen, disputes over theft, fistfights and barroom or brothel brawls in many ports, and a full-scale riot by merchant sailors ashore in Hawaii in 1852 all led to objections or protests by local authorities. In some of the more violent cases, U.S. merchant sailors were tried before U.S. consular courts and condemned to local prison or work gangs. The cultural contacts were often insulting to the local peoples, sometimes very contentious, and now and then bloody.[18]

When episodes of conflict between U.S. seamen (naval or merchant) and peoples abroad reached the U.S. press, ethnic and racist preconceptions created a natural tendency to place blame on the "natives." Even so, in terms of potential for armed conflict, the treatment of the U.S. flag on board merchant ships while at sea or in ports was far more crucial than the encounters of American tars with sailors from other nations or with local residents, whether primitive or modern. Journalists and statesmen were more likely to become engaged when the flag was challenged than when one or more American tars got in trouble ashore.

The Right of Search as Insult to the Flag

In a series of episodes involving the American merchant flag at sea in the 1840s and 1850s, Britain challenged U.S. national honor to the extent that it became a national concern. The protection the U.S. flag offered to merchant ships was tested when the British sought to interdict the continuing African slave trade from West Africa to Cuba, Santo Domingo, Puerto Rico, and Brazil in the 1840s. U.S.-owned and U.S.-flagged ships were active in this trade, and even Spanish slave traders, operating ships not regularly registered in any port, flew the U.S. flag in hopes of preventing British search and seizure of their vessels. The American response to the British challenge illustrated exactly how far the United States would go to protect its merchant flag at sea.

Howard Jones wrote, "Southerners protested British search tactics as an infringement of America's freedom of the seas—a reminder of impressment—and called on the Washington government to defend national honor. Their sincerity is impossible to determine, but some Southern papers argued for maritime rights and national integrity."[19] The southerners' outrage was also shared by politicians and journalists in the North, whose anti-British sentiment was aroused over both British treatment of the merchant ship flag on board suspected slave ships and the issue of the U.S. border with the British colony of New Brunswick.

At its height in 1841, the "right of search" controversy became one of several possible casus belli for a third war between Great Britain and the United States. After the issue had apparently been resolved with the signing of the Webster-Ashburton Treaty in 1842, it lay dormant for more than a decade, until it resurfaced in 1857 and 1858. Although the maritime issue was only one of several problems generating tensions between the United States and Britain, the controversy revealed that affronts to the flag and the honor due to the flag at sea continued to excite public, journalistic, and political outcry in the United States.

As noted earlier, the British exercise (and, in American eyes, misuse) of the right of search had been one of the reasons for the War of 1812. The British did not officially claim a right of search on a warship of a nation with which they were at peace, but even so, they did not officially apologize or make restitution for the violation of the principle in seizing deserters from the *Chesapeake* in 1807. The treaty that resolved the War of 1812 did not include a clause prohibiting the searching of ships in peacetime in the future. The British regarded such an explicit prohibition as unnecessary or redundant. Searching a foreign merchant ship in international waters during peacetime was a practice not even countenanced in British law unless the ship flew the flag of a nation that had entered a treaty allowing such a search. Therefore, the Royal Navy's detention and examination of merchant ships that flew the U.S. flag on the high seas in the 1840s and 1850s was indeed an extraordinary departure from commonly accepted international practice and Britain's own regular procedures.

Off the coast of West Africa and later in the West Indies, British warships did in fact stop and detain many merchant ships flying the U.S. flag; British officers then boarded the ships to inspect documentation to verify whether or not the ships were entitled to fly the flag. The British claimed that the detention, visitation, and searches of suspected slave ships were all done to determine proper documentation of the ships' right to fly the U.S. flag.[20]

During the Napoleonic Wars, seamen from U.S. merchant ships were impressed under the wartime right of search, but in 1839–1840 the United States and Britain were at peace. Americans believed that Britain had absolutely no right to permit or order its warships to detain, inspect, or board ships flying the U.S. flag in international waters during time of peace. The affront was manifest; the heated rhetorical responses to these episodes at the time repeatedly evoked the honor code. Editorialists and some officials urged the United States to reject "the insult to the flag." The searches, they claimed, showed British contempt and failure to treat the United States as an equal.

The right of search issue first arose at the same time that a simmering border dispute over the boundary between the British colony of New Brunswick and the state of Maine threatened to boil over into a full-blown conflict between Britain and the United States, known as the Aroostook War. The state of Maine prepared to send militia units into the disputed zone and unilaterally adjust the boundary by force of arms; the New Brunswick colonists also prepared their local militia. As this border issue loomed, the anti-British U.S. press focused on the British outrages at sea and linked the obscure local boundary question to the more nationally inflammatory issue of outrageous insults to the flag. As in 1812 the rhetoric of honor, as applied to maritime affairs, was used to enlist wide support for a war from which inland regions had more to gain. One U.S. resident in the disputed Maine–New Brunswick zone flew the U.S. flag; when New Brunswick authorities arrested him and confiscated his flag, the insult to the flag—this one ashore—became further fuel for the rising war fever in Maine and the United States.[21]

The United States had outlawed the importation of slaves into the United States in 1808. To prevent slave export from Africa by U.S. ships, U.S. naval ships, beginning with the *Cyane* in 1820, patrolled off West Africa. Blacks rescued from slavers by U.S. warships were taken to Monrovia, Liberia, where the American Colonization Society had established a colony for resettled African Americans. British captures went to Freetown, Sierra Leone, where commissions ruled on whether there was sufficient evidence of slave trading to condemn the ship and award prize money to the capturing ship.

Until the late 1830s, the British refrained from confiscating slave ships off West Africa unless there were actually slaves on board; that is, an empty slave ship, outfitted for the trade, flying the flag of Spain or Portugal, was not confiscated in this early period. In 1835 Spain agreed that ships outfitted for the trade under the Spanish flag could be seized even if they carried no slaves; Portugal agreed to the same principles in 1836. British naval officers immediately began stopping and seizing such suspected slave ships and taking them to Freetown, Sierra Leone, for adjudication.

By the late 1830s, some of the Spanish slave traders' ships had adopted the false use of the U.S. flag, especially when no slaves were on board, thereby hoping to avoid British inspection. As a consequence, in 1839–1841 at least five (and probably more) ships bearing the American merchant flag were stopped by the British West African Anti-Slavery Squadron and found to be in fact Spanish-owned slavers and slave-equipped ships falsely flying the U.S. flag. These five were the brigantines *Douglass* and *Iago*, searched by the HMS *Termagant*; the brig-sloop *Susan*, stopped by the HMS *Grecian*; the brigantine *Mary*, searched by the HMS *Forester*; and the brigantine *Hero*, searched by the HMS *Lynx*.[22]

The U.S. minister to England, Andrew Stevenson, protested vehemently against the British assumption of the right of search in these five cases, even though there had been no way to determine if the flag was legitimate without examining the ship papers. An exchange of diplomatic notes (often in not very diplomatic language) followed.

The right of search issue was divisive on both sides of the Atlantic, and the individuals involved contributed their personal tone to the debate. Among the most vehement defenders of the U.S. position were Andrew Stevenson, Daniel Webster, and Lewis Cass. On the British side, Lord Wellington and Lord Ashburton were conciliatory, whereas Lord Palmerston was intolerant of the U.S. position.[23]

For the British, the core question was this: How could British officers determine if a ship was fitted out for slavery or was flying the U.S. flag legitimately unless they searched the ship and inspected both it and the documents it carried? Traditional British practice accepted that the right of search existed only during war unless specifically conceded by treaty, as in the Spanish and Portuguese cases. In 1841 the United States took the position that only U.S. authorities had the right to investigate and punish false uses of the U.S. flag. The U.S. objection may seem rather technical now but simply illustrates the sensitivity over national honor that perceived insults to the flag could evoke during the nineteenth century. As a practical matter, the British held that searching suspected slavers was the best way to interdict the slave trade. Some U.S. officials and editorialists who opposed the British practice believed that Britain was exerting the right of search to interfere with legitimate American African trade, to impress naturalized U.S. citizens into the Royal Navy (no evidence of impressment in these cases exists), and to arrogantly and illegally insult U.S. national honor. Among the minority, William Lloyd Garrison's *Liberator* and other antislavery and pro-British U.S. journals argued that the British were simply being practical.[24]

For other editorialists, the issues of British arrogance and trampling on U.S. maritime rights were of far greater importance than stopping the slave trade. Some of these writers might have hoped to provoke a war with Britain during which the United States could seize portions or all of Canada; regardless of their motives, these editorialists used a rhetoric of honor similar to the rhetoric of 1812.

By 1844 Britain had treaties with Spain, Portugal, Brazil, Austria, Prussia, Russia, and some Spanish-American republics that either explicitly conceded the right of search or made arrangements for visitation to verify documents. However, Britain had no such treaty with the United States. The British acted as though they needed treaties with European and Latin American nations but could dispense with treaties when dealing with the United States. America's status as a nation among nations was being disrespected.

Decline of the Controversy

Beginning in 1842 the right of search issue rather suddenly subsided. William Henry Harrison died after thirty days in office in 1841; his successor, John Tyler, did not share Jackson's and Harrison's strong anti-British views, and neither did the members of Tyler's new administration. In fact, several of the most hostile individuals on both sides of the Atlantic were replaced with more conciliatory men, and this may have been the most striking contributor to the reduction of tensions. Under Tyler's more conciliatory leadership, the Webster-Ashburton Treaty was signed August 9, 1842. The treaty settled the Maine–New Brunswick border dispute, established reciprocity of extradition for crimes, and implemented cooperation between British and U.S. naval officers on antislavery patrol. Although the treaty did not explicitly concede the right of search in peacetime, it did take a step toward resolution of the issue.

The treaty was initially successful largely because it defined the new border between Maine and New Brunswick. Before the treaty was signed, members of the Maine state legislature had received copies of a "Red Line" map conveniently found in French archives by Daniel Webster's friend and fellow New Englander, the historian Jared Sparks. The map purported to show the British boundary claim more than conceded by Benjamin Franklin in 1783. Maine legislators who had threatened to fund a state militia to attack Canada backed down on being shown the map,[25] and the new border was included in the treaty. With the Aroostook boundary settled, those editorialists who had sought to invoke the right of search issue to win anti-British support over the land dispute no longer had a motive to make such appeals. More broadly, the resolution of the Maine border issue and the apparent agreement to cooperate in suppressing the slave trade was seen as a "vindication of national honor."[26]

For the British, there were several additional reasons for the controversy over the right of search to recede. Between 1815 and the 1860s, the British government faced major problems adjusting to a peacetime economy that was increasingly urban and industrial. Its response included the abandonment of the Navigation Laws in 1848 and nine major revisions of duties in 1860.[27] Eric Hobsbawm has pointed out, "The years from 1848 to the mid 1870s saw Britain involved in considerably more warfare than the preceding thirty or succeeding 40 years." These incidents were "either brief operations decided by technological and organisational superiority . . . or mismanaged massacres on which even the patriotism of the belligerent countries has refused to dwell with pleasure, such as the Crimean War 1854–6."[28] With such pressures, the British did not want a conflict with the United States in which Canada would be subject to invasion. Although the United States had attempted and failed to seize Canada in 1812, the disparity in population by 1840 and the ease of transporting troops by rail and road as compared with ship made an American conquest of some or all Canadian territory a more formidable threat by the later period.[29]

Tyler's administration was conciliatory in several ways. President Tyler replaced U.S. minister to Britain Andrew Stevenson. Stevenson was a hot-headed, slave-owning Democrat from Virginia who had been accused by Daniel O'Connell, the Irish leader and antislavery writer, of being a "slave-breeder." In typical fashion, Stevenson subsequently challenged O'Connell to a duel, but O'Connell did not accept the challenge and instead offered a backhanded "clarification" of his public statement.[30] Stevenson's replacement, Edward Everett, by contrast, was a pro-British Massachusetts Whig. If right of search cases came up, as a New Englander, Everett was not inclined to get involved; he had no interest in defending slavery.

On the British side, Lord Palmerston (who was rather contemptuous of U.S. claims to rights of various kinds) was out of office by 1842. Lord Wellington, who was very conciliatory to the United States, was now minister without portfolio. Alexander Baring (Lord Ashburton), sent to Washington to negotiate as a minister with plenipotentiary powers, was also more conciliatory, as was U.S. secretary of state Daniel Webster. Webster was, like Everett, a Massachusetts Whig and a leading advocate of North-South compromise. Furthermore, Webster had been an opponent of the War of 1812. Like other conservative Massachusetts Whigs, he sought to avoid war with Britain and was no defender of slavery. Thus, cooler heads prevailed on both sides of the Atlantic.

Even so, some spokesmen for a strong anti-British position on the issue continued in office. Lewis Cass served as U.S. minister to France into 1842. There he published a pamphlet that was intended to influence French deputies to reject the Quintuple Treaty, which conceded the right of search.[31] Lewis Cass was a "popular sovereignty" supporter of the rights of American slaveholders and a strong defender of American honor when it came to British insults. When the French did not include a distinct or explicit denial of the right of search in their negotiation of the Quintuple Treaty, Cass resigned his position as minister to France, claiming that the French negotiation of the treaty "compromised his position."[32] However, Cass' position prevailed, as the treaty was not ratified by France, and the French foreign minister, François Guizot, informed General Cass that France would never concede the right of search during peacetime. In further diplomatic notes in 1845, the French made it clear that they rejected any British claim to a right of search during peace.[33] That issue resurfaced in the 1890s with regard to the East African slave trade carried on under French flags on board dhows owned in Oman (discussed in chapter 5).

The British interpreted Clause 8 of the Webster-Ashburton Treaty, which established cooperation on the squadron level, as "conceding the Right of Search," but President Tyler declared emphatically that no such right was conceded. In the Senate, Thomas Hart Benton, an outspoken defender of national honor, roundly criticized Daniel Webster for giving in to Britain.[34] In response to Benton's criticism, Webster released to the press a letter he sent to Everett showing that he did not regard the treaty as conceding any "right" to search or visitation and that he thought the cooperation of naval officers on the scene would put an end to false flag uses.[35] In effect, Webster was claiming that the treaty resolved the issue, and at the same time he was publicly and officially stating to Britain that no right had been conceded. After Webster's letter was published, the right of search issue subsided. Over the following years, the U.S. press turned to other concerns—the admission of Texas to the Union, the war with Mexico, the California gold rush, the admission of California to the Union, the Compromise of 1850, and the burning issue of slavery in the federal territories acquired from Mexico in the 1846–1848 war.

From 1842 to 1860, the U.S. West African Squadron (and other U.S. naval ships and government vessels such as revenue cutters) successfully seized and condemned or destroyed more than fifty slave ships.[36] Some of them had been flying the U.S. flag as a false flag. Since U.S. naval ships were not allowed to detain any ships equipped for the trade but only those with slaves on board, often a slave transport ship so equipped would fly the U.S. flag as it approached the African coast, then, after the slaves had been loaded, the ship would be "sold" to a Spanish citizen and a Spanish flag hoisted. The ship would then sail past the U.S. squadron, which had no agreement with Spain to interdict slave ships. The Royal Navy could stop the Spanish-flagged ships, but U.S. naval officers were powerless to do so.[37] The U.S. record of slave-ship interdiction was far surpassed by the British antislavery squadron, which captured and condemned more than fifteen hundred vessels.

Few scholars have offered interpretations of the decline of the right of search issue from the mid-1840s to the late 1850s. Historian W. E. B. DuBois, writing in 1896, suggested that one of the reasons for the decline was that members of Congress would not come to the defense of U.S.-flagged slave ships because the detentions had "revealed so much American guilt that it was deemed wiser to let the matter end in talk." DuBois pointed out that in 1850 an investigation by the Fillmore administration showed that out of ten U.S.-flagged ships detained by the British, nine were proven to be slavers.[38]

Donald Canney, in his definitive work *Africa Squadron: The U.S. Navy and the Slave Trade, 1842–1861*, pointed out several factors that contributed to the decline of the issue from the mid-1840s to the late 1850s. With U.S. ships patrolling the coast, somewhat fewer slave ships resorted to the U.S. flag. There was a lull in the slave trade itself in the early 1850s. The gold rush of 1849–1855 drew many U.S.-built ships to the California route and away from the slave trade. Furthermore, legitimate U.S. traders were permitted to trade directly with Britain because of the British suspension of the Navigation Laws in 1849, also drawing ships away from the African trade.[39]

A thorough study of the debate over the British exercise of the right of search was written by Howard Hazen Wilson and published in the *Journal of International Law*. In this study, Wilson held that the Americans were correct to insist that there was no right of search in peacetime and to demand that the British inspections of potential slave ships displaying the U.S. flag not be conducted under some extension of the wartime right of search. Rather, he argued, the searches should have been justified in some other fashion.[40]

The Issue Revived and Resolved

After the issue had lain dormant for years, in 1857–1858 the British searched and detained several more ships flying the U.S. flag, and once again American tempers were raised.[41] In these two years, at least another fifteen U.S. ships were boarded or visited by British officers, off West Africa and also in the West Indies, and numerous U.S. ship masters filed complaints or reports in the United States. Again, Lewis Cass, now secretary of state under President James Buchanan, took the lead in protesting the infringement of American rights, clarifying once again that the United States had not conceded the right of search in the Webster-Ashburton Treaty. On April 10, 1858, he sent the following note to Lord Napier, the British minister in Washington: "To permit a foreign officer to board the vessel of another power to assume command of her, to call for and examine her papers, to pass judgment upon her character . . . to send her in at pleasure for trial, *cannot be submitted to by any independent nation without injury and dishonor* [italics in original]. The United States deny the right of the cruisers of any other power whatsoever, for any purpose whatsoever, to enter their vessels by force in time of peace."[42] The relative disappearance of the issue after 1843 and its sudden reappearance in 1857–1858 are striking, as is Lewis Cass' evocation of the issue of honor.

Several developments together account for the revival of the issue in the mid- and late 1850s. First, there was another change in personnel. Not only was Cass secretary of state, but in Britain, Palmerston, back in the cabinet, was more aggressive on this score than others, and he was reputed to be emboldened by the British election results of March

1857.[43] Second, slave transportation in the West Indies had recently resurged owing to increased prices for slaves in the United States and Cuba.[44] Third, news reports showed the outfitting of an estimated forty to eighty-five U.S.-built ships a year through the 1850s to engage in the trade; simply raising the number of ships involved led to more episodes.[45] Fourth, the equipping of the Royal Navy with steam-powered warships meant that they could effectively overhaul sailing vessels, particularly during the frequent calms off West Africa, within reach of their coal depot in Freetown, Sierra Leone. Fifth, the British decided to dispatch part of the antislavery squadron to the West Indies and to operate there as well as off Africa.[46] And finally, the issue may have received more attention because of exaggerated complaints by slave traders themselves, reflecting a movement in the slave states to repeal the prohibition on the Atlantic slave trade. This effort to repeal the ban on the slave trade was itself a part of the 1850s effort of slaveholders to claim that slavery was a "positive good," a development well treated in the literature surrounding the coming sectional crisis in the United States.[47]

The increased tension over the issue was grounded in a series of specific detentions on the high seas. The British boarded at least fifteen U.S.-flagged ships in 1858, and probably more.[48]After the flurry of press concern over repeated affronts to U.S. honor in the spring of 1858, the issue once again subsided, and there were only scattered further reports of British searches of ships flying (honestly or not) the U.S. flag. The settlement of the revived dispute came on June 17, 1858, during a discussion in the British Parliament of U.S. concern over the right of search. Several members of Parliament made it clear that Britain recognized no right of search in time of peace but that inspection of papers to ensure that a flag was legitimate had to be accomplished or all sorts of pirates and smugglers would use false flags, knowing they could never be boarded to determine if the flag was legitimate. Although this had always been the British position, the explicit recognition in Parliament that there was no right of search in time of peace satisfied some northern editorialists and, according to reports, also President James Buchanan and even his testy secretary of state, Lewis Cass.[49] At least, the U.S. politicians who had been outraged by the British insult could now correctly assert that the British had conceded that they had no right of search in peacetime.

The British indicated that while they accepted the U.S. position, they hoped to work out some practical means of determining the legitimacy of the flag, without giving offense. The United States rejected a British suggestion that a man-of-war's boat could approach alongside the suspected vessel and request the papers to be handed down (without boarding).[50]

Secretary Cass, in his complaint to the British, stated that like police approaching a suspect on a public street, naval officers could only visit a ship to confirm the legitimacy of the flag, and only if there was reasonable suspicion that the flag was misused.[51] Cass admitted that the legitimacy of the flag could be determined only by examining papers, but if a ship was wrongly boarded, the boarding officer and the British government would be liable for the financial damage from delay and a full diplomatic apology would be expected. This communication provided a final way through the impasse—indicating that officially the U.S. government would not object if a search revealed that a flag had been falsely employed but would expect an apology and restitution for any damages in cases of error. Although U.S. editorialists believed the British had stopped many innocent vessels, such complaints greatly diminished after the exchange of notes. For students of international law, the concession of inspection, especially when it revealed a false use of the flag, without conceding a right of search—Cass' solution—was entirely correct and fully justified, according to Wilson in his modern analysis of the issue. The fact that several British parliamentarians had agreed that Britain could not claim a right of search in peacetime also helped put the issue at rest.[52]

The Buchanan administration began to use steamers, and the U.S. Africa Squadron was much more active in 1859–1860 in apprehending ships, taking twelve vessels with more than three thousand slaves on board.[53] The number of reported English-on-American-flag incidents declined, although from time to time one would still make the news. One of the last was in 1859. The *New York Times* reported a "British Outrage" (noting the phrase with quote marks in the headline and thus mocking the concept) when the steamer HMS *Viper* overhauled, examined, evacuated, and burned the brigantine *Rufus Soule* off West Africa on October 11 or 12, 1858, later landing the crew on a beach. A ship of the U.S. West African Squadron rescued the stranded mariners. The news of the event did not reach the United States until February 1859. In that case, the master of the brigantine had tossed his papers overboard, certainly an indication they were fraudulent, according to Lieutenant Commander Austin B. Hodkinton, commander of the British steamer. No doubt the fact that the ship was obviously a slaver contributed to the mocking tone of the headline. In the growing antislavery climate of the North in 1859, it was hardly an "outrage" that the British interdicted an obvious slave ship.[54] The few continuing episodes of inspection to determine the legitimacy of registration no longer raised the specter of war, and the U.S. press turned its attention to the internal impending crisis with John Brown's raid on October 16, 1859.

The right of search controversies of the 1840s and 1850s demonstrated several underlying facts about the official and public attitudes toward the maritime flag at sea. First, the maritime code of honor was still strongly in place, despite the decreasing acceptance of the practice of dueling, especially in the Northeast. Second, the symbolic nature of the flag remained firmly entrenched in the public mind. The flag was flown proudly on exploration ships to the Arctic and Antarctic and, in 1846–1848, was planted in Chapultepec and throughout the new territories gained from Mexico. Third, at least some Americans regarded infringement of U.S. sovereignty at sea, as represented by the merchant flag, as an outrage sufficient to threaten armed conflict. Yet diplomacy prevailed. Even the strongly anti-British U.S. secretary of state, Lewis Cass, who saw the British actions as clear infringements of U.S. maritime rights, was willing, in the interests of maintaining peace, to find a diplomatic pathway through the issues. The U.S. Civil War, however, would bring further nuances to the relationship between the merchant flag and U.S. national identity.

3

Flagging-Out in the U.S. Civil War

During the U.S. Civil War, hundreds of shipowners in the North decided to operate under a foreign flag because of the depredations of Confederate cruisers, including *Sumter*, *Alabama*, *Florida*, *Shenandoah*, and *Georgia*. Together the cruisers destroyed 237 ships registered under the U.S. flag, but more than a thousand other American merchant ships switched registry to foreign flags.[1]

These transfers-out reflected a reciprocal principle to the issue of attacks on, or infringement on the rights of, U.S. ships during the prior six decades. Instead of offering protection, the U.S. flag opened ships at war to capture or seizure by a declared enemy. Although the Lincoln administration refused to recognize the Confederacy as a national entity but insisted on referring to secession as an act of rebellion, the Union military in fact applied the rules of war to Confederate soldiers, sailors, and ships. That is, while the Union government officially regarded the Confederacy as simply an area in rebellion, it treated captured soldiers and officers not as traitors but as prisoners of war. Furthermore, although the United States had not ratified the 1856 Declaration of Paris, which set up rules regarding blockade, the nation announced in 1861 that it would abide by the terms of the declaration and instituted a blockade of Southern ports, as if the Confederacy were a foreign nation. By doing so, the Union was de facto recognizing the Confederacy as a belligerent, not an area in rebellion, for maritime purposes. Confederate officers, both army and navy, also applied the rules of war. The Confederate cruisers sought out and destroyed U.S. merchant ships, while at the same time being careful to preserve the lives of crews and passengers. U.S.-flagged ships were suddenly at risk of destruction or seizure by Confederate cruisers. So hundreds of U.S. shipowners decided to reregister their ships abroad to avoid seizure by the cruisers.[2]

Portions of this chapter, reproduced here with permission, appeared in "Flagging-Out in the American Civil War," *Northern Mariner* 22, no. 1 (2012): 53–65.

In many articles and texts, the decline of the American merchant fleet in the 1860s has been attributed to the combined effect of cruiser sinking and flagging-out. Commentary during the war predicted such a result, and subsequent works repeated the claim. A scholarly treatment by George Dalzell in 1940 titled *The Flight from the Flag* made this argument.[3] In a modern and well-researched treatment, historian Chester Hearn reiterated the claim that the cruisers destroyed Union commerce.[4]

During the Civil War, Confederate cruiser commanders, including Raphael Semmes and James Waddell, would always check the documentation of commercial ships they encountered, stopped, and boarded on the high seas. If the master of the detained merchant ship flew a British or other foreign flag, but the design of the ship and the New England accents of the officers and crew suggested the ship was actually American and simply flying false colors, the Confederate officers would carefully examine the merchant ship papers, including the ship's log, and interrogate the crew to ensure that the vessel was legally entitled to fly the foreign flag. If all was in order, and the evidence proved the ship was not American, the Confederates would release the vessel; otherwise, if the ship was demonstrably Union-owned, the crew would be taken off the ship and the ship would be set afire and destroyed. In some cases, the ships were seized and operated with a prize crew. The application of the rules closely resembled the British practice of right of search a few years earlier. In time of war, the right of search, applied even to neutrals, was understood to be necessary to inspect documentation, uncover contraband, or detect false flag usage. In the light of the methods of later naval warfare, especially submarine sinking of merchant ships in World Wars I and II, it is remarkable that the Confederate cruisers destroyed so many private, commercial Union vessels without a fatality among any of their crews or passengers.

Under these circumstances, during which the ship's papers would be subject to inspection, it was not sufficient for an American merchant shipmaster to avoid destruction by hoisting a foreign flag as a *ruse de guerre*. Obtaining the protection of a foreign flag required that the ship be legally transferred through re-registry abroad and carry the proper papers to prove the transfer. In the case of British registration, the transfer had to entail an actual sale to a British subject and had to include the issuance of registry documentation, which could be accomplished through a British consul abroad.[5]

The Civil War practice set a precedent for the later use of flags of convenience. The term "flag of convenience" did not come into common usage until 1949 and 1950, when U.S. labor leaders used it to describe the transfer of U.S.-owned ships to Panama and Liberia. However, even in 1863 at least one reporter described the practice as "transfer of ships to a foreign flag for convenience and safety," anticipating by some eighty-six years the later common use of the term "convenience."[6]

Early in 1861, in the months before the war, British observers noted the likelihood that ship transfers would take place, and the Liverpool press obligingly published accounts of the proper procedures required to seek shelter under the British flag. The *Philadelphia North American and United States Gazette* quoted from the *Shipping and Mercantile Gazette* of Liverpool:

> The transfer of American shipping to the British flag can only be effected by vesting the property *pro tempore* in a British subject or subjects. To enable a ship to claim the protection of the British flag (supposing that protection to be sufficient during the impending hostilities) she must belong *bona fide* to natural born British subjects or to persons made denizens by letters of denization, or to be naturalized; and such persons must, moreover, during the whole period of their being owners, be resident within the Queen's dominions, or members of a British factory or partners in a house actually carrying on business in the United Kingdom, or within the Queen's dominions, and must have taken the oath of allegiance subsequently to the period of their being so made denizens or naturalized.[7]

The Philadelphia paper went on to editorialize:

> It would seem therefore that the transfer of a foreign ship to British owners must be by absolute sale—a fact which probably, many American owners who may contemplate registering under the British flag would not be aware of. . . . It would be humiliating to have to resort to a foreign flag for protection in our own waters, though if such a thing must be, we doubt not that England who throughout this melancholy crisis, has maintained the noblest sympathy for the Union, would render us

every assistance. She would do this as well for her own sake as for ours, for it is manifestly to her interest that her vast trade with this country should not be impeded.[8]

The editorial comment that "it would be humiliating to have to resort to a foreign flag" captured the contradiction between the business logic of such transfers and the traditional association of the maritime flag with national honor. In the code of honor, gentlemen studiously avoided humiliation.[9]

Within days of the firing on Fort Sumter, the practice of transfer began and was reported in both Britain and the United States. Some accounts noted quite openly that the transfers, entailing a sale for one dollar, were a "ruse."[10] In Britain, the practice had critics and supporters who engaged in publicly reported debates. Some shippers feared it would set a precedent harmful to Britain. In future wars, they argued, British ships might transfer out and thus diminish the British merchant marine.[11]

In Liverpool, those owners who had purchased U.S. ships defended the practice, claiming the sales were bona fide. Those British shipowners who had not engaged in the nominal purchase of U.S. vessels argued that most or all of the transfers were fraudulent and represented a corrupt usage of the British flag; they called the purported British owners "godfathers." A correspondent to the Liverpool Chamber of Commerce provided a clipping of a U.S. ship broker advertisement as evidence. In the advertisement, the ship broker offered to make transfers to the British flag, while allowing American owners to retain their interest. Others denounced that particular practice as an atypical fraud, asserting that 90 percent of the transfers had been entirely legitimate. Even so, another correspondent to the Liverpool Chamber of Commerce warned that the transfers "involved a species of evasion of the law which could only be carried out through misrepresentations on the part of those making the declarations of ownership." Of course, such "misrepresentations" would become the norm in twentieth- and twenty-first-century usages of flags of convenience by shadow corporations in Panama, in Liberia, and later, in small, mostly island countries around the world. The delicate language of 1863 suggesting "a species of evasion" reflects the underlying premise behind seeking a favorable foreign jurisdiction for legal, taxation, diplomatic, or other purposes.[12] The modern establishment of tax-shelter states like Bermuda, Andorra, and Monaco is perfectly described as "a species of evasion," and moving personal citizenship offshore reflects a similar underlying premise that an individual or business can seek the shelter of a foreign sovereignty. Thus, the British flagging of U.S. ships during the Civil War should be viewed as a clear precedent for the later practices, including those of corporations and individuals, as well as those of shipowners.

Other flags besides the British drew some Union-owned ships. When the *Alabama* cruised into the Indian Ocean, U.S. shipowners found that insurance companies refused to write policies for any U.S. ships trading in the region. As a consequence, the *New York Times* reported, American owners sought transfers to "Peru, Prussia, and Portugal."[13] With less hyperbole, the U.S. consul in Curaçao, in the Dutch West Indies, reported that the U.S. bark *Venus* reflagged under the Dutch flag to avoid capture by Confederate cruisers, and the consul expected many other U.S. ships plying between that port and New York to do the same.[14]

Statistics demonstrated, even in the war, that the cruiser attacks were diminishing the size of the U.S. fleet, not just by attacks but by the process of flagging-out. In 1863 a *Journal of Commerce* editorialist suggested that shipowners and others should petition the Navy for better protection.[15]

After having reviewed statistics, a large group of New York shipowners and insurance company officers did in fact protest to the Navy Department that the process of flagging-out was destroying the U.S. merchant marine. The group respectfully asked the Navy for greater efforts in tracking down the Confederate cruisers in order to protect the U.S. flag. In addition to shipowners, a number of others signed the petition, including bankers, New York mayor George Opdyke, and U.S. senator from New York E. D. Morgan, who was also a shipowner and chair of the Republican National Committee.[16]

Little noticed in the Union press at the time, an unknown number of ships in the South also flagged out. Indeed, that aspect of the topic has not been widely discussed in the voluminous historical literature regarding the Civil War and life in the Confederacy. In New Orleans, a cooperative marketing arrangement led by Texas shipowner Charles Morgan established a scheme in which ships would sail halfway to France under the Confederate flag and then would be reflagged and enter French ports under the French Tricolor.[17] Thereafter, they remained under the French flag. The blockade-running steamer *Tennessee*, when captured in the New Orleans harbor, "had a French flag flying."[18]

When Union forces took New Orleans, they discovered a number of French-flagged ships at the dock. Some were no doubt legitimately French-owned and -registered ships, but an unknown number may have been reflagged Confederate-owned ships. Moving up the Mississippi River, Union forces often found French flags flying on ships, which "from build and register they were not entitled to." From the scattered accounts, it was unclear how many of the schooners and other vessels flying French flags on the river had been officially transferred to French registry and how many were simply flying the flag in hopes that their vessel might escape destruction or confiscation.[19]

In Louisiana, along the Mississippi River, Union officers sometimes reported French flags even over churches and homes along the shore. Although Union officers thought such flags might have been intended for protection, it is possible that the Tricolor was adopted by some Confederates as an emblem of their rebellion, echoing the French revolutionary flag, or that local French-descended families sought to stress their continuing affiliation with their ancestral home.

The French Tricolor's resemblance when furled to the three-striped Confederate flag led to several episodes in which Union officers ordered their men to fire on a locale and then later apologized for the action upon discovering the flag was French, not Confederate. One officer noted that it was inappropriate to fly a foreign national flag over private property on land, although he admitted that had he known the flag was French, he would have refrained from attack.[20]

Many blockade-runner ships owned by Confederate entrepreneurs, mostly built in Britain, were legitimately and originally flagged in the United Kingdom and thus were not part of the flagging-out story. However, when U.S.-registered ships sought to engage in blockade-running into the Confederacy, they would sometimes adopt new flags. Even though records are fragmentary, it appears that some, perhaps numerous, Confederate ships reflagged under the British flag to avoid capture on the high seas.

However, whatever their flag, all ships would be subject to detention at the blockade line. In July 1863 a Union officer detained four "secession vessels," three of which had been reflagged through the British consul in Galveston. The ships were the three-masted *Ponchartrain* and the *Joseph Buckhart*, *Cecilia*, and *Lena*. According to another report, a Charleston shipowner reflagged his whole fleet in Britain.[21]

Lasting Effect of Civil War Transfers

In 1866 Secretary of the Treasury Hugh McCulloch clearly did not include the flagging-out of numerous ships from the South to French and British flags in his tally of 1,061 ships transferred to other registries.[22] Not only was the information from the Confederacy difficult to obtain, but in the immediate postwar period, Congress and the administration were more concerned with the decline in U.S. shipping engaged in international commerce than in the coastwise vessels that had previously dominated Southern fleets. Before the war began, the vast majority of sailing ships and steamers engaged in transatlantic trade were home-ported in the North, while the numerous shallow-draft steamers and small schooners based in Southern ports most often engaged in riverine and coastal transport. Thus, many of the transfers of Southern vessels to French or British registry probably had little impact on the postwar position of the United States in the competition for the international carrying trade.

On the other hand, even as the flagging-out of Northern commercial ships to avoid cruiser depredation flourished, some Northern observers feared that the practice would result in a lasting decline in the U.S. merchant marine, removing U.S. ships from the lucrative transatlantic trade and the commercial carrying trade between foreign ports. Even before the war ended, some maritime writers had predicted that the effect would be lasting and deleterious. One *Journal of Commerce* commentator noted, "It must be evident that the fear of depredations on our commerce, by the Confederates and privateers, has driven a large part of our foreign trade to neutral vessels."[23]

Some accused the British of perfidious conduct. After all, several of the Confederate cruisers, in particular the *Alabama*, *Rappahanock*, *Shenandoah*, and *Georgia*, had been built in British yards, and most of the merchant ships transferred out were transferred to British registry. If it had not been for U.S. representatives, including U.S. minister to Britain Charles Francis Adams, still other, more powerful British-built ships, the Laird Rams, would have entered Confederate service. These ships were planned not to be blockade-runners or high-seas cruisers but rather to provide the weaponry to break the blockade. The British maritime support of the Confederacy via provision of warships and a thriving trade with blockade-runners only heightened the Union government's resentment of the British. In this context, the permanent transfer of numerous previously U.S.-registered merchant ships could readily be viewed as part of a British scheme to dominate the world's ocean trade.

In the war's immediate aftermath, some Republican leaders saw the British construction of raiders and the transfer of American merchant ships to British flags as part of a larger British plan to destroy the U.S. fleet in the long term. President Andrew Johnson, Lincoln's successor, who was noted for making impolitic remarks, made such an accusation in his 1865 State of the Union address:

> The materials of war for the insurgent States were furnished, in a great measure, from the workshops of Great Britain, and British ships, manned by British subjects and prepared for receiving British armaments, sallied from the ports of Great Britain to make war on American commerce under the shelter of a commission from the insurgent States. These ships, having once escaped from British ports, ever afterwards entered them in every part of the world to refit, and so to renew their depredations. The consequences of this conduct were most disastrous to the States then in rebellion, increasing their desolation and misery by the prolongation of our civil contest. It had, moreover, the effect, to a great extent, to drive the American flag from the sea, and to transfer much of our shipping and our commerce to the very power whose subjects had created the necessity for such a change.[24]

In the immediate postwar period, the matter of interpretation soon surfaced. On the one hand, some political leaders, like Andrew Johnson, continued to blame the American merchant fleet's decline on both the British outfitting of cruisers and the practice of flagging-out. Under the law, a U.S. ship that had transferred to another flag was ineligible to reregister under the U.S. flag. When individual shipowners sought permission to reflag their vessels in the United States by special act of Congress, opponents voted down such measures. For example, in 1869, when the owners of the *Agra* sought congressional dispensation, Senator James Warren Nye of Nevada strongly opposed the measure. The *Boston Daily Advertiser*, however, thought such re-registry would be a good idea, even though transfer-out had "a bad taste." After all, the editorialist opined, the problem grew out of the Union's failure to protect its shipping.[25]

Together with the restriction on reflagging in the United States once registered abroad, only U.S.-built ships could register in the United States. Both of these legal factors—the prohibition on return from foreign registry and the requirement of U.S. construction—no doubt contributed to U.S. shipping's inability to recover after the Civil War.[26] The raw statistics suggested that something had happened in the 1860s to reverse the growth of the U.S. merchant marine and send it into decline, as shown in Table 1.

TABLE 1. RISE AND DECLINE OF THE AMERICAN MERCHANT FLEET IN FOREIGN TRADE, 1830–90

Year	Gross registered tonnage (millions)	Deadweight tonnage (millions)
1830	1.42	.80
1840	2.19	1.14
1850	3.54	2.16
1860	5.35	3.56
1870	4.24	2.17
1880	4.07	1.97
1890	4.42	1.39

Source: Data from *Nautical Gazette*, January 22, 1921, 107.
Note: Figures rounded to the nearest 10,000 tons.

Even as this point was being made at the end of the war, some analysts doubted whether this diminution could account for the long-term decline of U.S. shipping that set in during the postwar period and continued into the 1880s. Close analysis of the statistics in 1866 by Secretary of the Treasury McCulloch suggested that the loss to flagging-out during the war was about 800,000 tons. Destruction and transfer of commercial vessels to the government for use as warships and transports accounted for the additional decline. Some small fraction of the decline was also due to "natural causes," such as the retirement or scrapping of older vessels, loss to the hazards of the sea, and other events unrelated to the war. However, the overall immediate decline was certainly a consequence of both the losses to the Confederate raiders and the transfers to foreign flags. U.S. shipping in foreign trade had been reduced from about 5.35 million gross tons to about 4.24 million gross tons.[27]

However, from the 1870s into the 1880s, the size of the U.S. fleet continued to decline. The failure to rebound and to again challenge

Britain for a major share of oceangoing trade was a separate issue, although many writers of the period blurred together the issue of war-time decline and postwar failure to recover. The popular and iconoclastic *Frank Leslie's Illustrated Newspaper* joined the discussion, suggesting that the long-term decline was due to the failure of U.S. shipbuilders to remain competitive in the cost of building new ships. The paper estimated that it cost $100 per ton to build a ship in the United States but only $40 per ton to build one in Canada. Furthermore, the paper argued, the decline in U.S. shipping was already evident several years before the war began.[28] Similar arguments were presented at the same time by others, such as San Francisco's *Daily Evening Bulletin*.[29] This position, based on a clearheaded analysis of costs, however, was not shared by others, who continued to blame the decline of U.S. shipping on British support of Confederate cruisers and the British flagging of U.S.-owned ships during the war.

The British finally agreed in 1872, after a process of arbitration, to pay $15.5 million in claims for the losses inflicted on U.S. shipping by British-built cruisers in the *Alabama* claims case. As that case was being debated, the scale of the British damage to U.S. shipping was magnified by linking the flagging-out to the cruisers' activities, an argument first made during the war and reiterated after by both Secretary of State William Seward and President Andrew Johnson. If the long-term decline of U.S. shipping could be attributed, even in part, to the practice of flagging-out, that enhanced the legitimacy of the claims against Britain and escalated the scale of the British damage. The arbitration decision, however, rejected such claims for "indirect losses."[30]

Thus, in 1865–1872 the claim that a long-term decline had been inflicted by British practices and by flagging-out in particular was seen as a propaganda position of the United States as it sought to press the *Alabama* claims for a larger amount. Senator Charles Sumner argued that Britain's liability for prolonging the war and destroying U.S. maritime commerce cost the United States $2.125 billion. The neutral arbiters from Switzerland, Brazil, and Italy, however, limited the compensation to the demonstrated loss of particular ships and cargoes.

Certainly, the decline of U.S. shipping in sheer tonnage persisted for decades after the war. More significant, U.S. shipping continued to decline as a percentage of the world trade; in absolute numbers, the tonnage of the British fleet began to far outdistance the tonnage of the U.S. fleet. One recent study shows the percentage of U.S. tonnage in world trade declining from about 10 percent in 1870 to just over 3 percent in 1890. Over the same period, the British proportion of tonnage in world trade climbed from 44 percent to more than 47 percent.[31]

The United States did not compete in transoceanic steam lines for decades, and the cost of construction of both wooden ships and iron or steel ships in the United States remained high. As previously noted, because the United States still employed sailing vessels for transatlantic trade, U.S. steamships were not present to engage in port-to-port European trade in competition with steam-powered European vessels, all on shorter-leg voyages that allowed recoaling. U.S. schooners and larger sailing vessels continued in transoceanic trade even into World War I. So the development of steam-powered ships, at first most efficient and economical in coastal and riverine trades but not economic on transoceanic voyages, was an additional factor in preventing a resurgence of U.S. shipping in these years.

With the westward expansion of the United States, labor costs stayed high, attracting an increasing flow of immigrants from Europe and Asia and driving up the cost of ship construction. Import duties on foreign-manufactured machinery and rigging that had been passed in Congress in a vain attempt to protect those U.S. industries also increased the cost of U.S.-built ships, a classic case of unintended consequences.

For shipbuilders and other advocates of the U.S. merchant marine, the issue of flagging-out receded into the past, and suggestions for reform of the present conditions required an analysis of those conditions. However, for writers who reflected on the Civil War itself, on the depredations of the cruisers, and for those who retained suspicions of British motives, the flagging-out during the war years still loomed large as an issue. An 1870 congressional report supported the claim that British wartime acts were responsible for the decline.[32]

Pro-British critics saw that position as strictly political, and some Republicans falsely blamed the British without addressing the current policy problems. "It is so much easier," wrote an editorialist for the avowedly pro-British *Albion*, "to bring a railing accusation against a nation which may for the time be unpopular than to study the causes of any social or commercial phenomenon, that we are not surprised to find both the Congressional Committee on Navigation and President Grant adopting this facile method of explaining the recent decline in American ship-building, and charging the conduct of Great Britain during the late

Civil War with many of the results now witnessed." The article went on to blame the protective tariff for the decline in U.S. shipbuilding.[33]

Because the two different analyses arose in different forums, two interpretations of the significance of the flagging-out process flourished, each with a different focus, a different point of departure, and a different audience. One might put the viewpoints in two camps: those with a presentist outlook on economic conditions and those with a historical focus. Those concerned with present policy and considering different methods of addressing the decline of shipping saw the flagging-out issue as dead, no longer pertinent in the 1870s, 1880s, and 1890s. Rather, they saw the problem as deriving from U.S. shipbuilders' inability to compete with Canadian and British labor costs. Editorialists, essayists, and economists hoping to influence Congress remained focused on contemporary aspects of the shipping decline, especially the issue of shipbuilding costs. However, the other group, seeking to unite avid anti-British voters with essentially historical arguments, continued to perceive the decline of U.S. shipping as the result of intentional British action. Both groups saw the decline as reflecting poorly on the status and honor of the nation.

Through the later 1870s and 1880s, proponents of various reforms to address the decline of U.S. shipping continued to focus on causes that went far beyond the Civil War flagging-out issue. The rise of steam propulsion and iron hulls that prevented U.S. competition in the European markets figured prominently in an analysis presented in the *Banker's Magazine and Statistical Register*.[34] A long analysis presented in the *International Review* in 1879 also attributed the decline of the U.S. fleet to the rise of steamers and the lack of U.S. focus on steamship construction.[35]

Book-length treatises arguing for improvements in protective tariffs or subsidies for the shipbuilding and merchant marine industries continued to be published through the era. These included books by Hamilton Hill (1869), Henry Hall (1878), Charles Marshall (1878), and Henry Peabody (1901).[36] Many journalists, essayists, and editorialists contributed further observations on the lack of government support for the maritime industries.[37]

As policy makers and policy writers sought to address the persistent decline in U.S. shipping even after the *Alabama* claims case was settled, the more immediate question was what to do about present conditions in the late nineteenth century. Clearly, the U.S. fleet continued to atrophy for reasons that went far beyond the dip in registry figures during the war. Rehashing of complaints about British aid to the Confederacy, the cruiser attacks, and the question of flag transfer no longer seemed pertinent to the economic problems and technological developments of the 1870s and 1880s, and gradually, more contemporary concerns with cost and government policy eclipsed the wartime issues.

The proliferation of articles, books, editorials, and reports agonizing over the decline of U.S. shipping in the post–Civil War period is significant in itself. The tone of many articles, even those examining economic and technological factors, showed that the reduction in number and proportion of U.S. shipping continued to be an emotionally charged issue. The statistics, the authors all claimed, reflected "decline," "depression," and "disease," and measures to address the concerns were seen as "remedies." Rather than simply addressing the decline of U.S. shipping as a dry economic development, the various writers all saw the dip as reflecting poorly on the status, honor, and international standing of the United States.

Because fewer American merchant ships were flying the U.S. flag, the presence of the U.S. flag overseas had diminished. To the extent that the nation's power was reflected by its merchant fleet, the decline was a matter of national honor and international respect. At the same time, the remaining but diminished fleet of merchant ships plying the waters of the Caribbean, the Pacific, and beyond continued to encounter challenges at sea. Even as the nation entered the age of enterprise— with railroad expansion; development of agriculture, mining, and timber resources; and a burgeoning industrial base—the issue of the respect shown for the merchant flag abroad remained very much alive.

Persistence of the Maritime Honor Code

The issue of national honor, evoked by editorialists and other writers critical of the practice of flagging-out to Britain during the Civil War, continued to shape debates over shipping in the years following the Civil War. During and after the war, naval officers in both the Confederate and Union navies conducted themselves in accord with the maritime *code duello* and honor code that had characterized the conduct of, and accounts of, ship-on-ship encounters during the War of 1812.

When the Confederate raider *Alabama* was finally destroyed by the U.S. naval ship *Kearsage* off Cherbourg, France, on June 11, 1864, Capt.

Raphael Semmes of the *Alabama* specifically complained that Capt. John Winslow of the *Kearsage* had violated the maritime *code duello* by protecting his ship with concealed chain armor. Research shows that Semmes himself had been lured into the battle by French officers who appealed to his sense of honor. Another indication of the persistence of the *code duello* was the immediate labeling of the battle between the *Monitor* and the *Virginia* (formerly, *Merrimack*), by the popular press, as the "duel of the ironclads."[38]

The issues of personal and national honor in shaping thinking about the international encounters of ships carrying the U.S. flag in the post–Civil War decades is further explored in the following chapter.

4

The Flag Insulted, 1865–95

Honor, the U.S. flag, the national identity, and U.S. ships at sea had become firmly linked together in the republic's early years. In the years following the Civil War, the cult of the flag developed even more strongly. This increased intensity of reverence for the U.S. flag was reflected in the sensitivities surrounding insults to the merchant flag at sea.

The cult of the flag in the late nineteenth century in the United States had roots in the firing on Fort Sumter, as Marc Leepson has shown in his cultural history *Flag: An American Biography*.[1] Following the fort's surrender, Maj. Robert Anderson removed the fort's flag and returned to the North with it. The Sumter flag was taken from city to city and auctioned; the funds from the auction went to the Sanitary Commission, the agency responsible for treating and caring for Union wounded soldiers. Suddenly, the U.S. flag appeared everywhere—in schools, in front of churches, in front of stores, and in pins worn on hats, lapels, and ladies' bosoms. Leepson quotes Edward Everett, statesman and president of Harvard University, as saying, "Why is it that the flag of the country, always honored, always beloved, is now at once worshipped I may say, with passionate homage of this whole people? Why does it float, as never before, not merely from arsenal and masthead, but from tower and steeple, from edifices, the temples of science, the private dwellings, in magnificent display and miniature presentment? The answer? 'Fort Sumter.'"[2] The *New Orleans Picayune* dubbed this phenomenon, replicated in the South with the Confederate battle flag, "flagmania."[3]

As Everett noted, the flag had always flown "from masthead" on American merchant ships. When ships were challenged or attacked at sea, those challenges were considered insults to be avenged under the

Portions of this chapter, reprinted here with permission, appeared in "The Flag Insulted: U.S. Merchant Marine Incidents, 1865–1895," *Northern Mariner* 20, no. 3 (2010): 267–82.

maritime code of honor. Precisely the same language was used in reaction to the firing on Sumter. In 1871 Adm. George Henry Preble wrote of Sumter, "The heart of the nation swelled to avenge the insult cast by traitors on its glorious flag. . . . One cry was raised, drowning all other voices—'War! War to restore the Union! War to avenge the flag!'"[4]

In the three decades following the Civil War, U.S. shipowners and other entrepreneurs extended the reach and influence of the United States abroad. In effect, the flag followed the dollar, as noted by historians of the era. With the tone and rhetoric of the maritime *code duello* and the flagmania of the Civil War era, journalists, politicians, and essayists roused public responses to episodes in which the flag was "insulted" or "affronted" abroad. The writers' motives varied: Some sought an expanded Navy or U.S. territorial or colonial expansion, whereas others simply wanted to discredit the incumbent administration with allusions to its failure to adequately respond to challenges in international or foreign waters. Still others, as the *Times Picayune* observed, might simply have caught flagmania, as if it were a contagious condition.

According to modern sociologists and group psychologists, as the cult of the flag emerged, the flag itself came to serve as a totem to be revered, honored, treated ceremoniously, and when affronted, avenged with blood sacrifice. Sociologists have compared this post–Civil War cult of the flag with similar phenomena in preindustrial societies, including Native Americans, Polynesians, Australian aborigines, and isolated groups in Africa. The episodes discussed here provide evidence of the cult in the United States; of course, in the same era, intense nationalism with a militaristic tone was prevalent in Europe as well, particularly in Germany, France, and Britain. The phenomenon was hardly unique to the United States.[5]

Historians, in contrast to the sociologists, consider the exaggerated reverence for the flag in the late nineteenth century simply a symptom of an emotional nationalism, or jingoism. Evidence of this new nationalism immediately after the firing on Fort Sumter, and continuing for at least the next three decades, was found in the ritualized singing, in schools and at public events, of three competing national anthems: "My Country 'Tis of Thee" (or "America") by Samuel Francis Smith, first performed in 1832; "The Star-Spangled Banner" by Francis Scott Key, first performed in 1814; and "Hail Columbia," first sung in 1789. "The Star-Spangled Banner," with its focus on the flag itself, did not become the official national anthem until 1931, although the Navy had endorsed it in 1889. The Pledge of Allegiance, first drafted in 1892 by Francis Bellamy, was widely introduced in public schools in celebration of Columbus Day and in honor of the 1892 Chicago Columbian Exhibition, which celebrated the four hundredth anniversary of Christopher Columbus' landing in the New World.[6]

This intensified nationality contributed to the mood that sparked the brief war with Spain in 1898 and a series of military engagements abroad in the first decades of the twentieth century, under Theodore Roosevelt, William Howard Taft, and Woodrow Wilson. Some historians treat the blue-water imperialism of those decades as an extension of the Frederick Jackson Turner thesis: the fishers, sealers, overseas planters, and China traders were much like the frontiersmen of earlier decades, pushing U.S. interests into lawless parts of the world.[7] Enlisting support for that expansion required a strengthened Navy and a heightened sensitivity to the treatment of U.S. interests abroad.

A close examination of the numerous, but mostly minor, incidents in which merchant ships were challenged or attacked in foreign waters in 1865–1895 suggests the degree to which the episodes evoked deep emotional responses, often far out of proportion to the events' actual severity. More than sixty episodes involving American merchant ships were reported either in the *New York Times* or in *Foreign Relations of the United States* in the period.[8] Journalists and others continued to describe such events using the rhetoric of honor, and with much the same fervor as in the period following the *Chesapeake* affair of 1807. A few of the encounters were violent, resulting in the death of U.S. seamen and the destruction or impounding of their ships. In other cases, U.S. ships were hailed with a warning shot, stopped, searched, and then released. In still other incidents, U.S. ships were commandeered by armed forces for use in a local conflict. The episodes varied in causes and consequences, but through the decades, officials and journalists described such events not simply as matters of maritime legality or the vicissitudes of trading in waters troubled by war or revolution but as insults to the flag or outrages.

The dozens of episodes and the reactions to them demonstrate several important facts about the position of American merchant shipping both on the international scene and in domestic affairs. The treatment of American merchant ships, fishing boats, and whalers in the period suggested widespread international disdain for the U.S. claim that it was a major world power. In the United States, navalists, attempting to win support for naval expansion, often employed strident language, the same rhetoric of honor that had been invoked regarding the Algerian, French, and British disrespect for the flag in the nation's first decades. More widely, the sensitivity to affronts to the flag was symptomatic of the undercurrent of jingoism in the era, or as sociologists would say, the emergence of the cult of the flag. The dozens of incidents, and the language of outraged honor, thus reflected both the actual inability of the United States to protect its merchant shipping abroad and the navalists' domestic agitation for a strengthened Navy to meet that need and to represent the nation as a world power.

Considering that the more than sixty incidents were minor and often involved ships with ambiguous legal standing, the contemporary concern of diplomats, journalists, and politicians is striking. Episodes involving just a few seamen and officers, often engaged in activities that others would consider smuggling, violation of port-state rules or fishing ground regulation, support of criminal or insurgent forces, or outright filibustering, usually received very generous treatment in the forum of American public opinion. The motives and purposes of the owners, officers, and crews were not as significant as the ship's flag itself. Even when a ship was on legitimate business, the fact that it ventured into waters troubled by war and revolution would suggest to a modern observer that the owners and officers, aware of the conditions, themselves put the flag at risk. Blame for damage should, to some extent, fall on the owners and officers in addition to the foreigners who offered the insult. But such arguments were almost never raised at the time.

One underlying reason that the episodes received such striking public attention was that they served the navalists' purposes. Mark Shulman has noted publishers' efforts to popularize the Navy and urge its expansion through vivid descriptions of expeditions launched to rescue stranded Arctic explorers and of the technical wonders of new ships and through appeals in youth magazines and books. As Shulman observed, "Newspapers, especially the 'Yellow Press' . . . found that the Navy commanded a large audience, especially if discussed in sensationalist language."[9] The incidents involving U.S.-flagged merchant ships, whatever their cause, provided rich material for the navalists. Shulman concluded, "Navalism spread across America between 1882 and 1893, not merely as the cause of a few scheming imperialists, but as a national movement growing up with the burgeoning nation. . . . By 1893, America was dressing, humming, and voting to the tune of the Navy."[10]

The reasons for the defense and sometimes outright glorification of some merchant seamen who were in fact scoundrels with dubious backgrounds reveal aspects of the American self-image of the era as well as the navalists' propaganda efforts. That self-image, when it came to maritime affairs, seemed characterized by an awareness of inadequacy similar to that of 1812. The press and official reaction reflected the Navy's genuine inability to do much about infringement on U.S. maritime rights abroad.

Furthermore, in the post–Civil War decades, U.S. statesmen and the broader public were quite familiar with the maritime heritage and history of the United States, far more so than are twenty-first-century Americans. Heroes such as John Paul Jones, Oliver Hazard Perry, and David Farragut were known by every schoolboy. The battles of the War of 1812 were refought in print, with close examination of each ship-on-ship encounter to demonstrate American bravery in defense of national honor. The glory days of U.S. clipper ships that had briefly carried easterners to California ports in the 1850s and a vast sail-powered merchant marine of the antebellum period were also well remembered. As that era receded into the past, it acquired a mystique and romance fueled by and reflected in the literary works of Herman Melville and Richard Henry Dana, in the works of less well-remembered British and American writers, in historiography, and in thousands of pieces of nautical art.[11] For a generation of citizens developing a nationalistic self-identity, in which a somewhat mythologized history played a central part, the decline of American merchant shipping and the relative impotence of the U.S. Navy following the Civil War were sources of dismay. As noted by Shulman, navalists sounded two "cultural chords" in compensation, a "popular diad" of "gigantism and heroism."[12]

However, while Congress considered remedies for the problem of a decline in merchant shipping, much of the voting public in the nation's interior had little sympathy for spending federal funds on businesses located in a few coastal cities. The slowly declining political power of the seaboard states, already notable by 1860, continued. By 1890 there were twenty-two seacoast states and twenty-two inland states, resulting in a tie in the Senate in representation of coastal or seaport interests.[13]

Any effort to rally support for commercial maritime interests was further hampered by the conflicting economic interests of shipowners and shipbuilding firms, shipowners and commercial importers and exporters, and shipowners and merchant mariners. Shipowners bought from shipbuilding firms and ship chandlers, sold their services to importers and exporters, and hired merchant mariners. In every case, the economic interests of these different groups were diametrically opposed, or "countervailing," as some economists would call them.[14] Even though all would benefit from a large and strong merchant fleet, special-interest politics made it hard to build one.

The merchant crews themselves were notoriously exploited, and the growing labor movement began to take note of their conditions. A few representatives of coastal states fought for shipping interests, most notably William P. Frye of Maine, who served in Congress from 1871 to 1881 and in the Senate from 1881 to 1911.[15] However, the conflicting interests of the constituents of Frye and other representatives from coastal states and the isolationism of the interior states stood in the way of effective congressional action on the issue of the declining merchant marine.

Because of these conflicts, there was no successful federal aid to the maritime industries until a postal subsidy was passed in 1891, and that aid had only minor results. Meanwhile, despite the efforts of several secretaries of the Navy to maintain and rebuild the U.S. Navy, Congress provided very little funding for new naval shipbuilding from 1865 to 1881, leading to the obsolescence of much of the fleet of warships. New ships included the *Nantucket*, laid down in 1873 and launched in 1876.[16] The Navy was also able to redirect some funding from authorized repair of four monitors to the construction of one new ship, the *Puritan*, launched in 1882.[17] The first four ships of the new steel Navy were built beginning in 1884, a herald of the stronger Navy that would follow in later years. Even so, the new ships represented a small and trouble-racked "squadron of evolution," hardly worthy of the name "New Navy" so often attached to them in the press and in history.

Alfred Thayer Mahan produced his thought-provoking *The Influence of Sea Power on History* in 1890, marrying naval and maritime arguments in an effort to reinvigorate the tie of maritime interests to national identity. The numerous studies of the causes of the merchant fleet decline (noted in chapter 3) reflected Mahan's argument for commercial sea power, and all expressed concern that the American merchant fleet had become inadequate to match the nation's position in the world.

With a declining merchant marine and a small and ineffective Navy, but with a maritime heritage of vigorous defense of the U.S. flag abroad, the sensitivity of some policy makers and maritime advocates to even minor encounters at sea as "insults," "affronts," or "outrages" is quite understandable. Even if the flag itself had not become an object of veneration, a concern with the protection of U.S. business interests around the world would be justified. Just as the nation was experiencing a domestic triumphalism with the opening of the West, the completion of the transcontinental railroad, and a booming expansion of industry, agriculture, and immigration, the U.S. flag overseas seemed to constantly run into indignities, and its protection abroad could be correctly depicted as shamefully inadequate.

The U.S. Navy was in reality rather powerless to protect U.S. ships in these incidents. The few times that U.S. naval forces engaged in punitive expeditions to exact retribution for offenses against U.S. commercial ships contrasted rather strongly with the repeated and aggressive assertion of power by the navies of Great Britain, France, Germany, Japan, Italy, and Chile during the same years. Although some U.S. presidents and secretaries of state dabbled with gunboat diplomacy through the three decades, they had very little naval force to work with. As a consequence, the rulers of and insurgent or criminal groups in weak nations, such as Korea, and even those racked by constant internal conflict, such as Haiti, the Dominican Republic, and Colombia, had little compunction in detaining U.S. vessels when it suited their purposes. Some even confiscated American merchant ships temporarily or permanently to use in local military conflicts. Despite the outcries of rage from certain politicians and newspapers, most but not all of the affronts went unavenged. The details of some of the episodes illustrate the dilemmas.

General Sherman Incident

The misadventures of the officers and crew of the trading ship *General Sherman* in 1866 at first drew little attention. The incident happened in Korea (known at the time as "Corea"), a remote, semi-independent kingdom under the nominal control of China. Like Japan, Korea had remained isolated from foreign influences by choice, and information about the 1866 incident in the "Hermit Kingdom" was sparse since all of the *General Sherman*'s crew members were slaughtered. U.S. officials did not even know what actions by the ship's crew had led to the incident. Whether the crew had violated Korean laws and customs, how the crew members met their demise, and whether British and French interests were also at stake—all remained unclear for several years. Some reports indicated that the U.S. ship had been engaged in a harebrained scheme to raid the Korean capital and kidnap the preserved and revered body of a former ruler.

In 1866–1867 the American press and public were consumed with the controversies of the Andrew Johnson administration and Reconstruction in the South. The death of a few adventurers who had apparently, in violation of local law, proceeded upriver in a remote and unknown region could hardly compete for public attention with possible presidential impeachment and Southern legislators' attempts to restore the power and position of the planter aristocracy. Nevertheless, the *General Sherman* episode merited investigation, and after several years, the Navy launched a punitive expedition against Korea in 1871. Emulating Matthew Perry's earlier opening of Japan, Adm. Robert W. Shufeldt eventually obtained a treaty opening the Hermit Kingdom to American trade in 1883. The treaty made no reference to the *General Sherman* affair, and no compensation was made for the loss of the ship.[18]

Incidents in the Reconstruction Era

During the Civil War, the United States was in no position to assert the Monroe Doctrine, which prohibited the extension of European-controlled territory or new colonies in the Western Hemisphere. Partly as a consequence of the U.S. preoccupation with its internal crisis, the Spanish engaged in a naval war with Chile and Peru over claims to off-shore islands, reestablished control in 1861–1865 over the eastern half of Hispaniola (now the Dominican Republic), and tightened their authoritarian rule over Cuba and Puerto Rico. Meanwhile, France, establishing Archduke Maximillian as ruler of Mexico, turned that independent republic temporarily into an informal French protectorate on the border of the United States. The State Department received complaints regarding the treatment of U.S. ships by France, and more especially by Spain, through 1866 and 1867. Despite his aspirations to extend U.S. hegemony through the Caribbean and North America, Secretary of State William Seward was in no position to do more than investigate the complaints and present objections to the imperial powers. Of course, he did succeed in acquiring Alaska from Russia by purchase in 1867, but his efforts to purchase the Virgin Islands from Denmark and Santo Domingo from Spain were defeated in the Senate.

In the three years following the Civil War, more than ten maritime incidents in Latin America and the Pacific attracted diplomatic concern.[19]

The press noted that minor powers, such as Ecuador and Korea, showed little compunction in interfering with U.S.-flagged merchant ships and their officers and crews. Among the ships involved in incidents reported as "insults" or "outrages" in 1865 were the *Apure* off Venezuela, the *Antioquia* off Colombia, and the *Washington* off Ecuador. The *William L. Richardson* was seized by the French off Mexico for carrying blasting powder in 1866. Shipowners alleged that Spain unfairly imposed quarantine on the *I. F. Chapman* in 1866 and on the *Canandagua* and *Young Turk* in 1867. Other minor incidents involved American merchant ships and Spanish authorities in the West Indies.

In 1867 shipwrecked survivors from the *Rover* were murdered on the island of Formosa (now Taiwan). Formosa was under the loose administration of China, and the inhabitants of the island treated all foreigners, especially westerners, with suspicion and hostility. The details of the incident and the language used by State Department officials, naval officers, and the press reflected not only the racial chauvinism of the era but also the emerging set of values that would coalesce into a belligerent form of nationalism. The Formosans who had attacked the sailors from the *Rover* were characterized as "savages," and the U.S. Navy conducted a forceful retaliatory expedition in August 1867 to avenge the insult to the U.S. flag on the ship.[20]

In 1869 Ulysses S. Grant took office as president, replacing Andrew Johnson. After some floundering around, Grant settled on Hamilton Fish as secretary of state and George Robeson as secretary of the Navy. Fish, unlike some of Grant's other appointees, was a competent statesman, and his management of foreign affairs was regarded then and by historians as a bright spot in an often corrupt and incompetent administration. As incidents involving U.S. ships plying the nearby waters of the Caribbean and West Indies came to his attention, Fish worked to resolve the difficulties and to avoid international conflict. Nevertheless, his handling of several incidents indicated some bedrock principles regarding the protection of U.S. interests abroad and affronts to the U.S. flag in foreign waters.[21]

Headlines in the *New York Times*, which often were relatively restrained, reflected a rhetoric of honor flavored by the rising temper of jingoism. In an article titled "The Florida Case: Affidavit of Her Officers Touching the Spanish Outrage," the *Times* reported that the "outrage" began in international waters off the Virgin Islands in the Caribbean. There a Spanish man-of-war, the *Vasco Núñez de Balboa*, fired first a blank shot and then a warning shell in the wake of the steamer

Florida. When the *Florida* stopped, a Spanish officer boarded the vessel, examined the ship's papers, asked permission to go below, confirmed that the ship was in ballast (carrying no cargo), and left. The *Florida*'s engine was inoperative, and she proceeded in sail and was again stopped by another Spanish warship near the Bahamas. Again she was examined by a Spanish officer, who first asked permission. It appears the Spanish suspected the *Florida* of filibuster operations.

The *Times* argued that it was an outrage that the ship, flying a U.S. flag, was stopped in international waters and searched, regardless of whether the Spanish had asked permission or not. The Spanish might have thought the exercise of the right of search outside Spanish territorial waters during the period of insurrectionary activities in Cuba was justified. But technically, since the Spanish had not declared the Cuban insurrection a state of war and had not imposed any blockades, no Spanish right of search recognized internationally existed during this period, that is, 1868–1897. The *Florida*, the *Hornet*, and another small U.S.-flagged ship, the *Fannie*, were all either known or suspected to be involved in shipping arms or filibusters to Cuba, but editorialists considered any interference with them on the high seas to be "outrageous."[22]

Virginius Incident

The *Virginius* incident of 1873 was the most serious of all the more than sixty maritime episodes characterized in the press as "outrages" or "insults" between 1865 and 1898. As historian Richard Bradford noted, the affair "boiled up suddenly. After some weeks of apparent indecision it subsided. And yet in long retrospect . . . it appears to have been one of the more remarkable, although perhaps least remarked, events of American history in the post–Civil War era."[23]

The *Virginius* was a former Confederate steamer nominally purchased from the U.S. government in August 1870 by John F. Patterson, a U.S. citizen. A group of filibusters set on invading Cuba and joining the rebellion against Spain operated the steamer. At the time the ship was purchased from the government, the law required that a U.S. citizen be registered as shipowner and that one or more sureties should give bond before the ship was registered. Patterson, working with Marshall Roberts and J. K. Roberts, owners of a shipping line, purchased the ship for Cubans Manuel Quesada and José Maria Mora, who represented the revolutionary junta and intended to use the ship to aid the Cuban insurrection.[24] John F. Patterson executed the bond on September 26, 1870, but failed to file the necessary sureties. J. K. Roberts told the ship's officers that the true owner was the junta, represented by Quesada and Mora.[25]

From 1870 to 1872 the *Virginius* operated in the Caribbean, helping Venezuelan rebels under Máximo Gómez and securing promises of assistance from them for the Cubans seeking independence from Spain. During this period, the ship sailed under the colors of the Cuban rebels, and in fact, it did not possess a U.S. flag to fly until April 1872. Through mid- and late 1872, some U.S. consuls and naval officers in the Caribbean and Central America believed that the ship was indeed properly registered in the United States and entitled to U.S. protection. At one point, the Navy's gunboat *Kansas* even prevented a Spanish naval ship from attacking the *Virginius* by escorting her off Aspinwall, Colombia (Colón, in present-day Panama).[26]

On October 30, 1873, with the engine and pumps failing and the ship in danger of sinking, the *Virginius* was captured off Cuba by the Spanish ship *Tornado*. The crew believed that the U.S. flag would provide protection.[27] It was a vain hope. Spanish troops boarded the ship, tore down the flag, and seized the crew. When the *Virginius* was brought into harbor, local Cuban authorities tried and executed by firing squad the shipmaster, thirty-six crew members, and sixteen rebels over the next few days. One hundred and two of those taken from the ship remained in prison, including thirteen Americans.[28]

The outrage, as reported in the news, had two shocking aspects: the seizure of a ship flying the U.S. flag by a Spanish naval vessel and the hasty execution of filibusters and crew members, including some U.S. citizens. While the hasty executions were appalling, the affront to the U.S. flag held the potential to raise the episode to an issue of national honor and possibly lead to war. A great deal, therefore, hinged on the issue of the ship's right to fly the U.S. flag.

The reaction in the United States to the *Virginius* affair depended on the political orientation of the observer. Conservatives (such as former northern Whigs, now found largely among the Republicans) tended to oppose any effort to aid the Cuban revolution or use the episode as an excuse to annex Cuba. Importantly, Hamilton Fish belonged to this group of former northern Whigs. However, sentiment in favor of the annexation of Cuba and against Spain was strong among southern

Democrats and among some northern Democrats who had joined the Union Party during the Civil War. Two of the southern Democrats were Congressman Horace Maynard of Tennessee, who wanted "to see the outrage avenged," and Jacob Thornburgh, another Tennessean member of Congress, who advocated purchase of Cuba from Spain and who thought Congress would "favor a vigorous policy and protect the national honor."[29]

Bradford wrote of the press reaction, "Already the sensationalism that would mark the yellow press of the 1890s was present in James Gordon Bennett's *Herald* and Charles A. Dana's *New York Sun*." Some papers supported intervention, but others, such as the *New York Times* and *New York Tribune*, were "more restrained." However, "men everywhere now bestirred themselves over what they regarded as an insult to their country and joined those few individuals who hitherto had worked for intervention out of sympathy for the Cuban cause or to enrich themselves."[30]

The term "outrage" was applied to both the insult to the flag and the executions. For the more conservative press, including the *New York Times*, the outrage was the execution. For the more radical, and overtly anti-Spanish, pro-Cuban, or "annexationist" papers, including the *New York Herald*, the attack on the U.S. flag was itself a major outrage and was presented in inflammatory terms that smacked of the rhetoric used following the *Chesapeake* affair and during the right of search controversies of the 1840s and 1850s.

However, several strategic considerations militated against the *Virginius* incident leading to war with Spain in 1873. First, the U.S. Army was greatly reduced from its Civil War strength and had difficulty even maintaining enough force to control routes through Native American territory in the West. The U.S. Army was no match for the experienced Spanish army, which had been engaged in suppressing two separate rebellions in Spain. Second, the U.S. Navy was in no shape to engage the Spanish fleet.[31]

Although some newspapers sought to stir war sentiment, Hamilton Fish was well aware of the nation's military unpreparedness, and he innately preferred a negotiated peace to war as long as national honor could be preserved. Fish found his diplomatic pathway through the imbroglio by emphasizing that the ship did not have proper registration in the United States, that its use of the flag was improper, and that, therefore, U.S. national honor was not at stake. Bradford described the evolution of Fish's thinking:

> Fish's reaction passed through three phases. When he first received word of what had taken place, he regarded it as another incident in a long line of outrages by Spanish against Cubans. Belief that the *Virginius* was an American vessel seized either in British territorial waters or on the high seas caused him to view the capture in terms of an affront to national honor. Then came news of massacre of the crew. He had recoiled from the barbarity of this action and nearly swung to intervention. . . . Finally, based on his conversation with Parne and reports from Hall and Polo, his doubt about the right of the *Virginius* to fly the American flag reasserted itself.[32]

The Spanish ambassador, José Polo de Barnabé, met with Fish, and together they worked out the pathway through the crisis that would avoid the necessity of going to war over a question of national honor. "Would it be possible," Polo asked, "for the United States to make inquiry into the status of the *Virginius* if the ship and men were given up, and [if the result of the investigation required it] punish those individuals who had violated laws of the United States, reserving until further information, the Spanish salute to the flag?"[33] Fish responded that if the ship did not have the right to fly the flag, a Spanish salute to the U.S. flag on restitution of the ship would not be required.[34]

After an investigation into the ship registry had found that Patterson was not the true owner and that no sureties had been paid, Fish sent Polo a note about "the satisfaction of the United States that the *Virginius* was not entitled to carry the flag."[35] After a peaceful surrender (with no salute to the flag), the *Virginius* sank as it was towed back to the United States by U.S. naval ship *Ossippee* on December 26, 1873.

Secretary Fish, the "respectable" press, and conservatives in Congress were relieved that the nation had escaped war. Fish wrote to his son, "There *is* a national evil worse than war, but unless the national honor, or the national existence, require war . . . then the nation should do all that it can to avoid the terrible evil. That is what I have endeavored to do."[36] Note that even though Fish was quite relieved to have avoided war, he clearly thought it would be worse to accept national dishonor in the form of a foreign naval attack on an American merchant ship legitimately flying the U.S. flag. Although war had been averted, nearly all the ingredients for a genuine affront to national honor by a major European state that could lead to war had been present.

Minor Incidents during the Grant Administration

Through the two Grant administrations that lasted from March 1869 until March 1877, American merchant ships continued to run afoul of local authorities as they traded through the Caribbean and into the South Pacific. A typical news story, this one describing an incident involving the *Tybee* in 1876, called it "another outrage upon the American flag."[37]

An odd assortment of legitimate traders, gunrunners, adventurers, whalers, and others believed they had cause to complain of the lack of respect shown the U.S. flag on their ships. Incidents involving U.S. ships continued around the world, with an insult to the flag on the *James Bliss* in 1872, the misuse of the U.S. flag on the *Generalissimo Conquistador* (ex. *Sherman*) in 1873, and the outrages involving the *Virginius*, *Tybee*, and *Florida*.

Incidents in 1877–91

During the administrations of Rutherford Hayes (1877–1881) and James Garfield (1881), Secretary of State William Evarts and his volatile successor, James G. Blaine, confronted a highly risky situation that could easily have involved the nation in a war with Chile. The fact that the Chilean navy was far more powerful and well-equipped and had better morale and training than the U.S. Navy made such a prospect daunting. Chile fought a three-year war with neighboring Peru and Bolivia, effectively defeating both and gaining control over the disputed provinces of Tacna and Arica, rich in nitrate deposits. The War of the Pacific engaged no direct interests of the United States, and official U.S. policy was one of strict neutrality. Neutrality, by U.S. standards, meant that American traders had the right to continue trade with both sides, subject to interdiction by any effective blockade. As the war continued, the danger that U.S. neutrality might lead to conflict (as it had in 1812) remained imminent. Several maritime incidents tested the limits and boundaries of the policy, and Blaine's stumbling efforts to intervene, plus the missteps of U.S. ministers to both Peru and Chile, created a set of foreign policy debacles.[38] Among the maritime incidents were an

1877 "outrage" involving the *Rising Sun*, a whaler detained off Cuba, and the detention of the *Eva*, a guano schooner, in 1878. Incidents in 1879 and 1880 in ships off Chile and Peru and four ships boarded and detained off Cuba also aroused the press. The year 1881 saw an "outrage" in Japanese waters, when the U.S.-flagged schooner *Diana* was fired on.[39]

The War of the Pacific between Chile and Peru and the numerous maritime incidents in the fifteen years following the Civil War bolstered arguments for rebuilding the U.S. Navy. A congressional report of 1881 advocated the building of new naval ships that would take advantage of the new technologies of steam and steel. Meanwhile, naval officers and their civilian advocates founded institutions, such as the U.S. Naval Institute, that provided information and publicity for the New Navy movement. Alfred Thayer Mahan's *The Influence of Sea Power on History* is only the best remembered of many publications urging, directly or indirectly, a strengthened navy. That work, and other navalists' speeches and writings, asserted that a strong nation needed a strong navy to protect its international commerce. Insults and affronts to the maritime flag abroad proved the need for a larger naval budget. Compounded with the obvious inferiority of the U.S. Navy even to the navy of Chile, the arguments carried weight, and the "squadron of evolution" was launched in 1884–1889.[40]

During the administrations of Grover Cleveland (1885–1889, 1893–1897) and Benjamin Harrison (1889–1893), the efforts of U.S. settlers, planters, and merchants to strengthen their position in Samoa, Hawaii, Cuba, and Central America often resulted in further affronts to the flag, many of which occurred on merchant ships. Through the 1880s, minor episodes on the high seas around the world continued to receive bellicose reaction in segments of the American press.

When insurrection movements in Panama sought independence from Colombia, it was almost inevitable that U.S.-owned and U.S.-flagged ships would become involved in the conflict. Ships seized or impounded in that conflict in 1885 included the *Colon*, the *Gamecock*, the *Albano*, the *Ambrose Light*, the *City of Mexico*, and several river steamers of the United Magdalena Steam Navigation Company.[41]

Fishing cases in Canadian, Russian, and Portuguese waters, together with continuing cases in Latin America, led to at least ten more maritime affronts to the flag (see table 2). A tone of indignation ran through news reports and shipowners' complaints about the various incidents.

TABLE 2. AMERICAN SHIP INCIDENTS, 1886–95		
Year	Ship(s)	Incident
1886	*Adams*	Canada, fish and bait case
1886	*Marion Grimes*	Canada, fishing issue
1887	*Merida*	Nicaragua
1887	*William S. Moore*	Nicaragua, forcible search
1888	*Haitian Republic*	Haiti, confiscation
1888	*Mary Frazer*	Portugal, fishing episode
1889	*Julian* and *Willie*	Colombia, both vessels seized
1891	*James H. Lewis*	Russia, seizure for fishing
1894	*Henry Crosby*	Dominican Republic
1894	*Loring Haskell*	Canada, fired on
1895	*Allianca*	Cuba, fired on by Spanish naval ship

Sources: Data from *New York Times*, May 21, 1886, December 25, 1886, February 7, 1889, December 24, 1889, December 29, 1891, June 10, 1894, March 1895; *FRUS* 1887, 1888, 1894.

The language of the news reports and magazine articles closely echoed the rhetoric of honor that had surrounded the maritime flag earlier in the nineteenth century. The *Scientific American*, which followed naval and maritime affairs, noted in an 1890 editorial that the weakness of both the U.S. merchant and naval fleets was a cause for concern. Even this sedate publication echoed the language of humiliation and insult: "We have allowed other nations to monopolize the principal routes and vehicles of ocean commerce and at the same time overshadow us with superior naval establishments. . . . It is hoped that we shall never have occasion to resort to hostilities with any nation. Still it is humiliating to feel that, in case of insult or attack, we have little or no means of naval offense or defense."[42]

Naval Expansion

Although Congress was ineffective in developing a policy to support merchant shipping expansion, the agitation of navalists did succeed by 1890.

The Navy's perceived inadequacy was addressed through the vigorous building and commissioning of warships in the 1890s. Although Secretary of the Navy Benjamin Tracy recommended building some two hundred ships in that year, the Navy Act of 1890 authorized building three battleships: the *Indiana*, *Massachusetts*, and *Oregon*. These three, designated BB1, BB2, and BB3, were all launched in 1893, followed by the *Iowa* (BB4) in 1896. As Mark Shulman noted, the dual appeal of "gigantism and heroism" had resulted in naval expansion, but "the cost of emphasizing the big may have been an inflexibility of construction that led to five decades of over-reliance on battleships."[43] However, the rapid expansion of naval forces in the early 1890s no doubt contributed to an even more bellicose press and public reaction to the *Allianca* affair of 1895.

Allianca Incident

The *Allianca* incident raised, in a serious fashion, the specter of war with Spain in 1895. According to Marcus Wilkerson, in the classic study *Public Opinion and the Spanish-American War*, the Spanish were "aggravated by the manner in which the news reports were handled by a part of the American press."[44] The *Allianca*, a U.S.-flagged merchant steamship, was headed to New York from Colón. Six miles off Cape Maysi in Cuba, the Spanish gunboat *Conde de Venadito* signaled the *Allianca* to stop, but when the *Allianca* ignored the signal and continued on its course, the Spanish ship fired several shots at the steamer. The Spanish claimed that the *Allianca* was off-loading munitions to fishing vessels to be taken ashore for use by the rebels, but the master of the *Allianca* denied the charges.[45]

The incident involved several aspects of international law. The United States claimed that even where the Windward Passage came within the territorial water limits of Spain, it was a natural route for ships sailing between ports of the United States and the Caribbean Sea, and it was wrong to forcibly stop ships passing there since no formal state of war existed between Spain and the Cuban rebels. Spain had not recognized the rebellion in Cuba as a state of war even during the Ten Years War of 1868–1878 or the Guerra Chiquita (Little War) of 1878 and, thus, had no claim to a right of search.

Secretary of the Navy William Whitney called the *Allianca* affair "a willful insult," a remark broadly reprinted in the press.[46] The press response to the 1895 episode reflected the growing clamor over Spanish suppression of the rebel movement in Cuba in 1894–1898. However, although the Pulitzer and Hearst newspapers actively competed in exaggerating Spanish atrocities in the suppression of the rebels, the reaction to the *Allianca* incident was not confined to the yellow press. It extended to more conservative papers across the country. The *New York Sun* commented, "The American flag has been insulted and the lives and property of American citizens have been placed in jeopardy." The *Chicago Tribune* pointed out that the *Allianca* incident was not the first of "outrages of this sort [that] have been committed by the hot-blooded Spaniards, but it is high time they should be stopped." The *Milwaukee Sentinel* noted that the "tendency to support Cuba's desire for independence is incalculably strengthened in this country by the late indignity offered our flag." The *San Francisco Chronicle* called the episode "a manifest outrage on the American flag." The *New York Times* even joined in condemning the "insult."[47] An unsigned editorial in the *New York Observer and Chronicle* stated that the firing on the *Allianca* "must be regarded as a gratuitous insult to the American flag."[48] The *New York Herald* had a long history of supporting filibuster activity, and one of its readers wrote to the editor, "Old Glory must not be so outrageously insulted like this by any foreign nation." If Spain did not apologize, then the U.S. fleet should "go to Spain and let her smell a little of our Yankee smokeless powder."[49]

Press reaction to other episodes involving U.S. ships stopped or confiscated by Spanish authorities off Cuba became part of the growing response to the Cuban situation. Another major incident was the seizure of the U.S.-flagged schooner *Competitor* in May 1896; the crew was subsequently sentenced to be shot. The *New York Herald* and the *San Francisco Chronicle* reminded readers of the parallels to the *Virginius* affair, twenty years before.[50] After formal complaints and a barrage of press reports, the queen regent of Spain finally pardoned the *Competitor*'s crew in November 1897.[51] Meanwhile, the press kept the activities of U.S.-flagged filibuster ships before the public through 1897, reporting rumors of their departures and voyages even when they did not encounter Spanish naval vessels.[52]

Resentment of Spain's authority over Cuba and Cuban waters brought the nation to the verge of war, and of course, the destruction of the *Maine* in 1898 in Havana Harbor did in fact precipitate the Spanish-American War later that year. The new battleships played a crucial role in that war. The *Indiana* departed Key West, led the North Atlantic Squadron to bombard San Juan, Puerto Rico, and moved on to Santiago, Cuba. The *Massachusetts*, *Indiana*, *Oregon*, and *Iowa* all participated in the blockade and battle of Santiago Bay.

Three Decades of Merchant Ship Incidents

The rich documentation of dozens of incidents involving American merchant ships between 1865 and 1895 suggests several patterns in the responses to the episodes. Whether a "willful insult" or a "gratuitous insult," an "affront to the flag" or simply an "outrage," the episodes invariably evoked official and journalistic language echoing the vocabulary of the honor code that had prevailed in the 1812 era. The State Department and the Navy Department were under pressure from segments of the press and the public to provide diplomatic or naval support to shipowners and crews in foreign waters. Such support was generally demanded by the more jingoistic press even when it seemed possible or even certain that the U.S.-flagged ship was violating local or international law.

With an average of more than two nationally newsworthy maritime episodes a year during the thirty-year period, the plight of unprotected American merchant mariners overseas was constantly before the public. The attacks were common knowledge in the era. Most of the events faded from public memory after a few years. Even so, the frequency of such episodes proved useful to navalists and others in reminding the American public of the nation's low international standing and its lack of a competent navy to defend its interests.

The rhetoric and flag-waving aside, it was true that U.S. ships, engaged in fishing off Canada, in the Pacific, or off the Azores and in trade in Latin America, were exposed to claims of foreign jurisdiction, some of which were legitimate and others entirely unjustified. The *Virginius* had been engaged by rebels against the Spanish government; fortunately, because the ship did not have the right to fly the U.S. flag, Secretary Hamilton Fish was able to resolve the episode through diplomacy. The *Virginius* incident and others like it revealed that the U.S. Navy indeed lacked bases or sufficient ships to do much about any infringements on legitimate trade or fishing and other challenges to the American merchant flag at sea until the mid-1890s. However, by 1895, emboldened by a stronger Navy and caught up in the jingoism of the era, large sectors of the public were ready, if not eager, for war. When the *Maine* exploded in Havana Harbor in 1898, the press, much of the public, and Congress enthusiastically supported another war in defense of the flag's honor.

5

The New American Empire and the Muscat Dhows Decision

In the mid-nineteenth century, the competition among the imperial powers to establish colonies proceeded for the most part with only minor participation of the United States. In particular, the United States showed no ambitions to establish colonies or outposts in Africa or Asia, concentrating instead on the Western Hemisphere and a few outposts in the Pacific. Liberia, which had been established by the American Colonization Society on the west coast of Africa, became a self-governing republic in 1848 and was never administered by the U.S. government.[1]

In 1856 the Guano Act provided for the extension of U.S. territorial status to isolated and largely unpopulated small islands in the Pacific and Caribbean. The act provided that a U.S. citizen had to lay claim to the uninhabited "island, rock or key"; file the latitude and longitude of the island with the State Department; and provide evidence that the spot was previously uninhabited. Then, "at the discretion of the President," the United States could claim the land. The United States also took a long-term lease on Corn Island, off Nicaragua, but never exerted administrative control there. Some of the islands acquired under the act later became well-known, but for the most part, they remained lonely, uninhabited outposts: Howland, Jarvis, and Midway Islands in the Pacific and Navassa off Haiti.[2]

Following the acquisition of Alaska on October 11, 1867, and Secretary of State William Seward's failed attempts to acquire Santo Domingo and the Virgin Islands until 1898, U.S. blue-water territorial imperialism in the nineteenth century included only the scattered "Guano islands." The Navy had established coaling stations in Pearl Harbor, Hawaii, in 1860 and in Pago Pago, Samoa, in 1878. U.S. planters, traders, and

Portions of this chapter, reprinted with permission, appeared in "The Muscat Dhows Case in Historical Perspective," *Northern Mariner* 24, no. 1/2 (2014): 23–40.

missionaries took the lead in a revolt against the royal house in Hawaii and established the Republic of Hawaii in 1894.

American Empire and U.S. Shipping

In the ultimate maritime outrage of the century, the *Maine*, one of the nation's new battleships, blew up in Havana Harbor on February 15, 1898. Although the explosion was probably an accident, the failure of Spanish authorities to apologize or to facilitate an investigation into the causes of the explosion fueled public and congressional anger at Spain, already high over treatment of the Cubans and U.S. merchant ships. Still simmering after the *Allianca* affair of 1895, the United States declared war on Spain on April 25, 1898, and after a few months, Spain surrendered, on August 12. A treaty followed on December 10, 1898. Congress approved the annexation of Hawaii during the war, on July 7, 1898.

The broader pattern of concern with national honor and respect for the U.S. flag in this period suggests that much of the expansionism of 1890–1914 came not from economic pressure but rather from expectations of international respect and, ultimately, from the need to avenge the affront to the flag represented by the destruction of the *Maine*. Suddenly, the United States acquired an empire. Spain ceded Puerto Rico as compensation for expense and sold the Philippine Islands to the United States. The island of Guam was surrendered to the United States by its Spanish commander. In addition, Cuba gained its independence from Spain and granted the United States a permanent coaling station and harbor at Guantanamo Bay, as well as the right to intervene militarily in Cuba to preserve democracy, domestic order, and independence. That power to intervene in Cuba was announced in the Platt Amendment to the 1901 joint resolution of Congress that authorized the removal of troops from Cuba. Incorporated into the Cuban constitution in 1903, the Platt Amendment remained the document that governed Cuban-American relations until 1934, when a treaty was signed between Cuba and America more or less normalizing relations. Under the Platt Amendment, the United States intervened with troops in Cuba in 1901, 1906–1909, and 1912.[3]

In 1898 the new U.S. battleship *Oregon* had to steam around Cape Horn in a perilous and much publicized sixty-six-day voyage to participate in the Battle of Santiago, Cuba. That voyage made clear the immense distance naval vessels had to travel between the two coasts of the United States. Building a transisthmian canal became a matter of national security. The province of Panama declared its independence from Colombia on November 3, 1903. It was widely known that the United States supported Panama's secession from Colombia because the Colombian legislature was refusing to grant canal rights to the United States. The local rebels of Panama, however, had promised to be much more amenable to the U.S. plans. Panama immediately signed a treaty with the United States ceding a swath of territory to U.S. control for the construction of the Panama Canal. The independent nation of Panama also immediately signed agreements with the United States that made it a virtual protectorate of the larger country. That is, the United States, by treaty, acquired the right to send military forces to Panama to ensure the democratic regime and the peace and order of the nation, terms very similar to the Platt Amendment rules that applied to Cuba.

Work on the canal began in 1904 and was completed in 1914. The canal zone, some 553 square miles in a belt across the nation, while still part of Panama, was granted to the United States to govern as if it were sovereign there. The United States administered the zone as a territory until 1979, with U.S. troops, civil government officials, and twenty-one military bases, some retained until 1999.

Thus, in 1898–1903 the United States joined England, France, and Germany as an imperial power. Overseas territories rather suddenly included not only Alaska and Samoa but also Hawaii, Puerto Rico, Guam, and the Philippines. In addition, the United States had administrative control of the Panama Canal Zone and a protectorate relationship with the nominally sovereign countries of Cuba and Panama. The age of blue-water imperialism had arrived for the United States.

In the first decade of the twentieth century, the U.S. Navy grew to meet the need. Twenty-one battleships, twenty destroyers, and nineteen cruisers were launched between 1901 and 1910.[4] During Theodore Roosevelt's administration, two squadrons of U.S. Navy battleships, totaling sixteen ships and called the Great White Fleet, made a round-the-world tour from December 1907 to February 1909.[5] One result of the tour was the realization of how dependent the U.S. Navy would be on the goodwill of other nations in allowing refueling. With Caribbean and Central American stations in Cuba, Puerto Rico, and Panama and Pacific bases in Pearl Harbor (Hawaii), Pago Pago (Samoa), and Subic Bay (Philippines), the U.S. Navy could steam independently to the Far East and around the Caribbean and the Gulf of Mexico. But there was a severe lack of U.S. holdings and coaling stations in the Indian Ocean, Africa, and South America. Fueling concerns added even more urgency to the opening of the transisthmian canal, already under construction when the Great White Fleet steamed around South America.

The United States had become a major imperial power with these new commitments in the Caribbean and Pacific and an offshore establishment that required a strong blue-water Navy. Theodore Roosevelt, a great admirer of Mahan, of course played a central role in both the acquisition of the "empire" and the linked growth of the Navy. Less heralded in this period of imperialism was the related growth of the U.S. merchant marine.

The American Merchant Flag and the Empire

The United States had leased foreign-flagged ships to provide the cargo shipping necessary in the Spanish-American War, demonstrating the need for a domestic fleet of merchant ships as a matter of national security. Cabotage rules restricted shipping between U.S. ports to U.S.-flagged ships; with the acquisition of the new overseas territories, cabotage restricted shipping to U.S.-flagged vessels that plied from the continental United States to Hawaii, Alaska, Puerto Rico, Guam, the Philippines, and other U.S.-controlled islands. The little empire quite suddenly led to the expansion of existing U.S.-flagged shipping.

The U.S.-flag-registered merchant marine expanded about 50 percent in one decade. The fleet went from 5.164 million gross registered tons in 1900 to 7.508 million gross registered tons in 1910. Most of the fleet was engaged in coastal, lake, riverine, or U.S. port to U.S. port territorial trades, rather than in international shipping in competition with Britain.[6] Nevertheless, the acquisition of an overseas empire led to a much larger merchant fleet under the U.S. flag, to the growth of existing shipping companies, and to the establishment of new ones with new ships. Along with numerous ocean-crossing schooners, the new steel, coal-powered freighters, bearing the U.S. flag, represented a partial rebirth of the U.S. merchant marine.

Mahan reasoned that historically, great nations built great merchant marines that required great navies to protect them, which in turn required far-flung naval bases and coaling stations. The supposed sequence was as follows: first, merchant fleets would require a naval fleet; then, a naval fleet would require coaling stations; and finally, colonies would be needed to back up and protect the coaling stations. Theodore Roosevelt helped the United States acquire all three but, perhaps ironically, in a different order. That is, the United States started building its Navy first, then acquired some colonies, and only then built a larger Navy and, last, a larger merchant marine.

In the years between the Spanish-American War and the outbreak of World War I in Europe (1898–1914), more than a dozen new U.S.-flagged shipping lines formed, most of them to service the new outlying territories of the nation. The expanding merchant fleet also included proprietary lines devoted to carrying the products of a single company in the steel, petroleum, and banana trades. Table 3 lists the major shipping companies formed in the period. Smaller, one- and two-ship companies and those with schooner fleets are not included. Most of these companies survived for decades.

TABLE 3. U.S. SHIPPING LINES, 1899–1914		
Shipping line	**Year founded**	**Area of trade**
American-Hawaiian	1899	Hawaii
Barber & Co	1902	West Africa
Bull Line	1902	Puerto Rico
Eastern Steamship Co.	1901	New York and New England
Gulf Oil	1901/1907	International (proprietary, petroleum)
Insular Line	1904	Puerto Rico
Isthmian Line	1910/1914	International (proprietary, steel, U.S. flagged 1914)
Matson Navigation	1882/1901	Hawaii
Moore and McCormack	1913	Latin America, esp. Brazil
Munson Line	1899	Cuba, Gulf Coast
North Pacific Steam-ship Co.	1902/1904	Northwest and Alaska
Peninsular and Occidental	1900	Florida, Cuba
Robert Dollar Line	1903	Pacific Northwest
United Fruit	1899	Central America (proprietary, bananas)

Source: Data from Joe McMillan, "House Flags of U.S. Shipping Companies," Flags of the World, August 19, 2001, http://flagspot.net/flags/us~hf.html, accessed June 2, 2014. *Note:* Two founding years, for example, 1902/1904, indicate the year of the company's origin and the year of its later reorganization.

In addition to the new lines, existing shipping companies expanded. Among the expanding lines were the Savannah Line, founded in 1873, with routes from the East Coast to the Caribbean, and the Ward Line, established in 1840–1841, with passenger and freight routes to Cuba. The Ward Line's official name was the New York and Cuba Mail Steamship Company, and it was finally liquidated in 1954.[7] The Morgan Line, established in 1881, also expanded in 1901, acquiring the British-founded White Star Line. Standard Oil, founded in 1870, by John D. Rockefeller, had a proprietary petroleum shipping line, with overseas subsidiaries and sixty tankers by 1900. The Standard Oil fleet thrived with some twenty-five new tankers by the end of 1914, most built and added to the fleet in 1910–1914.[8] Similarly, the Texas Company (Texaco), founded in 1897, expanded after a gusher came in at Spindletop, Texas, in 1901 and added a small fleet of oil tankers in the pre–World War I years, reaching a total of three by 1916. The intricate tale of the various freight and passenger lines that flourished in the early twentieth century is beyond the scope of this work.[9]

The Spanish-American War and the new American empire had thus led to a rebirth of the U.S. merchant marine, and in the first decade of the twentieth century, new and expanded fleets of U.S.-flagged merchant ships regularly plied routes across the Atlantic and Pacific as well as the waters of Latin America. Ironically, in this same period, a dispute over the issuance of the French merchant ship flag to slave traders in the Indian Ocean laid the legal groundwork for the system of flags of convenience that would eventually nearly sweep the American merchant flag from the seas.

The Muscat Dhows Dispute and Decision

Like several other aspects of the history of the flagging of merchant ships, crucial events and developments that led to the practice now known generally as open registry, or the use of flags of convenience, have been largely ignored in the historical literature of maritime affairs. However, prominently cited in legal literature as a justification for the practice is an international law case, the Muscat dhows decision of the Hague Permanent Court of Arbitration (PCA), issued in 1905.[10]

The Muscat dhows controversy at the time seemed remote from American affairs and was barely mentioned in the U.S. press and in historical literature. Later regarded by maritime law and international law experts as a crucial decision justifying the practice of registry of ships under foreign flags, the episode and its outcome are key to understanding the legal framework under which the U.S. merchant ship flag went into decline in the mid- and late twentieth century.

The Muscat dhows decision came out of the well-known nineteenth-century struggle between the European powers, particularly Britain and France, for colonial domination in the equatorial regions of the world. Through the late nineteenth century, France established a string of colonies around the world. One of the richest of these colonies, French Indochina, included the provinces of Tonkin, Annam, Cochin China, and Cambodia; Laos was added in 1893. To reach Indochina from Europe, French coal-fired warships proceeded through the Mediterranean Sea and Suez Canal; across the Indian Ocean, from a French-controlled coaling station at Obokh at the mouth of the Red Sea, to India; and then southward to Singapore, the South China Sea, and finally, Indochina. By 1890 the French had established two enclaves in India (Pondicherry and Karaikal) on the eastern side of that subcontinent. However, the trip from Obokh to Pondicherry or Karaikal was an intimidating 2,900 nautical miles or more, nearing the outer limit of the cruising range of the French warships of the 1890s.[11] Among possible spots for a coaling station between the two French outposts at Obokh and Pondicherry was the self-governed Arab sultanate of Oman (also known then by the name of its capital, Muscat) on the northeastern tip of the Arabian Peninsula. Oman was almost exactly 1,500 nautical miles from both Obokh and Karaikal, conveniently halfway between the two established French enclaves. However, by the 1860s the British had established an informal protectorate in Oman and regarded that ill-defined and loosely governed Arab territory as within their sphere of influence. Thus, Muscat was a focal point in the Anglo-French rivalry of the 1880s and 1890s.

In 1888 Faisal ibn Turki took power as sultan in Muscat. Although the Atlantic slave trade was almost entirely eliminated by the late 1860s, the Indian Ocean slave trade continued to flourish throughout the last decades of the nineteenth century and into the twentieth century. Slave traders operating from Zanzibar and nearby regions exported slaves by Arab dhows to the Arabian Peninsula, the small states of the Persian Gulf, and India. The British, who had combined their effort to suppress the Atlantic slave trade with territorial aggrandizement in Africa, led the effort to suppress the eastern or Indian Ocean slave trade. In Britain, many writers were convinced that the French willingly consented to the use of the French flag to shelter the slave trade carried on by Oman.[12] Published accounts of the efforts to suppress the slave trade in the Indian Ocean pointed to the operators of Omani dhows, especially those in the town of Sür, sailing under the French maritime flag, as key villains in the trade.[13]

In 1889 eleven European powers, plus Turkey and the Congo Free State (a personal colony of the king of Belgium), met at a conference in Brussels, Belgium, to discuss the suppression of the slave trade. The result was an international convention, signed by the thirteen countries on July 2, 1890, known as the General Act of the Brussels Conference Relative to the African Slave Trade.[14] Britain acceded to the convention in 1892. The convention recognized an established practice of granting the use of the European powers' maritime flags to local boats and ships owned by non-European peoples, regarded as "protégés" of the Europeans, in the Indian Ocean region.[15]

However, the Brussels Act declared that European powers could only extend a right of flag use to protégés that had been under the protection of the European power before 1863.[16] The intent of the agreement, from the British perspective, was to eliminate the grant of protection of the flag. In particular, the British knew that much of the slave trade from East Africa to the Persian Gulf was conducted on native dhows. However, if the owners of the dhows claimed French protégé status and flew the French flag, the British could not exercise the right of search on their ships. French-flagged dhows would be immune from the British antislavery patrols because, in their rejection of the 1845 Quintuple Treaty and in subsequent correspondence with Britain, the French explicitly denied the right of search during peacetime.[17] Furthermore, the dubious status of French protégé could readily extend to other forms of allegiance, legal relationship, or affinity with the French in the midst of the British-claimed sphere of influence.

Soon after the Brussels Act was signed by both Britain and France, British resident agents and officers on board the Royal Navy antislavery patrols in the Indian Ocean reported numerous slaves being shipped to the Persian Gulf on dhows that flew the French flag. The reports suggested that the numbers of such slaves per year carried on dhows from Sür, under the French flag, may have been as many as a thousand.[18] Considering the size of the dhow fleet and the carrying capacity of the dhows, the estimate was probably low. One report showed specifically that the twenty-three dhows from Sür that claimed the French flag could easily transport many more than a thousand slaves per year as the voyage took only a few weeks. The larger dhows could carry as many as two hundred slaves.

In 1895 the Omani sultan formally offered to the French the right to establish a coaling station at a port near the city of Muscat, at the small settlement of Bandar Jissah.[19] British complaints about French-flag protection of the slave trade were to some extent motivated by evidence of growing French influence in the British informal protectorate in Oman. Despite the imperial motives for the British complaints, there was plenty of concrete evidence that the British claims about dhow slavers were based in fact.[20] The French informed the British that they did not intend to stop the practice of issuing French flags to Omani dhows.

In 1899 the British terminated their cash subsidy to the sultan of Oman on the grounds that the sultan had improperly agreed to let the French establish the coaling station.[21] This issue was resolved on February 27, 1899, when the French ambassador to Oman said the French were willing to accept a "coal depot" next to the existing British wharf on the same terms that the British had for their wharf. That is, the coaling depot would be granted "on sufferance," and not with the special extraterritorial rights that would accompany a full-fledged coaling station or enclave like the larger outpost at Pondicherry in India or the Obokh enclave on the Horn of Africa.[22]

Reports indicated that the only reason the sultan backed down from his original agreement to grant a full-fledged coaling station to the French was that he was forced to board the British flagship in the Muscat harbor under threat that his palace would be bombarded if he did not do so. It was a classic threat of gunboat diplomacy in the era.[23] The sultan, realizing his independence had been virtually destroyed and that he was, in effect, subject to British control, resigned. However, Lord Curzon, the viceroy of India, whom Faisal notified of his resignation, rejected the resignation and told the sultan he must continue in office. The sultan simply retired from active administration, leaving affairs of state to two deputies.

After the coaling station problem had been resolved, the British and French began moving toward a resolution of their competing colonial claims around the world, yet this minor dispute in a backwater of the Indian Ocean threatened to remain an issue. The two powers resolved many of their other small border claims and issues in the Entente Cordiale signed in April 1904 but kept confidential many of the terms of the agreement. Historians consider this Anglo-French agreement a response to the rising threat of German expansion and one source of the World War I Franco-British alliance.[24]

The Dhows Dispute Resolved at The Hague

Not all the French-English colonial conflicts were settled in the confidential terms of the Entente Cordiale. As part of the resolution of colonial difficulties, the British and French agreed, on October 13, 1904, to submit the Muscat dhows dispute to the newly formed PCA.[25]

Established in 1899, the court was not really a court. Instead, it was a formal setting in which nations could submit disputes for arbitration by independent jurists. The nations in dispute would select independent international law experts to sit on a panel to hear the arguments and issue a decision, and they agreed in advance to abide by the panel's decision. If the nations could not agree on a full panel, each would appoint one (nominally neutral) arbiter from a permanent group of international jurists, and those arbiters, in turn, would select a third to serve as umpire. If the two could not decide on a third party, the representatives of the signatory governments to the Hague Convention resident in The Hague would assign an outside party (the king of Italy, for example) to nominate the third arbiter. In effect, the Hague court simply provided a formal setting for a long-standing practice of agreeing to arbitration of international disputes.[26] It varied from earlier arbitration agreements because there was a "permanent" body of highly respected jurists, monarchs, and legal authorities in third countries from which to select panels.

The dhow case was only the fourth case brought to the PCA. The first of the prior cases involved funds related to the California missions, disputed between Mexico and the United States. The second case dealt with a blockade of Venezuela, and the third case with the Japanese house tax as applied to foreign residents. The Muscat dhows case was the first test of the permanent court to resolve an issue between major European powers. Not surprisingly, the small quasi-independent state of Oman was not a party to the conventions establishing the PCA, nor was any representative of the sultan invited to provide testimony, evidence, or documentation.

While the court was assembling, on March 25, 1905, the French submitted to the sultan the names of the dhow owners to whom they had issued permission to fly the French flag. Acting under British orders, the sultan replied that he could not recognize that the French flag had any jurisdiction over his subjects whatsoever, and he referred the whole matter to the upcoming Hague tribunal decision.[27]

At The Hague, three arbiters reviewed the documents submitted by the British and French. Their sessions ran July 25–August 2, 1905. The three arbiters for the dhows case were H. Lammasch, a member of the Austrian parliament who had served on the Venezuelan case; Melville Fuller, chief justice of the U.S. Supreme Court; and Alexander de Savornin Lohman, a respected Dutch aristocrat and professor of law who had served on the California missions case. Fuller had been chosen by Britain and de Savornin Lohman by France, and since they had not agreed on a third member, the king of Italy had selected Lammasch.[28] The story behind the selection of the third member, or umpire, provides some insights into Melville Fuller's position and the outcome of the arbitration.

The Arbiters and the Award

Although Fuller and the other members of the arbitration panel sought to present themselves as impartial, there are several indications that Fuller took his selection by the British to mean that to an extent he would represent their interests. Evidence for his tendency to see his role as advocate for the British side rather than as an entirely impartial arbiter surfaced even before the hearings began.

In February 1905, by way of transatlantic cables, Fuller and de Savornin Lohman sought to select the umpire. The British quietly suggested to Fuller that it would be important to name as umpire an arbiter who spoke English. The British ambassador to the United States, H. M. Durand, wrote to Fuller on February 17, 1905: "It would look better if the selection of an Umpire could be made by the Arbitrators by the date specified. Either Count [Constantine] Nigra or Monsieur [Gregor] Gram, on account of their knowledge of English would be very well fitted to act, but His Majesty's Government add that they will be content with any choice that may recommend itself to you."[29] Count Constantine Nigra was the former ambassador of Italy to Great Britain; Gregor Gram was the former prime minister of Norway (1889–1891, 1893–1898) who was currently serving as governor of a Norwegian province.

Three days after Durand wrote his letter, Fuller wired de Savornin Lohman: "In compliment to the King of Italy, who chooses if we fail, I suggest that we select Count Nigra." Fuller did not mention to de Savornin Lohman that Nigra's name had been suggested to him by the British ambassador to the United States. Count Nigra apparently declined, so on February 23, Fuller sent a cable to Jonkheer L. H. Ruyssenaers, secretary general of the PCA: "I propose Gram Consider knowledge of English of vital importance." Again, Fuller made no mention that Gram's name had been suggested to him by the British embassy.[30]

When an umpire was not agreed on within a month of Fuller and de Savornin Lohman's notification that they needed to nominate an arbiter, Ruyssenaers explained to Fuller that the Permanent Court Council thought it proper to give the choice to the king of Italy. The king, in turn, nominated Lammasch, who accepted the post.[31]

Although there was nothing improper in Fuller's forwarding of the British suggestions for the third arbiter, the details of the episode demonstrated Fuller's propensity to perceive himself as an advocate for Britain, rather than as an independent judge or arbiter, a view in keeping with his background. When Fuller had been selected as U.S. Supreme Court chief justice, the press had remarked on the fact that unlike most Supreme Court nominees, he had a strong prior career at the bar and not on the bench—that is, he had never served as a judge but always as an attorney representing one or another side in legal disputes.[32]

A review of his notes from the arbitration shows that Fuller went over a carbon-copy draft of the decision, and later, over printed page proofs, carefully inserting phrases, clarifying details, and correcting errors of style. Fuller introduced one of his most significant changes in a key passage later cited in defense of flags of convenience, a passage that would be entirely satisfactory from the British viewpoint: "Whereas generally speaking it belongs to every Sovereign to decide to whom he will accord the right to fly his flag and to prescribe the rules governing such grants . . ." Fuller twice—once in the transcript and then in the page proofs—insisted on the insertion of the phrase "generally speaking." He first inserted the phrase himself on the transcript, and then on the page proofs, he reaffirmed his earlier edit by correcting the transcript from "generally spoke" to "generally speaking."[33]

With this addition, Fuller made it clear that he wanted to stress the flags of convenience principle as one of existing international law and he wanted to clarify that although the principle was general, it was limited in particular cases, such as the Muscat dhows situation, by existing treaties and agreements. The phrase helped clarify that in this situation the general principle did not quite apply because of treaties. But with the insertion of "generally speaking," the passage took on the quality of a pronouncement. Fuller's editing notes make it clear that it was he who insisted that every nation had the right to issue its flag to whomever it chose. Fuller also made many other minor corrections and additions, showing that he took the writing of the final decision very seriously and that he wanted to ensure that the final decision read logically and accurately.

The British objected to the misuse of French protégé status to shelter the slave trade but, at the same time, issued their own red ensign to citizens of other nations, either directly to British subjects in Canada and elsewhere in the empire or indirectly to foreigners who incorporated firms in Britain. The British wanted to deny the French protégé claim in the dhows case but also sought to preserve a nation's right to issue its maritime flag to nonnationals, just as the British had done during the U.S. Civil War to merchant ships from Union states. The British wanted the French claim denied without damaging the principle. Fuller's phrase "Whereas generally speaking" was thus exactly in compliance with the British position.

On August 5, 1905, the arbiters ruled on the dhows case after a week of hearing evidence and deliberating. Although the arbitration pronouncement offered by the three jurists only addressed the specific right of Omani dhow owners to use the French flag, it was often referred to in later years as a "Hague" decision or "Hague" ruling, as if the arbitration award were in fact a court decision on a matter of international law, requiring adherence by other countries. Although the arbitration decision did acquire that status by default, in fact, it was no such thing when it was rendered. It was simply a ruling in a particular arbitration by three specially selected jurists, presumed to be impartial.

The decision noted that any country could grant its maritime flag to anyone it wanted to, subject only to treaties or agreements limiting that right. However, the arbiters stated, in this case the right of France to grant her maritime flag to native vessels was limited by the 1890 Brussels Act, signed in 1892. Until 1892 France could issue the flag to protégés in Oman, and after that date, it could issue the flag only to protégés that had been under its protection before 1863.[34] Thus, to be entitled to the flag under the Brussels Act, the dhows would have had to be the same dhows owned by the same individuals who either had been already been granted the status of French protégé before 1892 or, if newly asserted after 1892, could demonstrate such status as of 1863. With the passage of more than a decade, changes of ownership and fuzzy documentation left very few, if any, dhows legitimately under the French flag in 1905.

With the sultan's government siding with the British in this dispute and the French conceding this practical point, Omani dhow owners were no longer in a position to use the French flag to prevent inspection by the ships of the British Indian Ocean Anti-Slavery Squadron. Probably more to the point, the French, having accepted the Muscat dhows decision, would not come to the assistance of any dhow owner claiming wrongful exercise of the right of search. Furthermore, the decision made clear that French influence in the British quasi-protectorate of Oman would not be extended through French granting of new protégé status. Meanwhile, the French had accepted the grant of the coaling wharf with no claims to French control in Muscat/Oman.

Melville Fuller's Principles

Although Melville Fuller left no published memoir, some insight into his legal thinking and viewpoint can be gained by looking at the major U.S. Supreme Court opinions when he sat as chief justice (1888–1910). Among the more famous cases were *Caldwell v. Texas* (137 U.S. 692 [1891]) and *Plessy v. Ferguson* (163 U.S. 537 [1896]). Fuller produced the memorable phrases "equal justice under law" in the first and "separate but equal" in the second. "Separate but equal" was used to provide a legal basis for racial segregation until 1954.

We can see the outlines of precedents for the Muscat dhows decision in some of Fuller's other Supreme Court positions. In *Western Union Telegraph v. Commonwealth of Pennsylvania* (129 U.S. 39 [1888]), the Court decided that corporations incorporated in one U.S. state were not subject in their interstate business to the rules of another state. The Muscat dhows decision held that a shipowner was subject only to the rules of the flag state when on the high seas because, as Fuller insisted, "Generally speaking, it belongs to every Sovereign the right to issue its flag." The parallel between these cases is clear.[35]

Fuller was well-known as a "Copperhead Democrat," that is, a northern Democrat who had opposed the Lincoln administration and supported the right of the Southern states to secede. This position was consistent not only with his support for racial segregation (on a supposedly "equal" basis) but also with his extreme support for states' rights—that is, for the separate sovereignty of each state within the United States over questions of domestic law. The theoretical underpinnings of his support for states' rights were entirely consistent with the view that each nation was equally sovereign when it came to issuance of its flag, just as every state in the United States had equal rights with every other state with regard to incorporation, as noted in the *Western Union* case. A major twentieth-century legal justification for flags of convenience had been established by applying states' rights logic on the international level.[36]

The Muscat dhows precedent asserting that the practice of flagging-out was "generally speaking" acceptable had no immediate effect on U.S. shipping. During World War I, the ships of the Texaco, Ward, Savannah, Gulf, and Standard Oil lines, all flying the American merchant flag, put the American flag at risk, and they were among those that would create the casus belli for U.S. entry into that war, as shown in chapter 6. However, the precedent and legal principle established by the Muscat dhows decision would prove quite valuable to a variety of American shipowners in the 1920s and later decades, either for avoiding diplomatic or military incidents that would involve the United States or for getting around various requirements of U.S. law.

6

Attacks on the American Merchant Flag as Casus Belli in World War I

By 1910 three modes of thinking about international maritime rights had emerged in the Western world and in the United States in particular. Not altogether incompatible, they lay one atop the other. That is, some leaders reflected one mode of thinking more than the other two, whereas other leaders applied two or all three of the modes simultaneously. The three modes were represented by three types of rhetoric: the rhetoric of international law; the rhetoric of the honor code and the maritime *code duello*; and the rhetoric of the cult of the flag, defended by force.

Those leaders relying particularly on international law hoped that the emergence of a formally approved code of international practices could avoid war in many cases by taking disputes to arbitration at either The Hague or another forum. They worked to ensure that if war broke out, established and agreed-on rules could ameliorate the horrors by protecting noncombatants, establishing practices for the treatment of prisoners of war, and requiring respect for hospitals and religious institutions. International organizations could be formed, they hoped, to regulate and adjust international differences. The body of institutions and specialists in international law continued to grow during and after the Muscat dhows decision.

Leaders who valued the maritime honor code expected individual naval officers to treat maritime war with the same punctilios that applied in duels between gentlemen. Furthermore, many governmental leaders tried to practice, in governmental exchanges, the kind of diplomatic

---

The maritime roots of U.S. entry into World War I discussed in this chapter are the subject of the author's monograph *Sovereignty at Sea: U.S. Merchant Ships and American Entry into World War I* (Gainesville: University of Florida Press, 2009). The findings are summarized in "The Attacks on U.S. Shipping That Precipitated American Entry into World War I," *Northern Mariner* 17, no. 3 (2007): 41–66.

behavior that governed personal interchanges among polite people. Some took this concept to the extreme of expecting nations to make certain promises or pledges; national honor required that a nation stand by its official international commitments. Thus, the honor code could supplement and support the system of international law.

Leaders who favored jingoism, intense nationalism, or the cult of the flag relied on force to address affronts to a nation's sovereignty. In one sense, this reliance on force can be considered an extreme application of the honor code. A nation insulted or damaged would use force to avenge the wrong and to subdue and discipline the offender. In the United States, Theodore Roosevelt, among others, was an advocate of using force. Roosevelt's rhetoric of force is captured succinctly in "Walk softly and carry a big stick." The "big stick" image itself conjured America's potential to thrash misbehaving inferiors.

Although Theodore Roosevelt and Woodrow Wilson both employed the rhetoric of honor, Roosevelt believed that commitments must be backed by a strong military; Wilson preferred to rely on international law and the commitment of other nations to honorably respect that law and their pledges. In the parlance of a later generation, both hawks and doves shared underlying values of national honor, but hawks relied more on a willingness to employ force, whereas doves relied more on the workings of international law and honorable behavior of nations.

President Woodrow Wilson sought to keep the United States neutral in the Great War. He expected foreign leaders to adhere to the rules of war and to behave honorably. He worked to avoid the bluster and resort to force that had characterized the Theodore Roosevelt administration; in fact, even after war had broken out in Europe, Wilson resisted calls to institute a military draft or to otherwise build up the Army and Navy. This approach outraged Roosevelt, who openly criticized Wilson for his less than "manly" approach to the issue.

When Wilson was inaugurated as president in 1913, he appointed to his cabinet two renowned pacifists: William Jennings Bryan as secretary of state and Josephus Daniels as secretary of the Navy. Wilson's first secretary of war, Lindley M. Garrison, by contrast, was more willing to opt for force than Wilson preferred; the president replaced Garrison with another well-known pacifist, Newton D. Baker, in 1916.

The Outbreak of War and the Rules

World War I began in Europe following the assassination of Franz Ferdinand, the archduke of the Austro-Hungarian Empire, in Sarajevo, Bosnia, on June 28, 1914. The Austro-Hungarian government, which ruled Bosnia, suspected Serbian government officials of funding and planning the killing (a charge later admitted) and thus demanded that Serbia allow a full investigation. When Serbia refused, Austro-Hungarian forces bombarded the Serbian capital, Belgrade, and then invaded the small country. In this case, of course, the chastisement of an offending inferior was extremely dangerous thanks to a number of international agreements and alliances that engaged the Great Powers in the conflict.[1]

Within weeks, the major nations of Europe were at war, with Russia, France, and Britain (and later, Italy and Japan) siding with Serbia, while Germany (and later, Bulgaria and Turkey) sided with the Austro-Hungarian Empire. Germany, Russia, France, and Britain all entered the war because of various prior treaty commitments. The United States remained neutral until April 1917, and President Woodrow Wilson worked to bring the opposing parties, particularly Germany and Britain, to negotiate a truce and a peace. Because the major powers soon developed other war goals beyond the resolution of the question of the Serbian role in the assassination, including readjusting the boundaries of Europe and rearranging the colonial empires in Africa and the Middle East, as well as fixing blame (and costs) for the war, the warring nations were not genuinely responsive to Wilson's efforts.

U.S. neutrality between 1914 and 1917 allowed American merchant ships to trade with both sides, subject to blockade. Britain used mines to enforce its blockade, whereas Germany used submarines known as *Unterseeboote*, or in the Anglicized version, "U-boats," to enforce its blockade of Britain and France. The technologies of both blockade systems, each relying on "infernal" devices that violated the maritime code of honor and its surrounding values, presented the United States with a series of dilemmas and then crises that eventually forced Wilson into war.[2] The particular pathway of the United States into World War I was a direct result of the value system surrounding the U.S. flag and the conduct of international affairs. Previous historians have detailed the diplomatic exchanges and the ship losses that generated those exchanges. Extended discussions of the principles of neutrality and the underlying pro-British bias of the president and his advisers characterize some of those works. Other works focus on factors that influenced public opinion, such as the sinking of the British liner *Lusitania* in 1915 or the German offer of an alliance with Mexico revealed in the Zimmermann telegram. However, German attacks on U.S.-flagged merchant ships were in fact what finally precipitated Wilson's decision to ask Congress for a declaration of war.

International Law and Blockades

In an effort to codify the internationally accepted practices of maritime warfare to make it more humane, ten European nations, Japan, and the United States had met in London from December 1908 to February 1909 and issued in 1909 the Declaration of London. Although the declaration was not ratified as a formal treaty or multiparty convention, at first the warring nations of Europe adhered to the principles spelled out in its terms, treating them almost as rules of maritime war. Those rules allowed destruction at sea of neutral vessels carrying contraband to an enemy under certain procedures. That is, a warship could hail and stop a merchant ship on the high seas, inspect the merchant ship to determine her nation of registry, and if a neutral, then board her to see if she was carrying a cargo of contraband to the enemy. If the ship did carry contraband, she could be confiscated and taken to port for adjudication. If the warship could not seize the merchant ship for safety reasons, the merchant ship could be sunk after all crew members and any passengers had been safely evacuated. The neutral shipowners and cargo could seek compensation for their loss. Collectively, these procedures were informally known as cruiser rules. Enemy warships, of course, were not shown such courtesy and were subject to unannounced attack. When merchant ships were armed, they were treated as warships.

The laying of mines at sea violated the Declaration of London, but since the general locations of the World War I minefields were announced, very few ships hit the mines. In fact, before U.S. entry into the war in April 1917, only five or six U.S. ships had been damaged or sunk by mines. The British, who laid extensive minefields in the approaches to European harbors, provided pilots for ships through the minefields. The British also provided a clearly delineated neutral zone through the North Sea to the Netherlands, a nation that remained neutral in the war. But to get a minefield pilot for a ship sailing to a German port required checking in with the British and getting the cargo examined and possibly confiscated. In effect, the British minefield-enforced blockade worked for the most part without extensive surface patrols off Europe. The British did allow cotton to go through to Germany for a period; then they interdicted both cotton and food. The blockade of food was regarded by Germans as inhumane and a violation of the standard rules of war. Britain, on the other hand, justified the embargo of food because Germany, through strict control of the domestic economy, was explicitly importing food in order to free up the agriculture workforce for participation in the war as troops or industrial workers. By the Germans' own logic, food was a war resource and hence contraband, and the British used this point as the rationale for violating this particular aspect of the Declaration of London.

Submarines, by their technology, tended to violate the maritime *code duello*. That is, a submarine had to act surreptitiously, like a bushwhacker or an infernal machine, when attacking either an enemy warship or an enemy merchant ship. Lacking armor, they could easily be sunk when they surfaced with one or two small-caliber cannon shells or by being rammed. The fact that submarines had to act with stealth had delayed their adoption by the navies of the world, largely dominated by officers imbued with the maritime honor code, who saw stealth in itself a violation of honorable war conduct. During the U.S. Civil War, Union officers as well as journalists had labeled Confederate mines, submarines, and semisubmersible vessels infernal machines. But by World War I, with the emergence of the doctrine and rhetoric of force, objections to submarines gradually declined. Nevertheless, surprise U-boat attacks on merchant ships, whether armed or not, were viewed in Britain and in the United States as dishonorable in themselves. And in fact, the Declaration of London had submarines operating under cruiser rules, that is, stopping, inspecting, and safely removing all personnel from a merchant ship before sinking her, just as the Confederate commerce raiders had done during the U.S. Civil War.

The War on Merchant Shipping

At first, the Germans did not attempt to impose a full blockade with U-boats against Britain or France because the German navy was unwilling to use submarines against merchant ships and also simply did not have enough submarines with enough range to be effective. In 1915 and 1916, as Germany deployed more submarines, it used them mostly against British, Canadian, and other Allied ships, many of which carried deck guns and could be treated as enemy warships. Americans were horrified when a German submarine sank the unarmed British passenger liner *Lusitania* on May 7, 1915, off the coast of Ireland, causing the deaths of 1,126 passengers and crew members, including some 129 Americans.[3] The Germans claimed, correctly, that the passenger ship had taken evasive maneuvers, that it was under orders to ram and sink German submarines, and that it carried weapons cargo and thus could "legally" be regarded as open to unannounced attack. These arguments counted for little in Britain and the Unites States against the fact that literally hundreds of women and children had died in the disaster.

In response to the *Lusitania* tragedy, President Wilson sent a rebuke to the German government. The message was so strongly worded that Secretary of State William Jennings Bryan resigned rather than sign the note. His replacement, Robert Lansing, was far more pro-British than Bryan.[4] In fact, over the next months, Lansing grew impatient with Wilson's attempt to adhere to a strictly neutral position in the war and pushed for a more determined stand against German infringement of U.S. neutral rights.

Robert Lansing came to the office of secretary of state with an extensive background in the growing field of international law. The son-in-law of a former secretary of state, he had served as associate counsel for the United States in the 1892–1893 arbitration of pelagic (open-sea) sealing in the Bering Sea and then as a U.S. government attorney before the Alaskan Boundary Tribunal in 1903. He then served as counsel for American Fisheries in the seventh case that came before the Hague PCA, in 1909–1910, regarding the right of American fishermen to land and dry fish in British-controlled Canada. Wilson appointed Lansing to serve as legal adviser to the State Department at the outbreak of World War I and when Bryan resigned appointed him as secretary of state. To a great extent, the official U.S. reaction to German submarine warfare over the next two years was governed by Lansing's view of the issue as one of international law, and both Wilson and Lansing used legal rhetoric and thinking in dealing with the issue of the treatment of U.S. ships at sea. However, Wilson personally directed the tone, content, and even the specific language of the most important diplomatic notes and policies.

Both Lansing and Wilson expected Germany to behave within the established principles of the relationship between nations at sea during time of war, as if such behavior were subject to a legal framework. Some practices had become customary in the treatment of neutral shipping at sea, and the unratified 1909 Declaration of London embodied those practices. However, if one or another country violated those rules, the offended party had no legal recourse, and there was no agency that could enforce the rules. Instead, to attempt to obtain compliance with the rules or standards, a nation could send diplomatic notes of protest, and if the notes did not result in agreement, the recourse could escalate to implementing economic sanctions to breaking diplomatic relations to threatening war to going to war. For these reasons, although some of the maritime issues between the United States and Germany could be couched or discussed in legal terms, ultimately the attempt to remain neutral in the face of German use of the submarine against shipping headed for Britain and France resulted in such a progression of escalation from diplomatic protest to war.

Specific U.S. Ship Losses

From 1915 to January 1917, seven American merchant ships flying the U.S. flag were severely damaged, sunk, or captured by Germany.[5] In all of these cases, however, Germany claimed that its submarines obeyed the rules of war as they had been encapsulated in the unratified 1909 Declaration of London. In each case, the State Department, at first under Bryan and then under Lansing, protested what could be seen as minor infractions of the rules or as matters of interpretation. Although sectors of the U.S. press continued to term these events outrages or insults to the flag (especially the more pro-Ally press, following the established honor rhetoric), the official position, as directed by Wilson and Bryan and then Wilson and Lansing, was that none of the events constituted a cause for war. Details of each of these seven events show why the attack on the U.S. flag did not constitute a legal reason to go to war from the Wilson administration's point of view.[6]

Frye. The German armored cruiser *Prinz Eitel Friedrich* stopped the *William P. Frye*, a large U.S.-flagged four-masted sailing bark, on January 27, 1915, in the South Atlantic off the coast of Brazil. The German crew inspected the ship and discovered she carried a cargo of wheat bound for Britain. After an attempt to throw the cargo overboard, the German sailors removed the *Frye*'s crew members to their own ship and then sank the bark. The cruiser later brought the *Frye* crew and many other captives to Newport News, where the United States impounded the German warship. Although the United States protested the destruction of the *Frye*, the apprehension of the ship, the first attempt to destroy the cargo, the evacuation of the ship, and the safe and courteous treatment of the crew were all in strict accord with the accepted principles of maritime war and of the unratified Declaration of London. The Germans offered compensation for both the ship and cargo, and discussions about the proper forum for adjudicating the proper amount dragged on for months.

Gulflight. Off the southwest coast of Britain, German submarine *U-30* launched a single torpedo against the Gulf Oil tank ship *Gulflight* and severely damaged her on May 1, 1915. Two sailors fell overboard and drowned, and the master later suffered a fatal heart attack. The damaged ship was taken in for repairs in the Scilly Isles off Britain. In this case, the Germans openly admitted that the submarine commander was mistaken and notified the State Department that the German government would be willing to pay for the damage to the ship if a cost could be negotiated. The official German position also indicated that the master had not made clear that *Gulflight* was a U.S. ship by properly displaying a U.S. flag. The three fatalities from the *Gulflight* attack were the only deaths incurred on a U.S.-flagged ship by naval action before 1917.

Nebraskan. *U-41* torpedoed the *Nebraskan* on May 26, 1915, off the British coast. Again, the ship was damaged, and again, the German apology made mention that the U.S. flag was not clearly displayed. After this incident, U.S. ships began to take more care to prominently display a U.S. flag, usually painted directly on the hull, and to illuminate the flag at night. Thereafter, there were no more cases of mistaken identity. Even though they involved the American merchant flag, all three of these events received far less press coverage than the contemporary loss of the British-flagged passenger liner *Lusitania*.

Pass of Balmaha. *U-36* captured the U.S. sailing bark *Pass of Balmaha* on July 24, 1915, north of Scotland and put on board a petty officer who directed the bark's sailing as a prize to Cuxhaven, Germany. This vessel later became the famed German naval sailing vessel commerce raider *Seeadler* (Sea-Eagle), which captured some sixteen merchant ships without inflicting any casualties.[7]

Leelanaw. The *Leelanaw* was stopped off the coast of Scotland on July 25, 1915. On inspection, the U-boat commander determined that the ship carried a load of contraband (flax for linen). He evacuated the crew and then sank the vessel. The *Frye* precedent applied; the Declaration of London rules had been scrupulously followed.

Lanao. German submarine *U-63* stopped the *Lanao*, carrying a cargo of rice from French Indochina to France, off the coast of Portugal.

Commander Otto Schulze, who spoke perfect English, had ordered the crew safely evacuated before his sailors planted charges and sank the ship on October 28, 1916. As the U.S. State Department formulated a protest, investigators discovered that the master of *Lanao* had simply raised a U.S. flag at the last minute, and the ship turned out be registered in the Philippines. The U.S. flag had been raised in a ruse, a vain attempt to prevent a German attack; the State Department decided not to press the matter. Although the Philippines was a U.S. territory at the time, Philippine-registered ships were not entitled to fly the U.S. flag.[8]

Columbian. U-49 stopped the U.S.-flagged *Columbian* on November 8, 1916, off the northwest coast of Spain. German sub commander Richard Hartmann safely evacuated the crew and then sank the ship. He held the merchant shipmaster, Frederick Curtis, as prisoner for a few days in the submarine before he released him. The German government later pointed out that Curtis had used his wireless to attempt to notify Allied warships of the location of the German U-boat. Thus, by Declaration of London rules, the merchant ship lost all its immunity from attack by acting in an unneutral fashion. Curtis complained that he was fed only "a few morsels of black bread." Nevertheless, Hartmann released all the crew members, and eventually Curtis, unharmed. Again, although segments of the U.S. press treated the event as an outrage, the State Department could offer only mild protests. The action conformed to the Declaration of London rules.[9]

Although each of these seven events had risen to the level of either lengthy or perfunctory diplomatic protests, none of them was treated by the U.S. government as a casus belli. Despite Lansing's growing concern, Wilson insisted that the United States adhere to the strictest interpretation of all such events and continue to remain neutral. Through the winter of 1916–1917, Wilson renewed his efforts to bring the warring parties to a peace discussion with no success; however, there were no major attacks by German U-boats on U.S. ships between the *Columbian* incident of November 1916 and February 1, 1917.

German Sinking of Allied Merchant Ships

The U.S. government also protested the use of submarines against British and French vessels when there were casualties. One of the most important such protests came in the wake of a German submarine attack on the French ship *Sussex*, employed in the English Channel as a

passenger vessel. On March 24, 1916, *U-29* torpedoed the ship, destroying its bow. The ship did not sink but was towed into Boulogne. Some
fifty passengers, none of them American, died as a result of the attack.
The commander of the sub reported that he mistook the passenger ship
for a British mine-laying ship.

Lansing and Wilson disagreed on how to react to this event. Lansing
suggested that the United States break diplomatic relations with Germany on the grounds that the Germans had earlier pledged not to attack
passenger ships. But instead, Wilson insisted on a strongly worded note
of protest, warning that unless Germany abandoned "its present method
of warfare against passenger and freight carrying vessels," the United
States would "have no choice but to sever diplomatic relations" with
Germany. The German reaction to this scolding tone was an agreement
that Germany would not sink any unarmed civilian ships of any nation,
without warning. That had already been official German policy; officials
were simply reiterating it. However, they also stated that in obeying this
aspect of the rules of war, they expected the United States to pressure
the Allies to also obey the rules, by lifting their embargo on food and
their blockade of the neutral ports of Denmark and the Netherlands.[10]

Wilson ignored the counterconditions, icily responding that it was
not a regular international practice for one country to agree to commonly
accepted practices only on condition that other countries do so. The
U.S. press and the administration claimed that Wilson had obtained a
"pledge" not to attack merchant ships without warning, the so-called
Sussex pledge. Perhaps inadvertently, Wilson had painted himself into
a corner by noting that he would have no choice but to break diplomatic
relations if Germany began to attack civilian merchant ships without
warning. Although Wilson did not attempt to appeal to public opinion
through the use of the rhetoric of honor, it was clear that he believed
nations should adhere to pledges as gentlemen did.

Unrestricted, Ruthless Submarine Warfare

In late 1916 the German High Command recognized that the war with
France and Britain had ground to a standstill on the western front. After
a meeting at Pless Castle in German Silesia, the German High Command decided that it would launch "unrestricted submarine warfare"
on February 1, 1917. The German leaders recognized that the United
States was now openly sending not only food but contraband of war

(including chemicals, machinery, trucks, horses, petroleum, and even munitions) to Britain and that Britain was using mines to prevent even food from reaching Germany. As a consequence, the Germans believed the only way to bring Britain to the negotiating table was to interdict *all* seaborne trade with Britain. In fact, in a careful calculation, the Germans estimated that if submarines could sink between 800,000 and 1 million tons of shipping a month, Britain, deprived of food imports, would be forced to negotiate a peace settlement before the fall harvest. Germany announced on January 31, 1917, that henceforth *all* shipping in designated war zones around Britain, France, and Italy would be sunk on sight. Specified passenger ships would be allowed passage on a weekly basis, but all other ships, whether schooner, bark, cargo steamer, or passenger liner, would be subject to unannounced attack; crews and passengers would not be evacuated. The announcement itself, the Germans suggested, constituted fair warning. For any ships already on the way across the ocean on the date of the warning, the German announcement stated, U-boat commanders would still exercise the care to inspect for contraband and to evacuate the crews. After that, ships would be sunk on sight with no effort to identify the nation of origin, the propriety of the flag employed, or the nature of the cargo or to ensure the safety of those on board. The policy, in German wording, would be "*rücksichtslos*"—that is, "ruthless."[11]

The German policy went into effect on February 1, 1917, and was immediately announced in the press. Across the United States, newspapers responded with rhetoric that reflected the values that had shaped the press reaction to attacks on ships in the late nineteenth century, as well as the attacks on passenger liners like *Lusitania*, *Sussex*, and others. The German policy evoked the sense of outrage and insult to "the honor" and "manhood" of "red-blooded Americans." A few examples suffice to demonstrate the persistence of the honor imagery:

- *New York Tribune*: "We have submitted to outrage long enough. Peace with Germany would be purchased at too dear a price if it is to be purchased by compliance with the Kaiser's latest insulting instructions as to how we shall conduct our commerce with the Entente nations. . . . The United States fought one war—the war of 1812—in behalf of the principle of the freedom of the seas. We cannot believe that it has so far lost its manhood as to hesitate now that the challenge has come which may compel it to fight another."

- *Baltimore American*: "The United States will not abandon its rights on the sea or abandon its carefulness for the rights and lives of its citizens because Germany chooses to go rabid, and make indiscriminant warfare upon mankind."
- *Worcester Telegram*: "It is a declaration of war against the United States, sent in the form of an insult which red-blooded Americans cannot stand for."
- *Minneapolis Tribune*: "That our own commerce in our own ships should be barred from Europe by the arbitrary decree of one of the belligerents whose only means of suppressing it is to destroy it on the high seas is a matter which the people of America will expect our Government to deal with in accordance with our rights as neutrals and with due regard to the maintenance of our national honor."[12]

President Wilson, however, moved deliberately. After two days of considering the matter, he dismissed the German ambassador to the United States, Count von Bernstorff, just as he had committed himself to do when releasing the Sussex pledge and the associated notes to the press. At the same time, Wilson announced to Congress that he doubted Germany would actually act so rashly and that the United States would go to war *only* after an "overt act." Because the Germans held back from full implementation of the "ruthless" policy for a period to allow ships already in transit to reach port and because most U.S. shipowners hesitated to send ships into the war zone in the face of the German announcement, there was no immediate overt act or casus belli. In fact, there was no "act of war" by Germany against the United States after the German policy had been announced for a period of about six weeks. Even so, in that period, three U.S.-flagged ships were sunk by German submarines. Some historical accounts of the origin of the war suggest that these three vessels were part of the casus belli, but they were not so regarded by Wilson at the time for specific reasons.

Housatonic, Lyman Law, the Zimmermann Note, and *Algonquin*

The *Housatonic* was stopped on February 3, 1917. When the German commander of *U-53*, Hans Rose, discovered that the ship was carrying contraband, he made sure that the ship's crew members safely evacuated and then sank the freighter by cruiser rules. Rose even ensured the crew members were safe by towing their lifeboats on the surface for several hours. When he sighted a British patrol vessel, he cut the towline, and the submarine submerged again only after Rose was sure the rescue ship had spotted the lifeboats. Rose had visited Newport, Rhode Island, on his submarine earlier in the war, and he was well-known to readers of U.S. newspapers for his exploits, good looks, and perfect manners.

The U.S.-flagged schooner *Lyman Law*, carrying an innocuous cargo of wooden shooks for making lemon crates, was stopped off the coast of Sardinia in the Mediterranean on February 12, 1917. The submarine commander safely evacuated the crew, set charges on the schooner, and sank her in full conformity with cruiser rules.

These two attacks were completely in line with the practices that had gone on before; that is, they both followed the *Frye* precedent of conformity to the Declaration of London rules. Wilson was in no position to claim that either one constituted the overt act that he hoped Germany would not take. In fact, the attacks on the *Housatonic* and *Lyman Law* conformed not only to the Declaration of London rules but also to the Sussex pledge. Elements of the press, particularly *Outlook* magazine (known to reflect the viewpoint of Theodore Roosevelt), were outraged.[13] But Wilson demurred. In fact, in his inaugural speech for his second term, delivered March 5, 1917, he specifically stated that the sinking of neither the *Housatonic* nor the *Lyman Law* represented an overt act of war.

Meanwhile, on February 17, 1917, Wilson was shocked to learn of the Zimmermann telegram. In this famous case of decryption, the British had decoded a secret message, sent by the German foreign minister to Ambassador Bernstorff in the United States, asking him to relay instructions to the German ambassador in Mexico. The instructions included an offer to form an alliance with Mexico in case the United States and Germany should go to war. Wilson was appalled, not only at the suggestion of a German-Mexican alliance but also at the fact that the Germans transmitted the secret message via a secure undersea cable that Wilson had personally authorized them to use in order to carry on correspondence regarding his efforts to arrange a negotiated truce. When Lansing told Wilson that the Zimmermann note had been sent over the provided cable, the president, Lansing noted, said, "Good

Lord," two or three times. Lansing had never heard Wilson use such an expression, and he made note of it as indicating the president's shock at the German behavior. Not only were the Germans admitting they would violate the rules of war, but in taking advantage of his offer of cable access for peace purposes, they were behaving in an ungentlemanly fashion.[14]

Clearly, Wilson reacted to the German issues not only as violations of legal principles (as did Lansing) but further as a matter of dishonorable behavior. By treating the Germans' restated commitment to the Declaration of London rules as a pledge, Wilson, on one level, clearly thought that international affairs could be conducted by the rules under which gentlemen conducted polite and proper personal relations. A pledge had no force in affairs of state between nations unless honored. Wilson regarded the violation of a pledge as almost unthinkable, and he viewed the use of the cables for encoded diplomatic communications as entirely inappropriate. Whereas Virginia-born Wilson applied the honor code that had characterized much of nineteenth-century U.S. diplomacy in a tempered and measured fashion, the German High Command had already made it clear that they did not regard warfare as subject to any such honor code and that, for the sake of victory, the war would have to be conducted in a ruthless or unrestrained fashion. In fact, the Germans regarded their note on the *Sussex* not as a pledge but as a statement of an existing policy that could be changed if they chose to publicly announce such a change—which they had planned to do if Britain persisted in violating the Declaration of London principles with mines on the high seas and embargos of neutral ports. Although Wilson applied the honor code to his thinking, he largely refrained from using any exaggerated rhetorical appeals to honor in public statements, except in his cool references to "pledges."

A German U-boat stopped another U.S.-flagged ship, the *Algonquin*, a week after Wilson's second inauguration, on March 12, 1917. The *Algonquin* was carrying contraband and was sunk without inspection or warning. The sinking of the *Algonquin* might have represented an overt act of war from Wilson's viewpoint, except that the ship was a recent transfer from Canada and thus not subject to U.S. flag protection under a strict reading of article 56 of the Declaration of London. According to article 56, recent transfers from a belligerent to a neutral flag did not give a ship any protection from attack. Such transfers to neutral flags were transparent attempts to avoid damage to a belligerent ship, like transfers of U.S. ships to the British flag during the Civil War for protection from Confederate cruisers.

The German officers on the subs involved in the *Housatonic* and *Lyman Law* sinking both had reputations for scrupulously obeying cruiser rules, and they did so in these cases. And the *Algonquin* sinking could hardly be protested under the standard set in the Declaration of London regarding recent transfers. Thus, the United States maintained its neutrality for a full nine weeks after the German announcement of unrestricted submarine warfare despite the sinking of three U.S.-flagged merchant ships. Unless these particular facts are considered, it is impossible to explain why the United States was able to remain neutral for two months after the German announcement of unrestricted submarine warfare at the beginning of February 1917.

Meanwhile, Wilson had attempted to have Congress pass a law authorizing the placing of U.S. naval gun crews on merchant ships, but a number of senators filibustered the bill to death. Wilson, in a rare display of pique, referred to the die-hard, convinced neutralists as "a little group of willful men, representing no opinion but their own." The president's advisers insisted that he order the arming of merchant ships by executive order, but Wilson had first sought congressional approval. After the filibuster had prevented legislative approval, Wilson took the advice to go ahead by executive order, and the outfitting of some American merchant ships with guns and crews began in mid-March 1917, after the president's second inauguration.[15]

Thus, the first three losses of U.S. ships after the declaration of unrestricted submarine warfare and the release of the Zimmermann note did not push Wilson to ask for a declaration of war. The ships were lost more or less in conformity to the Declaration of London rules, as previously discussed, and the Zimmermann note, while shocking, was not technically an act of war but only an effort to line up an ally in the event of war. However, the Zimmermann note and the ship losses clearly had important effects on public opinion.

Loss of Merchant Ships as Casus Belli

Over the weekend of March 16–17, 1917, the loss of *Vigilancia*, *City of Memphis*, and *Illinois* became the United States' casus belli. According to both Wilson and Lansing, each of the three ship losses constituted a separate overt act of war against the U.S. flag. There was no possible way that the president could honorably ignore these losses.

The U.S.-flagged *Vigilancia*, carrying a mixed cargo of war goods, was torpedoed without warning, and fifteen seamen, including six U.S. citizens, drowned during the evacuation of the ship. Although there were no casualties on the Savannah Line *City of Memphis*, nor on the Texaco tanker *Illinois*, those two vessels were sunk without any examination to determine if they carried contraband. In fact, both were returning to the United States in ballast—and thus were empty. Ships in ballast were never fair prey under Declaration of London rules, which allowed destruction only of ships carrying contraband cargo. Across the nation, newspapers pronounced that the overt act had occurred not once but three times in quick succession. Although the more testy and bellicose Theodore Roosevelt had found U.S. honor affronted and outraged much earlier, even the more idealistic Woodrow Wilson had to admit that the only honorable course at this point was war.

Wilson met with his cabinet the following Tuesday, March 20, and at that meeting, all cabinet members, including even the convinced neutralists Josephus Daniels and Newton Baker, agreed that Germany had committed acts of war against the United States. They all agreed that Wilson had no alternative but to ask Congress to declare that a state of war existed between the United States and Germany. Clearly, even the pacifists in the cabinet viewed German government–approved surprise attacks on U.S.-flagged merchant ships as acts of war against the United States. Wilson refused to commit himself publicly to that position, but he did ask Congress to convene early, on April 2, 1917, in a special session.

When President Wilson asked for a declaration of war, he was first motivated by the *Vigilancia* and two later attacks on the U.S. flag, violations of the rules of war, the Declaration of London, and the Sussex pledge. On a second, personal level, he was angered because of the Germans' dishonorable behavior. Still, before Congress, he chose to speak on a higher plane. Wilson's war address had the long-range effect of obscuring the technical, legal reasons for a declaration of war in favor of a more idealistic call to arms over issues of world peace, democracy, and self-government. When Wilson addressed Congress, he mentioned the ship losses only in general terms and devoted most of his speech to broader concerns.[16]

Wilson was a firm believer that the democratic process lent legitimacy to governments, and he vigorously attacked the autocratic leaders of Germany on the grounds that they did not represent the German people. He also believed, in accord with the international law approach, that at the conclusion of the war, an international league of nations should be established to permanently work to resolve problems between nations and to prevent war. He also supported the aspirations of various European ethnic groups, including the Slavic peoples under the Austro-Hungarian Empire, to form their own nations and elect governments of their own choosing. His logic of democratic self-determination in Europe was implemented to an extent at the Versailles Peace Conference at the end of the war.[17] The well-known tragedy of Wilson's career was that he could not convince the U.S. Senate either to agree to the Versailles Peace Treaty that he had helped craft or to join the League of Nations, established in 1919. However, when he addressed Congress in 1917, those disappointments were in the future, and he chose to present the argument in a Wilsonian way that focused on grand democratic ideals, such as human decency and the right of peoples to peace and democratically elected governments. He did not mention the handful of outrages or specific acts of war against U.S. sovereign jurisdiction on the ships attacked.

Robert Lansing had confided in private correspondence that not only did Wilson want a "bill of particulars" to indict Germany, but he needed more profound causes than a simple overt act to make a convincing case for war both to Congress and to the people.[18] Perhaps this practical concern partially explains Wilson's oratorical venture into the realms of idealism that overlooked the small number of merchant ship incidents and the violations of trust that had provoked him and even the pacifists in his cabinet to the final decision. Headline writers reduced the arguments of Wilson's speech to a set of slogans: a "war to end war" and a war "to make the world safe for democracy."

Even so, when Congress debated the motion to declare war after Wilson had made his address, the members had a list of specific events in hand, provided by Lansing to several key pro-war members, as well as detailed newspaper reports on all the ship losses. And in fact, those specifics saw far more discussion and debate in Congress than did the grand ideals Wilson had articulated. Most congressional representatives and senators discussing the justification were fuzzy in their remarks about the particular ship losses, sometimes getting the facts and statistics slightly or grossly wrong, despite all the publicity that had surrounded the events. At least fifteen congressional representatives and senators mentioned one or more of the recent ship losses and focused on them as causes of war. An examination of the debate as reported in the *Congressional Record* indicates that the specific legal grounds, that is, the presumed and actual violations of international law, although a bit garbled, resonated with Congress.

This observation applies not only to those who supported the declaration of war but to its opponents as well. Some opponents of the declaration argued, correctly, that the U.S.-flagged merchant ships that were sunk in 1917 went into harm's way knowingly and that if businessmen had not sought to profit from trading with the Allies, the nation would not have been at risk. Senator George Norris asserted that by their actions, shipowners had "put a dollar sign on the flag." His statement outraged some critics, and his opinion was a minority view, although one that gained popularity in later years. In effect, Norris was saying that the flag should be defended but not if it had already been dishonored by profiteers. After more than a day of debate, the House of Representatives voted 373 to 50 for war, and the Senate voted 82 to 6 for war.

The 1917 Decision for War and the Rhetoric of Honor

In the weeks leading up to the decision, supporters of former president Theodore Roosevelt and others who argued for U.S. engagement in the war were impatient with Wilson's stance of continued neutrality in the face of the German announcement and practice of unrestricted submarine attacks on shipping. For many, earlier German actions on the high seas and the mere announcement of the unrestricted submarine policy constituted outrages. For many, U.S. honor required a firm response in the twentieth century as it had throughout the nineteenth century. The advocates of an armed response to Germany used the rhetoric of honor; the confirmed pacifists and neutralists like Wilson himself understood the rhetoric and its power and shared the values but sought to take a higher and more measured approach.

Many advocates of action employed the traditional rhetoric. For example, Gifford Pinchot, who had served under Roosevelt as chief of the Forest Service, wrote in late 1916, "Unless the American people find a way to emphasize the truth that neutrality is not indifference, that they are not absorbed in their own National interests and do not think that National safety is more important than National duty and

National honor, should our own land be imperiled, we shall have no right to expect anything but the same indifference to our welfare which we have officially expressed when other nations were imperiled."[19]

Franklin K. Lane, Wilson's secretary of the interior, one of the hawks, pointed out in a cabinet meeting on February 23, 1917, that honor required an armed response to the German indignities reportedly heaped on U.S. legation members (especially wives and women staff) after the breaking of diplomatic relations. Wilson dismissed the charges, claiming "that Lane was appealing to the Code Duello."[20]

When Wilson's cabinet met on Tuesday, March 20, to discuss the sinking of the *City of Memphis*, *Illinois*, and *Vigilancia*, all members of the cabinet, including not only the confirmed hawks but also the die-hard doves, agreed there was no choice but war. Reporting on the cabinet meeting, the *New York Times* stated, "There was no doubt of the meaning of the Cabinet discussion and no doubt that if the President granted the appeal to move forward the date of the extra session, his action would mean that he had determined that war was the only course open to the United States to uphold national honor and dignity."[21]

For pro-war advocates, the traditional values of the honor code were at stake in the face of outrages. After the sinking of the *Vigilancia*, *City of Memphis*, and *Illinois*, Lansing sent a note to Wilson stating that the sinking of the ships without warning required U.S. action. He wrote, "It will be only a question of time before we are forced to recognize these outrages as hostile acts which will amount to an announcement that a state of war exists."[22]

Fifty members of Congress voted against the declaration of war. One of the leaders of that opposition was Representative Dorsey Shackleford from Missouri. In his minority report, Shackleford made it clear that one could oppose the war with honor. "It is no dishonor for an individual or a Government to overlook injuries which it has received," he said. As the *New York Times* noted, Shackleford raised this argument against those who claimed "we have been wronged and should fight to vindicate our honor."[23] The close resemblance to the choice of words and values in the debates of 1812 demonstrates the clear survival of the honor code in American thinking about international affairs and the respect due to the U.S. flag on board merchant ships.

Behind Wilson's public stance of idealism, it was clear that even in his case, the gentleman's code of honor shaped his decisions and behavior, and behind Lansing's legalistic language, there remained a sense that violations of international law were outrages. For the more bellicose supporters of Theodore Roosevelt, neutrality and pacifism were in themselves dishonorable.

Lessons for Preserving Neutrality

Supporters of the declaration of war believed that German behavior toward American merchant ships had led to the crisis and to acts of war and that the nation had no choice but to respond. Opponents of the declaration accepted the premise that German behavior had led to acts of war but placed the blame for those acts on the U.S. failure to adopt more neutral policies. Americans traveling on belligerent ships had been killed, and U.S. ships had attempted to run the submarine blockade. The lesson for opponents of war was clear: in the future, if American travelers were prohibited from boarding ships under belligerent flags and if U.S. ships were prohibited from trading with belligerents, Americans and the American merchant flag at sea would not be able to put the nation at risk of war. An armed response would be unnecessary because the flag would not be exposed. From the perspective of international law, such a neutrality would be far more "neutral." But by April 6, 1917, the damage had been done. When war loomed again in the 1930s, convinced isolationists and neutralists attempted to apply the lessons from these earlier events. The Neutrality Acts of 1933–1939 discouraged or prohibited U.S. civilians from traveling on belligerent ships during time of war and prohibited American merchant ships from trading with belligerent nations.

7

Danzig, the Missing Link in Flags of Convenience

For most practical U.S. shipowners, their ships' place of registry had little sentimental attachment. This fact had been amply demonstrated during the Civil War with the flagging-out of more than a thousand U.S.-owned ships, almost all to Britain. By the early twentieth century, U.S. corporations had begun to make use of the legal concept of the most favorable jurisdiction for incorporation, a practice pioneered by the law firm Sullivan and Cromwell and implemented with the incorporation of Standard Oil of New Jersey, oddly enough, in Delaware, not New Jersey. Between World War I and World War II, Standard Oil and a number of other U.S. and foreign corporations began to experiment with the economic, tax, and regulatory advantages of flagging-out their ships to more favorable jurisdictions.

For the managers of these corporations, the decision to flag-out was completely unrelated to matters of honor and patriotism. As in the U.S. Civil War, when Union ships sought safety from Confederate cruisers by reflagging to Britain, corporations reflagged in order to operate in jurisdictions free of threats of confiscation, restrictive legislation, high labor costs, or high taxes. According to the 1905 Muscat dhows decision, any sovereign country could issue a maritime flag under conditions it alone decided. The first major twentieth-century use of a flag of convenience by a major ship-owning corporation involved the small enclave of Danzig on the Baltic Sea.

Although largely German in population, Danzig (now Gdańsk) was given special status under the Versailles Treaty as a free city in order to provide newly constituted Poland with an outlet to the sea. Poland administered Danzig's foreign affairs and had certain special rights in

Portions of this chapter, reprinted with permission, previously appeared in "Danzig: The Missing Link in the History of Flags of Convenience," *Northern Mariner* 23, no. 2 (2013): 135–50.

the city and harbor, but Danzig was self-governing under League of Nations protection. The anomalous "free city" was one of many awkward results of the implementation of Wilson's principle of national self-determination based on ethnicity in Europe, where ethnic enclaves like Danzig were common.[1] From 1920 to 1939 Danzig remained a self-governing state with almost all the characteristics of an independent nation. Among these was the ability to offer its merchant flag to ships registered in Danzig.

During the reparations discussions at the end of World War I, Standard Oil of New Jersey (Esso) fought to keep ships of its German subsidiary, Deutsch-Amerikanische Petroleum Gesellschaft, Hamburg (DAPG), from being seized and transferred to Britain or France. The company successfully retained four ships in a new firm, the Baltic-American Petroleum Import Company (Bapico), established in the Free City of Danzig. A thorough (and semiofficial) history of the Standard Oil Company says that Bapico "had been organized in 1919 to take over the tankers being built for Jersey's German affiliate. Because of its domicile in what became the Free City of Danzig in January 1920, under the Treaty of Versailles, its tankers were immune from seizure under the reparations provisions of that treaty."[2] The Riedemann shipping company, based in Hamburg, operated the Danzig-flagged Bapico tankers, the *Zoppot, Gedania, Vistula*, and *Baltic*. The Reparations Commission, after considerable wrangling, decided that the ships, flagged as Danzig ships rather than as German, were not deliverable as part of the reparations to the victorious Allies.[3]

The law firm providing advice to Standard Oil at that time was Sullivan and Cromwell. One of the young attorneys with the firm was John Foster Dulles, who had served at the Paris discussions over reparations under his uncle, Secretary of State Robert Lansing. Allen Dulles, John Foster's brother, was in and out of the State Department in the period and was also an attorney for Sullivan and Cromwell; he later served with the Office of Strategic Services (OSS) in Switzerland in World War II and then as the first director of the Central Intelligence Agency (CIA). Sullivan and Cromwell had masterminded Standard Oil's recovery from the antitrust decision of 1911 and had an established reputation for finding the most convenient jurisdiction (in the United States) for state incorporations.[4] During the reparation discussions in Paris, John Foster Dulles reported that he met with F. D. Asche from Esso to discuss the company's reluctance to see its ships be part of reparations as required under the Treaty of Versailles.[5] The firm's previous work for Standard Oil and Dulles' discussion with Asche suggest that at the very least, Sullivan and Cromwell's legal advice played a role in the decision to escape confiscation under reparations by transfer to Danzig.

Under the reparations decisions, Germany had to surrender to the Allies all of its seagoing merchant fleet, some 625 ships, together with 91 interned in the United States and 121 embargo vessels originally of German registry but already confiscated and interned in Allied countries. The total tonnage of these ships was more than 4 million gross registered tons.[6] For Esso, the small four-tanker German-owned fleet of its subsidiary was also at risk, until the decision to reflag in Danzig.

Between 1920 and 1934 the Bapico fleet grew to a total of thirty-two ships. Seven of them were transferred out before 1935 to other countries: Belgium, Britain, France, Germany, Italy, and the United States. It appears that the profits from the trips of the Bapico line were plowed back into the purchase of new ships, most built in Germany. In 1935 Standard Oil transferred the remaining twenty-five Bapico ships to Panama.

The fact that the naming of ships at Bapico went through three distinct phases is suggestive. The ships in the first batch were named after geographic features in and around the Free City of Danzig, a practice rather common among ship-owning companies based in Danzig. This batch included the first four Esso-owned ships registered 1919–1921: *Baltic*, *Gedania*, *Vistula*, and *Zoppot*. The second batch registered in Danzig between 1923 and 1928 revived a pre–World War I practice at the Hamburg-based firm Waried of naming the tankers after figures from Greek mythology. These ships were the *Calliope*, *Clio*, *Leda II*, *Niobe*, *Penelope*, *Persephone*, *Phoebus II*, *Prometheus II*, *Thalia*, and *Urania*. The third batch, registered between 1930 and 1934 and reflecting more frankly the control by Esso of New Jersey, were named for American and international officers of Esso, ranging from historic figures to contemporary ones, all connected in one way or another to the firm's international trade. These ships included the *F. H. Bedford*, *Heinrich V. Riedemann*, *Harry G. Seidel*, *J. L. Mowinckel*, *J. H. Senior*, *Peter Hurll*, *F. J. Wolfe*, *Robert Hague*, *Orville Harden*, *Victor Ross*, and *George McKnight*. Most of the men after whom the ships were named held a contemporary position in international Esso operations; Robert Hague, for example, worked in the Esso Shipping Division.[7] The practice of naming ships for company executives was common to all ships operated by the Marine Division of Standard Oil under other flags and demonstrates the increasing role of the U.S.-based company in such decisions, as well as increasing confidence in the use of the Danzig flag.[8]

The first batch of ships seems intended to reflect affiliation with Danzig. The second batch made it clear that the ships were continuing the German connection; the Roman numeral "II" in a few of the names specifically echoed earlier Riedemann company names. The third batch abandoned any pretense of Danzig or German affiliation and stressed the Esso connection. In effect, the three phases of ship naming reflected a move from a pretense of Danzig affiliation to an admission of German affiliation to an outright assertion of the U.S.-based Esso connection.

Danzig Ships other than the Bapico Line

In addition to seven Bapico ships later transferred to other countries and twenty-five Bapico ships later transferred to Panama, twenty-five to thirty-five other ships belonging to other individuals and companies also registered in Danzig during the period. For the most part, these ships were owned and operated by local Danzig companies that operated in or from the port. Most of the companies had been established in Danzig long before World War I; most kept their ships in Danzig registry through the period of German takeover in 1939 and, if the ships survived the war, until the defeat of Germany in 1945.

The exception was the firm Artus Danziger Reederei & Handels-Aktiengessellschaft, a German company that, like DAPG, sought refuge in Danzig to avoid confiscation and was established there in 1919.[9] Hugo Stinnes, a well-known German industrialist with a reputation for sharp practices, founded the Artus line. His five ships were the *Artus*, *Danzig I*, *Danzig II*, *Holm*, and *Oliva*.

With the exception of the five ships of the Artus line, other ships registered in Danzig during the 1920s and 1930s appeared to be owned by just a few local Danzig companies with long histories in the city. These included F. G. Reinhold (owned by Hans-Gunther Siedler) with six ships, Behnke & Sieg with nine ships, and "Weichsel" Danziger Dampfschiffahrts-und Seebad-AG with four ships. Scattered and unconfirmed records suggest at least another eight or ten ships that may have been registered in the city for various periods during the two decades, some by these companies and others by one-ship firms.[10]

Esso's Departure from Danzig

After 1928, as new ships were acquired, Bapico transferred management of the fleet from Danzig to the Hamburg company Waried Tankschiff Rhederei GmbH as sole operators. Existing vessels in the Bapico fleet were transferred to Waried's management in 1928, and others acquired later, while still registered in Danzig, were also managed by this Hamburg firm. The Waried company maintained its own funnel emblem and company flag, which included the large *R* (for "Riedemann") that was on all the funnels of the Bapico ships. There were several variants of the Waried funnel emblem; photos of the Bapico ships, although in black and white, show these funnel emblems on the ships.

In 1933 Hitler came into power in Germany. A month after Hitler's election in Germany, the Nazi Party won local elections in Danzig. In 1935 the whole Bapico fleet of twenty-five ships was transferred to Panama under the ownership of a new firm, the Panama Transport Company. Whether the choice to relocate to Panama in 1935 was a business decision, a political decision, or a combination of the two is difficult to determine from publicly available records. The company-endorsed history attributes the decision to a mix of both factors. Citing correspondence from Standard vice president and Marine Department director Hague, the *History of Standard Oil* says, "Jersey's leaders saw in Hitler and his Nazi program a growing threat to Danzig—which could easily lose its neutral status and be taken over by Germany—and indeed a threat to the peace of Europe. . . . In making these suggestions, Hague was in effect proposing that Jersey follow the example of several companies in their search, after World War I, for a flag that would enable ships owned in the United States to compete on equal terms with ships of other flags."[11]

The German management of the tankers by Waried continued for a few years under the Panama flag, until 1937–1938, when Esso took over management directly.[12] The use of the Panamanian flag by companies through the 1920s and early 1930s is discussed in chapter 8.

The Danzig Registry as Flag of Convenience

To a small extent, other companies used the Danzig registry for illicit purposes. In the 1930s Sweden, Finland, and Lithuania, which all had strict laws concerning importation of liquor, faced a problem of smuggling, or rum-running. Danzig became a notorious departure point for the smugglers' ships. Records indicated that at its peak in 1930, some 1 million gallons of illicit alcohol were shipped from Danzig but that by 1934 the trade had greatly declined owing to Swedish and Finnish sea patrols. One ship, the 274-ton *Willy* from Danzig, was confiscated by the Lithuanians in 1936.[13]

Well before the transfer of Esso/Bapico ships to Panama in 1935, Danzig had the classic elements of what later came to be called a flag-of-convenience jurisdiction: it was a ministate; it needed sources of revenue; it provided flags for the Esso fleet, which was not owned by Danzig citizens but by a German company that was a subsidiary of a U.S. company; it also provided flags for the Artus company, a German-owned firm, demonstrating that the flag was more than a one-company service to Esso; it provided a tax haven for Bapico, which was not taxed in either the United States or Germany, allowing the company to build the largest Standard Oil fleet in Europe in 1925–1935; operation under Danzig's flag allowed a few ships previously under the German flag to avoid confiscation as part of the reparations agreement and protected newly built ships after 1923 from both the fluctuation of the German mark and social legislation enacted in Germany; and to a small extent, ownership in Danzig and possibly Danzig registry sheltered illicit trade. Danzig's relationship with Germany is noteworthy. As discussed in chapter 13, other flag-of-convenience states (and later, second-registry states) had special relations with the home country of major users of the flag.

Like later flag-of-convenience states, Danzig was a small national entity with some or most of the qualities of sovereignty, which it could market in the same fashion that Panama and other small nations with few sources of international income later marketed their sovereignty. J. B. Mason, writing on the issue of Danzig's status, noted that Danzig had a kind of quasi-sovereignty with some attributes of a state: "The independence of the Free City was restricted in several ways, but her character as a state was not thereby destroyed. . . . We conclude, therefore, that the Free City of Danzig was a state at international law and that it was in principle vested with the sovereign rights of a state, although these had been restricted by treaty agreements in favor of Poland."[14]

Danzig differed in one important respect from later flag-of-convenience states: it had a strong maritime tradition. It had a fairly large locally owned and flagged merchant fleet and was, as Gdańsk remains, a major port and shipbuilding city.

The Role of Sullivan and Cromwell

Given that Esso's law firm was Sullivan and Cromwell, the following observation from Peter Grose is pertinent:

> To call the Sullivan and Cromwell of the 1920s a law firm is to miss the point. The partnership of lawyers at 40 Wall Street constituted a strategic nexus of international finance, the operating core of a web of relationships that constituted power, carefully crafted to accrue and endure across sovereign borders. . . . The firm did offer legal associates to draft contracts, preserve estates, and argue in courtrooms, but this was not the profession of law as practiced by Foster and Allen Dulles. Their Sullivan and Cromwell sought nothing less than to shape the affairs of all the world for the benefit and well-being of the select, their clients.[15]

Sullivan and Cromwell closed its Berlin office in 1935 at the insistence of Allen Dulles and over the objections of John Foster Dulles. The office was closed because Allen Dulles was appalled at the Nazi regime, according to several sources. This closure of the office that represented Esso in Germany may very well have been a contributing factor of the switch of twenty-five tankers from Bapico ownership to the Panama Transport Company and the Panamanian flag. The prior separate transfers of seven Bapico ships to Britain, Italy, Germany, the United States, and France all appear to have been independent business decisions. Although Esso was later accused of maintaining friendly relations with I.G. Farben and the Nazi regime, the departure of the Bapico fleet from Danzig to Panama shortly after the Nazi takeover has been noted by some authors to suggest that Esso was antagonistic to the new regime.[16]

Later, when Germany launched its aggressions in Europe, Peter Grose noted, "the best that Sullivan and Cromwell could do for its European clients was to shelter their assets from war, preserving and concentrating property in neutral or otherwise secure hands."[17] Grose pointed out that Sullivan and Cromwell and others were simply working to keep industrial assets out of Nazi hands.[18] Although Germany had not started its geographical expansion by 1935, sharp observers like Allen Dulles might very well have foreseen the coming disaster of Nazi domination of Danzig, and thus, as Grose observed, the transfer to Panama was a way to shelter company assets.

Danzig's parallels and continuities with other open-registry systems have gone unremarked in histories of Danzig and Germany during the interwar years. Historical studies of the Weimar Republic have mostly concentrated on three specific issues of broader interest: the problem of hyperinflation and its relation to the reparations issue; the flourishing of "modern" culture in architecture, music, the arts, and film in the period; and the political environment that fostered the rise of Nazism and Hitler. Treatments of maritime issues, economic and social policy, and relations with Danzig are therefore of peripheral interest to most general studies of Weimar Germany. English-language historical studies of Danzig in the period have focused for the most part on relations with Poland and the efforts of the League of Nations to deal with that relationship and on local political issues, especially the rise of the local Nazi Party. Local business, shipping, maritime issues, and economic relations between Danzig and Germany are simply not discussed by most authors writing in English. Furthermore, since Danzig was totally destroyed and its German population forcibly removed at the end of World War II, there are few local records, making it difficult for researchers to study any aspect of local history.[19]

Danzig registry was the first twentieth-century flag of convenience for tankers, setting the precedent for later such registration in Panama and elsewhere. The short-lived Danzig registry thus represents a missing link in the evolution of modern open-registry and flag-of-convenience systems. The managers of the Esso Shipping Division learned several valuable lessons in Danzig. The ships there were relatively immune from the social, economic, and political upheaval in Germany until the mid-1930s. The profits from the operations, as long as they were not repatriated to the United States, could be plowed directly back into the business. The flag of Danzig was accepted internationally as a maritime flag, even though the country was a ministate without a navy and with only a small local fleet of merchant ships. As the names of the Bapico ships passed through their three phases—from names for Danzig landmarks to names for classical figures to names for company leaders—there was no international outcry about the legitimacy of the system. After all, as Melville Fuller insisted in the Muscat dhows ruling, "Generally speaking it belongs to every Sovereign to decide to whom he will accord the right to fly his flag and to prescribe the rules governing such grants." The rule applied to Danzig as a sovereign state, and no one challenged the system in any court. Quietly, outside the notice of the world press and behind the more momentous and newsworthy economic and political crises of the era, Esso established the values of a ministate flag for tanker operations.

Panama, 1919–39

Over the 1920s and 1930s, the maritime flag of Panama evolved into a flag of refuge for a wide variety of shipowners. An amendment to Panamanian laws in 1916 allowed shipowners to register their ships in Panama through a Panamanian consul in a foreign port. Perhaps the first foreign-owned ship to take advantage of this provision of the law was the *Belen Quezada*, owned by a group of Canadian investors who transferred the ship to the Panamanian flag through the honorary consul in Vancouver, British Columbia, in August 1919. Evidence suggests that the Canadian partners wanted to use the Panamanian flag to cover liquor-smuggling operations into the United States. At the time, the Volstead Act establishing Prohibition was pending in Congress. It passed over President Wilson's veto in October 1919 and went into effect January 1920. As in the case of the Danzig registry, sentiment attached to the flag played no part in these decisions; rather and quite the contrary, evasion of U.S. laws was clearly the smugglers' motive.

Although the *Belen Quezada* was never caught in liquor smuggling, or rum-running, as it came to be known, one of the owners of the ship, Enrique Clare, was later arrested on drug and liquor charges, and his partner, Browne Willis, was known to have purchased large quantities of liquor in Cuba with the probable intent of smuggling it into the United States. The ship had a rather adventuresome career both before and after Clare and Willis bought her. She had earlier been involved, under the name *Zafiro*, in the Spanish-American War as a dispatch ship for Adm. George Dewey and was later confiscated by Costa Rica during a short border war between Costa Rica and Panama in 1921. After a legal struggle over ownership, she was renamed the *Costa Rica*, operated for a few years in regional trades, and ended up being scrapped in Ecuador.[1]

Surplus Ships

The end of World War I left a shipping glut in the United States, which had excess shipping capacity largely because of the extensive ship-building program in 1917–1919. Fleets of recently built merchant ships and tankers lay idle in U.S. ports, slowly rusting. In addition, the United States had during the war confiscated numerous ships that had been owned by Germany and Austria-Hungary. The U.S. Shipping Board had chartered out these ships, but if the owners went bankrupt, as many did, the debts associated with the ships' voyages could be paid only if the ships, sometimes the last remaining asset of the bankrupt companies, were sold to satisfy them. Often the shipowners set up corporations organized around a single ship precisely so that accrued debts would not be charged to individuals or to larger corporate entities, a common practice in the shipping industry around the world.

In 1921 the U.S. Shipping Board offered for sale seven former German ships that had been the last assets of bankrupt corporations. These ships had been renamed the *Casco, Isonomia, Arcadia, Pawnee, Ida, Pequot,* and *Tunica*.[2] The U.S. government arranged the sale of the first six of these ships to the San Francisco–based Admiral Orient Line, which established a subsidiary, Pacific Freighters, to operate the ships. The total debt against the six ships was just over $148,000, and the company paid the government $325,000 for them, more than taking care of their outstanding indebtedness. The seventh ship, the *Tunica,* was sold to American Merchant and Forwarding Company in New York. As a requirement of the sales, the government insisted that the ships be removed from the U.S. registry so that they would not be in competition with the already bloated U.S. merchant fleet. In this case, the U.S. government itself hoped to recoup some costs that motivated the off-shoring of registry. The provision of the Panama code allowing foreign-owned ships to be registered in Panama through consuls abroad proved useful for continued operation of the ships by U.S. companies under a foreign flag.

Pacific Freighters transferred all six of the newly acquired ships to Panamanian registry. One of the company's officers, William Leslie Comyn, explicitly expressed the reasons for his decision to choose Panama over other possible flags: "The chief advantage of Panamanian registry is that the owner is relieved of the continual but irregular boiler and hull inspections and the regulations as to crew's quarters and subsistence. We are under absolutely no restrictions, so long as we pay the $1 a net ton registry fee and 10 cents yearly a net ton tax."[3] Comyn provided other details of the business arrangements, including paying salaries on the Japanese pay scale and hiring the same German merchant ship officers who had commanded the ships before the war. He noted that operations under the U.S. flag could not compete economically with Japanese shipping companies but that the Panama registry would allow competition with the Japanese in international trade. He also noted, in a droll remark, that he did not expect a war between Panama and the United States. He predicted other shipowners would follow the lead of Pacific Freighters for the same economic reasons. In short, Comyn made his decision not based on honor or sentiment but on strictly business grounds of seeking a favorable jurisdiction that would, in all likelihood, diplomatically align with the United States in case of conflict.

Comyn's accurate prediction, however, did not come true immediately because the Shipping Board did not regularly approve the transfer of U.S.-built and U.S.-owned ships to Panama or to other countries unless they were to be genuinely operated by a foreign firm in a trade that did not compete with U.S. shipping. Nevertheless, the shipping glut and the large numbers of German ships that had been either seized during the war or transferred from Germany to Allied nations as part of the reparations settlements created some anomalies in the world shipping picture that led to several new Panamanian registries. Panamanian registry was attractive to several owners in the United States and abroad.

Two German liners had been transferred from Germany to the Netherlands at the end of the war in partial compensation to Holland for the loss of neutral shipping to German submarines. Named the *Limburgia* (ex *Johann Heinrich Burchard*) and *Brabantia* (ex *Oswald*), they were planned for the Buenos Aires route. However, the Allies forced the Dutch to sell the vessels, and in January 1922 the American Ship and Commerce Corporation purchased them. That company, owned by W. Averell Harriman, operated the ex-German ships, along with several others in the United American Lines, under the U.S. flag and renamed the *Limburgia* as the *Reliance* and the *Brabantia* as the *Resolute*. When Harriman took over the ships, the Shipping Board accepted a clause that would allow transfer of the German-built liners from the U.S. flag to a foreign flag within three years. On October 31, 1922, the Harriman firm transferred the two ex-German ships to Panama.

At the time, the U.S. government prohibited the sale of liquor not only in the United States but also on U.S.-registered liners, even when they were outside U.S. territorial waters. Attorney General Harry M. Daugherty had aroused a storm of protest with this interpretation of the Volstead Act on October 6, 1922, and the Harriman company specifically linked the transfer of the two liners from the U.S. flag to the Panamanian flag to this Daugherty ruling. No doubt the publicity surrounding this protest against overzealous enforcement of the Volstead Act attracted passengers and was part of the business plan. Richard Robinson, president of United American Lines, explained that the liners could compete with those of other countries only if "passengers can be offered the same service and privileges," that is, the access to alcohol available on European-registered ships. Robinson also indicated that transfer to Panama "was most acceptable to the interests of the United States."[4]

The law firm representing the Harriman interests at this time was Sullivan and Cromwell. John Foster Dulles had visited Panama in 1917 to ensure that Panama would follow the United States in declaring war on Germany, and he had succeeded William Nelson Cromwell as the legal counsel for Panama in the United States. The firm continued to manage Panamanian affairs in the United States, including handling Panama's share of canal fees. United American Lines' letter of application to the Shipping Board for permission to transfer to Panama stated, "We have made a study of the laws of various countries which have no national aspirations to compete with the United States in the development of its merchant marine and its naval power. . . . The Panama flag will probably be the one most suited to our own necessities, and we believe, most acceptable to the interests of the United States both in the development of its trade and as regards availability in time of military necessity." This 1922 letter that summarily echoed Robinson's public remark that Panamanian registry would be in U.S. interests is striking in terms of later developments. As early as 1922, the Shipping Board saw both a strategic and a commercial value in Panamanian registry due to Panama's dependence on the United States and the likelihood that Panama would reflect U.S. foreign policy in war and peace. It is altogether possible that the study referred to in the letter was conducted at the offices of Sullivan and Cromwell; the letter certainly reflected the broad view of U.S. international interests that characterized the law firm's work and the Dulles brothers' opinions in particular. The combination of business advantages and Panama's political reliability became a hall-mark of later defenses of the practice of U.S. ship registry in Panama.[5]

It is also notable that the dual rationale, both business and diplomatic, in Robinson's letter to the Shipping Board bore a close resemblance to the dual rationale provided by Comyn of Pacific Freighters. That is, both statements reflected the identical reasoning: business reasons made the reflagging logical, and Panama was diplomatically, militarily, and politically reliable. The positions of Harriman's New York–based firm and the San Francisco–based Admiral Orient Line might have been so similar because the firms obtained the same legal advice; at the very least, the parallels showed that shipping company executives were driven by the same economic concerns, were well aware of merchant shipping's importance to the national interests, and were well aware of Panama's dependent status.

The Supreme Court overturned the Daugherty ruling regarding shipboard alcohol on April 30, 1923, and thereafter, U.S. ships could sell liquor once they left U.S. waters.[6] The Harriman firm sold the whole United American Lines fleet to the Hamburg-American Line in July 1926. By this circuitous route, the ships returned to the German flag after three years of voyages under the Panamanian flag.

Codifying Panamanian Maritime Registry Law

In 1923 the director of the U.S. consular service asked the U.S. consul in Panama, George Orr, to look into the Panamanian laws regarding ship registration. Orr reported back that pertinent passages were scattered through several different codes and that there was in fact at that time no single maritime code for Panama. The Panamanian legislature soon took up this very question and codified the relevant provisions in a new law in 1925, apparently in response to the Orr report. The exact details of who first requested the Orr report and how it may have been relayed back to the Panamanian legislature are unclear. Since, under a 1916 agreement, U.S. consuls represented Panamanian interests in ports where Panama did not maintain either a member of its diplomatic service or an honorary consul, the U.S. consular service may simply have wanted a clarification of the law for its own officers acting in that capacity.[7]

The new 1925 law required that at least 10 percent of the crew of a ship with a Panamanian flag be Panamanian citizens, but the law included an escape clause waiving the requirement if sufficient

Panamanian mariners did not apply for positions on a particular ship. There is no convincing evidence that this aspect of the law was ever enforced. The provision may have been included simply to help the Panamanian legislators claim that they had served national interests. The law also envisioned the creation of a maritime academy, which was not established until 1958.[8]

Under the streamlined registry law, the Panamanian registry began to attract a wide variety of international shipowners, many of them seeking to avoid legal, diplomatic, or economic restrictions on their businesses. Some of the operations were perfectly legitimate, some were designed to facilitate smuggling of one sort or another, and some were conducted in defiance of British and other restrictions on trade. The variety of maritime trades that developed under the Panama flag in 1926–1939 foreshadowed the vast proliferation of such trades after World War II.

Rum-Running

The *Belen Quezada* was probably registered in Panama to provide some legal protection against seizure at sea in liquor smuggling. Another ship, the *Taboga*, came to the attention of the U.S. State Department in 1923. While the *Taboga* was docked in Halifax, Nova Scotia, the master discharged a group of Chinese seamen who then approached the U.S. consulate to ask for repatriation to the United States. U.S. Consul General Edwin N. Gunsaulus reported to the State Department that some of the seamen had no proof of U.S. citizenship, and he sought instructions, noting in his report that the ship was "known to be involved in liquor smuggling."[9]

The Panamanian flag did offer some protection against U.S. liquor law enforcement. A convention signed in 1924 and ratified in 1925 by the United States and seventeen other nations, including Panama, gave the United States the right to board and search vessels on the high seas suspected of violating the liquor prohibition law. However, the convention limited the right of search to an area one hour's steaming time from U.S. territorial waters. Given the irregular coastline, the fact that territorial waters at the time extended only three miles to sea, and the differences in ships' steaming times, the Coast Guard and mariners debated the exact extent of the area legally open to search. If a ship flew the U.S. flag, of course, the Coast Guard could interdict it further out at sea.

Even as the exact area of Coast Guard jurisdiction remained unclear, smugglers knew they were safe from interdiction on the high-seas approaches to the United States from Canada and from Caribbean or Atlantic islands. A ship registered in Panama clearly had more freedom of operation than a U.S.-flagged ship. In fact, the smugglers believed that if they could outrun a Coast Guard patrol in a chase and get beyond an hour's steaming time from the territorial waters, they would be safe. Whether or not a continuous chase from within the three-mile limit to a point in international waters allowed confiscation was tested in a long-drawn-out set of legal battles over the *Federalship*, a rum-runner interdicted off the California coast.[10]

The Panamanian honorary consul in Vancouver, Maximo Morris, who had registered the *Belen Quezada*, helped facilitate the transfer of several other ships, including the *Federalship*, from various registries to that of Panama. The United States sought to get Panama to immediately cancel the registries of four of these ships on the grounds of suspicion of smuggling under a special law passed in Panama in 1926. However, when it was notified of the U.S. suspicions of smuggling, the Panamanian government proceeded cautiously, refusing to cancel the registries on suspicion alone. Panamanian authorities would examine the evidence, request a response from the shipowners, give a fair warning, and then either get voluntary cancellation of the registry or, failing an adequate response, cancel the registration. In the *Federalship* case, the U.S. Coast Guard confiscated the ship and the owners finally voluntarily canceled the Panama flag. In three other cases, those of the *Helori, Hakadata*, and *Chasina*, Panama canceled the registration after an investigation. Although the U.S. government had asked for immediate cancellation on notice of suspected smuggling, the Panamanians gave all the owners time to rebut the charges.[11]

Even so, whether Panama had yielded sovereign control over its ships became a sensitive issue in that country. The cancellations of the three ships' registries struck some local Panamanian observers as giving in to a U.S. overstepping of sovereign rights; on the other hand, Panama's procedural and deliberate approach, rather than immediate cancellation on suspicion, showed that the nation was protecting its rights. Panamanian politics in the period was focused on the ratification of the Kellogg-Alfaro Treaty, with which Panama would have sacrificed its autonomy by agreeing to automatically enter as a U.S. ally any war

the United States engaged in. Panama never ratified that treaty, but
the intense discussions over the issue in 1925–1927 in part prompted
the deliberate handling of the smuggling cases. Panama quietly dismissed Morris from his post in Vancouver. His motive for registering
the rum-runners may have been financial, as Panama allowed consuls to
retain half of collected fees to a maximum of $200 a month.[12]

Panama's slow but effective cooperation with the U.S. government
in the four notorious rum-runner cases became well-known in the
smuggling community. According to the U.S. Treasury Department, by
1928 of 113 known rum-runner ships, 89 flew the British flag, 8 were
Honduran, and only 2 were Panamanian—the rest were registered in a
variety of other countries or had no valid registration.[13] The brief flurry
of rum-running into the United States under the Panamanian flag had
dwindled to the vanishing point by the late 1920s.

As mentioned previously, a 1916 agreement between the United
States and Panama allowed U.S. consuls to represent Panama in those
ports where Panama had no representation of its own. This led to several
odd cases in the 1920s and 1930s in which shipowners of dubious reputations approached U.S. consuls around the world seeking Panamanian
registration. However, most of the transfers to Panama in the late 1920s
were quite legitimate. For example, three major vessels of the Pacific
Mail Steamship Line, doing business in Central America, were transferred to Panama with approval from the U.S. Shipping Board. United
Fruit Company, which had numerous ships flying under the British
flag, transferred some thirteen vessels to the Panama flag in 1928–1931.
Again, although freedom from British regulation and taxation may have
been factors in the transfers, the ships were legitimately involved in
Central American trade. Since they were previously British-flagged,
they did not represent a reduction in the U.S. merchant fleet.

Flag of Refuge

Although the precedents set by the Harriman line, Pacific Freighters,
and the handful of rum-runners in the early and mid-1920s showed the
potential for the Panama flag to be used to escape onerous economic or
political restraints, the flag remained largely devoted to perfectly legitimate shipping businesses, most of them operating in Central America,
through the 1920s. The expansion of the flag's use as a convenient
refuge flourished in the 1930s, partly because of European political

turmoil in that decade and partly for economic reasons, following the dual motivations originally noted by representatives of both the Harriman company and Pacific Freighters.

The major additions to the Panamanian fleet from the late 1920s to the outbreak of World War II were as follows:

- *Basque ships.* At least nine ships registered through the Panamanian consul in Bilbao, Spain, to escape from Spanish regulations in 1927–1937. Since there was a Basque movement to secede from Spain and adopt a separate flag, the adoption of the Panamanian maritime flag by Basque companies may have been a reflection of the desire for autonomy or a distinct national identity.[14]

- *Esso fleet.* Twenty-five large Standard Oil tankers transferred from Danzig to Panama in 1935 because of concerns over the political reliability of the Nazi regime, as discussed in chapter 7. In 1936–1937 Esso added three tankers to its Panama fleet: the *Motocarline, C. O. Stillman,* and *Esso Bolivar.*[15]

- *Norwegian ships.* Erling Naess, a Norwegian businessman and shipping expert, recommended the transfer of two Norwegian-owned whaling ships and their auxiliary vessels from British registration to Panama to avoid double taxation, that is, a corporate tax in Britain, where the corporation and the ships were registered, and personal income tax on dividends in Norway. Naess traveled to the United States and got advice and suggestions from Standard Oil Marine Department executives. The Rasmussen group and other Norwegian owners registered a total of more than thirty ships and small whale catchers in Panama in 1935–1940. If profits led to dividends, the companies would be taxed only on the dividends at the point of payment, as Panama did not charge a corporate income tax.[16]

- *Greek gunrunners to Spain.* Several Greek shipowners registered ships in Panama and used them to ship weapons to the Loyalist government in Spain during the Spanish Civil War (1936–1938). Britain, France, Germany, and Italy (along with all the other European countries except Sweden and

Switzerland) had signed a nonintervention agreement, pledging not to provide aid to either side in that war. Germany and Italy routinely violated the agreement to supply direct military assistance to the profascist insurgents, but England and France abided by the agreement, and the British even provided monitors to enforce the agreement.[17] Greece was also a party to the nonintervention convention, but no nations in the Americas had officially joined. The United States passed an amendment to its existing neutrality legislation prohibiting the sale of arms to either side during civil wars; U.S. firms were explicitly denied export permits to send aircraft or other war matériel to the Loyalists. The American consul in Piraeus, Greece, who handled Panamanian transfers in that port asked for instructions from the State Department on these cases, noting that some of those seeking to transfer from Greece to Panama were admittedly engaged in gunrunning to the Loyalists. He was instructed to raise no objections.[18]

- *Greek ships registered in Panama for business reasons.* Shipowners Aristotle Onassis (then located in Argentina) and Manuel E. Kulukundis in Greece transferred whole fleets to Panama to escape from Greek social legislation and wage scales or from British taxation (for ships previously registered under the British ensign) beginning as early as 1932. Onassis started his line with six ships declared surplus in Canada by the Canadian-Pacific Railway. Onassis and Kulukundis each later claimed the other emulated his example.[19]

- *Jewish refugee ships.* At least thirteen ships, from Greece, France, England, and Turkey and registered in Panama, were reported carrying Jewish refugees from Europe to Palestine in defiance of restrictions imposed by Britain (which administered Palestine under a League of Nations trusteeship) on the number of immigrants allowed there. This effort began early in the 1930s and was organized in 1938 under the local Jewish organization Mossad l'Aliyah Bet (the forerunner of Israel's foreign intelligence service, Mossad). The effort continued at a much lower level during the Second World War and was revived in the postwar years. The drama of the refugee ships was described in the documentary novel *Exodus* by Leon Uris. Panamanian registry may have somewhat protected the refugee ships from boarding by British authorities in international waters. By the beginning of World War II, some 24,000 immigrants had been brought to Palestine illegally.[20]

A few ships of other countries, including Germany and China, transferred to Panama in the 1930s.[21]

The only sizable registration of ships in Panama by U.S. companies in this period was the fleet of twenty-five Standard Oil tankers transferred from Danzig registry in June 1935. Then, later in 1935 and in 1936, Standard Oil of California followed the lead of Esso and transferred four other tankers from U.S. registry to a subsidiary in Panama and the Panama flag: the *R. J. Hanna*, *California Standard*, *Silveroak*, and *Silverspruce*.[22]

By June 1938 Lloyd's of London showed that Panama had a fleet of 134 ships with a gross tonnage of 611,207. By July 1939 the totals had risen to 145 ships with gross tonnage of 717,525.[23] Thus, although the Panamanian fleet had grown to be the largest in Latin America by 1938, that growth had not come at the cost of reducing the size of U.S.-registered shipping but from a variety of other fleets, including those of Danzig, Greece, Spain, Canada, Germany, China, and Britain.[24]

With all of these transfers, by 1939 it had become clear that the small Panamanian registry opened in the 1920s had rather rapidly become a flag of refuge. The Esso example was specifically emulated for economic reasons in Norway. Numerous Greek firms, most famously those of Aristotle Onassis and Manuel Kulukundis, set the pattern for later registration to escape from taxation, labor costs, and other disadvantages of registry in the home country of the owners or under other flags, such as the British. At least twenty Greek-owned ships had taken advantage of Panamanian registry by 1939; earlier in the decade, numerous Greek shipowners and managers had experimented with Panamanian registry, either setting up a firm in Panama or simply reflagging ships from home ports in Greece or Britain. Although Erling Naess, Kulukundis, and Onassis each later claimed to have pioneered Panamanian registry, it is apparent from the records that the advantages were perceived through the 1930s not only by those individuals and by the managers at Esso but also by many maritime attorneys, ship managers, and owners in Norway, Greece, Spain, China, and elsewhere.

In addition to the clear business and economic advantages of Panamanian registry, the diplomatic and political reasons for transfers were also precedent setting. The flight of Esso from Danzig because of the Nazi regime there and in Germany, the gunrunning to antifascists in Spain, and the transport of Jewish refugees to Palestine during the early Holocaust all represented diverse political uses that could be served by registry under the Panamanian flag, springing from the rise of fascist regimes in Europe.

Overlapping Factors of Flags of Convenience

By 1938 the short history of the open registry developed in Danzig and then more fully in Panama had demonstrated a group of factors that would underlie the evolution of flags of convenience in the post–World War II world. All of the factors, in one way or another, would explain why the use of the merchant flags of the United States and other traditional maritime states would later decline and why the flags of Panama and, later, of other small sovereign states with virtually no maritime traditions would come to dominate world shipping in the last decades of the twentieth century.

1. *Profits from registry itself.* The registry system could be a source of income for those arranging registry in foreign ports. The consuls in Vancouver and Bilbao, for example, took a share of the registry profits. Even though Panama treated both consuls as corrupt, they showed that the act of registration itself could be individually profitable. On a larger scale, of course, registry fees flowed into the Panamanian treasury. Ship registration was itself a business opportunity.

2. *Evasion of flag-state laws.* Various rules and regulations that reduced the competitive position of a ship in international service under the flag of a ship-owning firm or individual simply did not apply under Panamanian law. As William Comyn mentioned, Pacific Freighters found Panamanian registry profitable because the ships, although U.S.-owned, no longer had to conform to U.S. requirements as to manning or boiler inspections. Thus, operations could be conducted in competition with the Japanese. Similarly, Harriman's brief use of the Panamanian flag to allow U.S.-owned ships to serve alcohol on board on the high seas demonstrated the same factor: restrictions imposed by the country

where a ship was owned that reduced the ship's competitiveness did not apply in Panama.

3. *The lure of an offshore financial environment.* Several other business benefits derived from finding a favorable jurisdiction. The Danzig and Panama operations both showed that corporations, by registering ships abroad, could avoid the double taxation becoming common in Europe and America. Neither Danzig nor Panama had a corporate income tax, and this appealed to Esso, Erling Naess, Rasmussen, Onassis, Kulukundis, and numerous other Greek and Norwegian owners. In the Esso-Danzig case, it appears the profits were never distributed but simply plowed back into the acquisition of more tankers. Fewer taxes and lower operating costs, thanks to freedom from manning requirements that allowed the hiring of low-wage seamen, made registry in Danzig and Panama advantageous and represented the core motivations for later off-shoring of a wide variety of financial and business enterprises.

4. *Political and diplomatic motivators.* A variety of political and diplomatic factors made the registries of both Danzig and Panama attractive. As noted earlier, Danzig was initially attractive because it allowed ships to evade the reparations imposed on Germany by the Allies. Later, Danzig ships, although operated from Hamburg, were free of the economic and political turmoil of Weimar Germany. The Panama flag was similarly used as a shelter for ships smuggling arms to the Spanish government during the Spanish Civil War. Further, immigration rights were becoming severely restricted in these decades. When Britain started denying entry visas to Palestine, Jewish refugee immigrants had to be smuggled in. The Panama flag offered smugglers at least nominal protection from search on the high seas.

5. *Evasion of destination state laws.* The rum-running operations that had briefly flourished under the Panamanian flag (both in U.S. waters and in the Baltic) showed that when nations attempted to ban the import of some commodity, enterprising businessmen—by definition criminal smugglers—would turn to another country's flag in hopes of gaining some protection from search and seizure on the high seas. Panama's cooperation, without sacrificing the country's sovereignty, in deregistering several rum-runner ships soon put an end to that particular practice, but the attraction of a registration system for evading import restrictions had been demonstrated.

By the end of the Prohibition era in 1934, Panama had cooperated with the United States in canceling the registration of known smugglers, and rum-runners used the British flag extensively. Since the British ensign was issued in Bermuda, the Bahamas, Canada, and throughout the empire, and since the British would not consider deregistration on the mere assertion of suspicion by U.S. authorities, the British flag was far more convenient for smugglers. In fact, the British refused to stipulate that U.S. surplus ships transferred to the British flag would lose their registration if engaged in smuggling on the grounds that the operation of foreign laws had no bearing on British registration.

Although liquor, gun, and refugee shipments were treated by some states as smuggling, and even though the shipping of these illegal commodities was conducted necessarily by individuals with shady reputations or criminal records, it can be argued that the smugglers were simply conducting free trade. Jewish immigrant ships, smugglers, rum-runners, and gunrunners all drew members of the criminal class, but this does not diminish the fact that the trades they were engaged in had all been perfectly legal until they were interdicted by nations with powerful navies or coastal patrols. Decisions about which countries can receive weapons or whether immigrants or particular commodities can be imported were and remain serious matters of state policy and law.[25]

6. *Strategic considerations and national honor.* As demonstrated by William Comyn of Pacific Freighters, W. A. Harriman of the Harriman lines, and Esso Shipping Department executives (possibly all three following advice from Sullivan and Cromwell), transfers of U.S.-owned ships could be arranged comfortably with Panama, not only because of its more favorable business environment and lower costs but also because of its special dependent status in relation to the United States. That is, in time of crisis, Panama would presumably follow the U.S. lead in alliances and diplomatic affairs, allowing merchant ships under Panamanian flags to potentially be used as U.S. strategic assets. At the same time, if the ship were exposed to a hostile act by any nation, the U.S. flag would not be exposed; national honor would not require protection, retaliation, or even protest. Exactly that consideration led to a great expansion of the Panamanian fleet in 1939–1941, as discussed in chapter 9.

9

Neutrality and War

The U.S. political culture of the 1920s and 1930s reflected disillusionment with Wilsonian idealism and a commitment not to be sucked into another European war. Despite continued pro-British sentiment in some quarters, majorities believed that U.S. profiteers had engineered the entry of the United States into World War I. True, bankers had loaned millions to Britain and France and were invested in an Allied victory. And true, business as usual had prompted U.S. trade in petroleum, food, and war goods to Britain and France in 1914–1917. The historical literature first written about the war reflected the prevailing view of the U.S. entry: Walter Millis' *Road to War* (1935) and the Nye Committee investigations (headed by Senator Gerald Nye of North Dakota) confirmed the "merchants of death" thesis and contributed to the neutrality laws passed by Congress in the 1930s.

Because an isolationist mood dominated Congress and in order to avoid another war, the neutrality legislation banned loans to belligerents, ruled that American merchant ships should not go into war zones carrying cargoes to either side, prohibited U.S. citizens from travel on belligerent ships (to avoid *Lusitania*-type episodes), and said that the United States would embargo arms and other strategic materials to belligerents, no matter whose ships carried them. Slightly different variations of these prohibitions appeared in several iterations of neutrality legislation in the 1930s.

Given that World War I and World War II are often conflated in today's public memory, few realize the depth of Americans' interwar disillusionment with Wilson's proclaimed goal of "peace in our time" and with the other high-minded ideals in his 1917 appeal to Congress. That disillusionment pervaded American discourse in the 1920s and 1930s. It accounts for the expatriate movement of the era and helps put in context the escape from middle-class morality represented by resistance to Prohibition and the alienation of many intellectuals from the business class.

Before World War II, the vast majority of Americans preferred to stay completely out of the brewing cauldron of European conflict. Exceptions to this rule could be found in certain ethnic groups and in elite die-hard Anglophile quarters, and when the 1936–1938 Spanish Civil War pitted profascist Rebels against socialist and communist Loyalists, the appeal of the common front of the Left drew some U.S. volunteers to Spain to help. However, the official U.S. position on the Spanish Civil War was strictly neutral, with an arms embargo against both sides. And American majorities supported that position.

In 1937 Joseph P. Kennedy, chairman of the U.S. Maritime Commission, requested an analysis of the neutrality status of U.S. shipping in the event of war from the State Department's adviser on international economic affairs, Herbert Feis.[1] Feis, who later became well-known as a historian and published eleven major books on foreign affairs from 1947 to 1972 (as well as two posthumously), advised Kennedy in September 1937, "During a war in which the United States is a neutral, the existence of an American Merchant Marine gives the United States a measure of independence which it might not otherwise enjoy from certain inconveniences, hardships and losses. On the other hand, it may lead to incidents affecting American ships which may threaten entanglement of the United States in the war."

After he had detailed the dislocations that war might impose on the U.S. merchant marine, Feis commented, "The existence of an adequate Merchant Marine would give the United States a freer hand to maintain its neutrality with a minimum of commercial suffering and to assist in the maintenance of commerce by satisfying the merchandise needs and the Maritime transportation needs of the neutral part of the world. On the other hand, a war involving many of the large countries would almost certainly in its early stages mean a very substantial reduction in the volume of American foreign trade."

Regarding the risk that threats to the merchant flag might cause engagement in war, as they had in 1917, Feis noted, "As to the possibility of entanglement in hostilities between other countries because of incidents affecting American ships on the high seas, the Neutrality Act of 1937 endeavors to minimize the risk by prohibiting the transportation by any American vessel of arms, ammunition or implements of war to any belligerent state or to any neutral state for trans-shipment to a belligerent state. . . . These provisions tend to reserve American shipping for the peaceful commerce of neutrals and non-combatants during wars in which the United States is a neutral."[2]

In his cover note to Kennedy, Feis apologized that since the situation would "vary so tremendously according to what particular countries were the belligerents and what countries were the neutrals," it became "practically impossible to work out a comprehensive analysis upon which all responsible branches of the [State] Department would agree."[3] Nevertheless, Herbert Feis had put his finger exactly on the U.S. maritime dilemma. With a large merchant marine, the United States would be in a position to benefit economically from a major war in which it remained neutral, and at the same time, that large fleet would be in danger of involving the country in the war if U.S.-flagged merchant ships were interdicted or destroyed by one of the warring nations. In fact, precisely this dilemma faced Kennedy's successor as U.S. maritime commissioner, Adm. Emory Land, once war erupted in Europe.

When World War II broke out with Germany's invasion of Poland and Danzig on September 1, 1939, it was not just isolationists in the rural Midwest who wanted to remain out but firm majorities of the public, as reflected in polls of the era and in the lineup of congressional votes. All of these issues related to the underlying honor code that remained alive, although far less explicit, well into the twentieth century. A large sector of the U.S. public believed that Wilson's idealism in World War I had been hypocritical at worst and naive at best. The United States had become a tool of the Europeans, sucked into that war by trickery and special interests. "Never again" was the sentiment. The honorable course was to remain aloof, just as Wilson had tried to do from 1914 until his decision in March 1917 to ask Congress for a declaration of war.

However, a relatively narrow sector of the elite class remained pro-British, believing that the honorable course was to help the Allies. Among those who felt honor demanded assistance to, or even outright alliance with, Britain were many in President Franklin Roosevelt's class and administration. Others were anti-Nazi, either because they had Jewish connections or because Hitler's actions revolted them. The Far Left was thrown into confusion by the short-lived Nazi-Soviet Alliance, which was signed in August 1939 but which collapsed in June 1941 with the German invasion of the Soviet Union.

Thus, importantly, between September 1, 1939, and December 7, 1941, the country remained officially neutral, while some elements of the administration (Adm. Emory Land, but not Secretary of State Cordell Hull) moved carefully toward a pro-Allied position. Roosevelt, ever the consummate politician, did not want to alienate either his labor and Democratic urban base or his Republican and Progressive allies in Congress, most of whom were isolationist. At the same time, he wanted to prevent a German victory and aid Britain as much as possible within the constraints of official neutrality. For Roosevelt, that was the honorable course.

For the wider public, American honor was sorely tested, especially as families, gathered around radios, sympathetically listened to Edward R. Murrow broadcasting from London during the Blitz. Yet still for the majority, it was not "our fight." The result was the twisted foreign policy and innovative maritime policy of the era and a very uncomfortable neutrality until the Japanese attacked and simplified the issues. Then, there was no issue. On December 7, 1941, the Japanese solved FDR's dilemmas by what he called their "dastardly" attack. Honor and national pride switched overnight to wholehearted support for the war effort. The "stab in the back" was not only a technical and clear act of war against the United States, but by its nature, it served to "wake the sleeping tiger"; honor required a firm response. As volunteers flocked to recruiting stations to the tune of the pop song "Remember Pearl Harbor," it was clear that the outrage aroused national pride and offended honor.

However, to understand the impact of foreign-flag registry on the American merchant fleet, it is instructive to look closely at the two-year period of neutrality from September 1, 1939, to December 7, 1941. During that period, Admiral Land dealt with the dilemmas Feis had predicted with a series of innovative solutions that involved transfer of vessels to the flags of Panama and other nations.

Under Adm. Emory Land, the U.S. Maritime Commission from 1939 and, beginning in 1942, the War Shipping Administration (WSA) endorsed and greatly expanded the Panamanian flag fleet. The variety of ships transferred to the Panama flag in these years under Land's approval greatly expanded and changed the nature of the Panamanian flag fleet.[4]

Admiral Land found the flag of Panama convenient first to implement a pro-Allied neutrality policy and, after December 7, 1941, to help maintain effective control by U.S. officials over a sizable merchant fleet, much of it registered abroad, serving the nation's war goals. The association of Panama with clandestine and illegal trades faded, and the country gained legitimized and official sanction. The registry evolved into an extension of U.S. maritime policy, receiving endorsement from U.S. government shipping offices, from the State Department, and from the Office of the President.

Foreign ships reflagged in Panama during the war were frequently managed under contracts or agreements with existing U.S. shipping firms. In this regard, the policies that evolved regarding the Panamanian flag were part of the broader U.S. governmental approach during World War II to harness the skills of the U.S. free enterprise system largely without nationalizing enterprises or recruiting private managerial personnel directly into government service.

By 1943 various official practices and policies allowed ships registered under not only the flag of Panama but the flags of many other nations, including some occupied by Axis powers, to be operated as part of the U.S. war effort. As in other areas of industrial and commercial life, the government was able to set up a wartime command economy through a variety of bureaucratic and regulatory practices that only rarely included outright expropriation or nationalization. More often, the Roosevelt administration preferred methods short of confiscation, employing financial and tax incentives, regulatory procedures, procurement rules, and other measures to enlist industry and commerce to the war effort. Official U.S. policies contributed to the phenomenal growth of the Panama fleet from less than two hundred ships in 1938 to more than five hundred ships by 1948. These developments, crucial to the future history of world shipping, remained somewhat obscured from public view for several reasons: the grand military events of the war dominated the news; technical questions of maritime policy and administration were of interest to a limited audience; and some decisions and actions remained classified or at least not widely publicized.

Cash and Carry: The Neutrality Problem and the Panamanian Solution

When the German invasion of Poland led Britain and France to declare war on Germany in September 1939, the vast majority of Americans agreed that the United States should remain neutral. Even so, Roosevelt, some members of his administration, and a minority sector of the public believed that the United States should support the British and French to the extent possible without engaging in the war. In response, Congress debated amendments to the neutrality law that would permit at least some trade with Britain and France. Both nations were dependent on the United States, not for arms but for petroleum, and Britain also imported food from America.

As Herbert Feis had predicted, the U.S. Neutrality Act of 1937, still in force in September 1939, required the president to announce when a state of war existed abroad and to impose an embargo on weapons sales to either side. The act further required that U.S. citizens be warned that they traveled on belligerent vessels at their own risk, reflecting another of the lessons of the events of 1915–1917.[5]

The German invasion of Poland caused the administration to rethink the effects of the existing neutrality laws. Roosevelt argued for modification of the law to allow him to distinguish between aggressors and victims and to supply arms to the victims. Other critics of the acts pointed out that the embargo on arms was itself not "neutral" in the abstract, since in many respects Germany was better armed than Britain or France. Thus, a continued embargo would work against Allied interests and slightly favor Germany. After a national discussion and a month of debate, Congress finally amended the law early in November 1939. The new act, incorporating amendments introduced by Senator Key Pittman of Nevada and thus known as the Pittman Act, removed the embargo on weapons in cases of declared war. However, the 1939 law still prohibited U.S. vessels from entering war zones and also prohibited U.S. citizens from traveling on belligerent ships. Furthermore, the law prohibited the arming of American merchant ships. Congress' lessons learned approach to the 1939 neutrality legislation reflected the widespread disillusionment with Wilson's war goals and the sense that Wilson's neutrality policies had not been adequately thought through. This would be a more carefully structured and even more honorable neutrality than Wilson had overseen in 1914–1917.

Under the 1939 Pittman Act, also known as the Cash and Carry Act, the Allies or Germany could purchase goods and transport them in their own vessels or those of other neutrals. This form of neutrality, while legally quite impartial, clearly favored the British, who had control of sea surface transport.[6] Nevertheless, it would avoid putting U.S. ships in harm's way, the way the *Vigilancia*, *City of Memphis*, *Illinois*, and others had been put in harm's way in 1917. By requiring cash payments, the neutrality law was meant to prevent bankers from favoring the Allies because of loans or credits for their purchase of goods, as they had done in 1914–1917, reflecting the points made in Walter Millis' *Road to War*. The Pittman Act thus sought to prevent several possible casus belli, such as the loss of American lives on torpedoed ships and the loss of U.S.-flagged ships at sea, and to prevent the development of a creditor interest in seeing an Allied victory. Most important, it would prevent the U.S. flag from being attacked at sea, which would require an armed U.S. response.

From September 1939 to May 1940 (the period of the so-called phony war), little action took place on the western front since Britain and France could do little to aid Poland unless they were to launch an invasion of Germany or bomb German targets. Both countries felt unprepared for either course of action. According to William Langer and S. Everett Gleason, "phony neutrality" in the United States matched the phony war in Europe. The president and much of the U.S. public were clearly pro-Allied, and the cash-and-carry system, with its cloak of neutrality but tendency to favor the Allies and allow British purchase of U.S. goods, suited the national mood and seemed an honorable course.[7]

Even so, neither Britain nor France tried to buy many U.S.-manufactured weapons in this period, partly because they wanted to stimulate their own arms industries. Petroleum and food continued to be the main exports from the United States to the Allies, but they could no longer be carried on U.S.-flagged ships. For the British, the new law imposed difficulties. British shipping was in great demand to supply outposts throughout the empire, and with U.S. shipping suddenly banned from the northeastern Atlantic, the "carry" part of the legislation imposed more difficulties than the "cash" part. For U.S. shipping companies, Latin American, Asian, and Mediterranean trade could not absorb the tanker and dry cargo tonnage idled by the closing of the North Atlantic routes. Shipowners believed the prohibition of U.S. vessels from the trade had singled out one particular economic segment, the shipping industry, as the scapegoat for U.S. neutrality policy.[8]

Maritime Commission Reaction to the Pittman Act

Emory Land, who clearly sought to implement measures that would aid Britain as much as possible, approved a number of separate measures shortly after the Pittman Act was passed that technically conformed to the act but also fostered trade with the Allies. Several of the measures quietly worked, but one raised a firestorm of opposition. The approval of sale and transfer of ships to British companies involved no violation or evasion of the neutrality law, even though it was clearly a pro-Allied act. The British paid cash and then owned and registered the ships under the British merchant ship flag, completely avoiding the risk of a repeat of the events of February–April 1917, when German U-boats targeted U.S.-owned and U.S.-flagged ships. U.S. seamen on board such ships were dismissed and replaced by Canadian or Scandinavian seamen.

Another adjustment to conditions involved the quiet rerouting of British and Canadian flag vessels to take up the reduction in U.S. service. Thus, for example, Esso directed its Canadian subsidiary to carry a heavier transatlantic trade to substitute for U.S.-flag tankers removed from that route. In 1939 Esso maintained an international fleet of nearly two hundred tankers. Although seventy-five were U.S.-flagged, the non-U.S.-flagged Esso fleet available to supply Britain included fourteen tankers registered in Britain, twenty-one in Canada, twenty-eight in Panama, and almost sixty in various other countries.

Under Emory Land, the Maritime Commission could quietly approve the sale and transfer of ships from the U.S. flag to companies in Panama and other countries, and did so through the neutrality period. In addition to three U.S.-registered tankers shifted to the Panama Transport Company before September 1939, the company acquired another fifteen between September 1939 and February 1940 with full approval of the Maritime Commission.[9]

Esso faced a problem, however. All of the ships transferred from Danzig to Panama in 1935 still had German officers and crews. In August 1939, as it became clear that war neared, Esso ordered the German crews of sixteen ships paid off and dismissed. Twelve of the former Danzig-registered ships were recrewed with American seamen and four with British crews. In September German crews on the remaining nine former Danzig vessels were replaced. Once the war zones were declared under the Pittman Act, the crews on vessels sailing to Europe once again were changed: the American seamen were replaced by Danes, Norwegians, and Canadians.[10] The Pittman Act forbade Americans from traveling on belligerent ships; there had been no mention of forbidding American crewmen on board neutral ships in the war zone (the intent of the law had clearly focused on passengers, not crew), but to be safe, Esso replaced the American crews anyway.

The crew replacement did not always proceed smoothly. The German crew of the formerly Danzig-flagged *Calliope*, at anchor in Rio de Janeiro, at first refused to leave the ship. Esso anticipated further resistance and possible sabotage. Vice President E. J. Sadler of Esso called Adm. Harold Stark, chief of naval operations, and asked for naval or Coast Guard assistance in arranging the changeover in crews on the company's ships when they came into New York Harbor. Undersecretary of State Sumner Welles noted in a memo to Adolf Berle, assistant secretary, "The company now runs to us for help. . . . This is obviously a case of where the Standard Oil Company of New Jersey has deliberately evaded our shipping laws in order to obtain easier labor conditions and is now caught in a jam." Harbor authorities and local police in New York and New Jersey were alerted for possible trouble, but no further incidents were recorded as the German crews were quietly replaced.[11]

During the period of U.S. neutrality, Esso and Texaco both shipped petroleum not only to the Allies, by way of Panamanian-registered tankers, but also to the Axis, through shipments officially designated for Spain. As late as 1942, Esso supplied Tenerife in the Spanish Canary Islands. Ostensibly this petroleum was sold to the Spanish state monopoly, but the orders contained high percentages of naval-grade fuel. British and American intelligence agents suspected that Tenerife deliveries often found their way from Spain to Germany. On March 7, 1941, Panama Transport Company's *W. H. Libby* was observed transferring cargo directly to German and Italian tankers. Sales from Esso fields in Romania and Iraq continued more openly to Italy, which remained officially neutral through early 1941.[12] Esso's interpretation of neutrality as business as usual was more evenhanded than Emory Land's, in that, at least for a period, it allowed exports to *both* sides in the European war.

Another policy the Maritime Commission implemented to address the shipping problems generated by the Pittman Act smacked of outright evasion of the intent of the revised neutrality law: the transfer of registry of U.S.-flagged ships to Panama with ownership retained in a U.S. company. As early as 1937, when a cash-and-carry amendment to neutrality had first been considered, Gene Hackworth, the legal adviser to the State Department, had pointed out that such transfers of U.S.-owned ships to other neutrals posed no danger to neutrality, since the Maritime Commission, under powers retained in the 1936 Merchant Marine Act, could approve or disapprove all transfers. As he said then, ships would not be able to "scuttle to foreign flags because of curtailment of their activities under the Maritime Commission." At the time, Hackworth assumed that companies might attempt the device of flag transfer, but that the Maritime Commission could enforce neutrality by preventing any such transfers. By 1939, however, the commission, Roosevelt, and some of the president's closest advisers sought to find means to get around the restrictions on neutrality and to keep Britain supplied.[13]

In early November 1939, immediately after passage of the Pittman Act, the Maritime Commission announced approval of the transfer of a group of United States Lines ships from American to Panamanian registry, with ownership to be retained by United States Lines, a U.S. company. This decision provoked an outcry from a wide range of opponents, including isolationists, church groups, labor unions, and editorialists. The move was seen by opponents as a clear and dishonest attempt to evade the intention of the Pittman Act. U.S.-owned ships, if registered under the flag of Panama, would conform to the letter of the law, but reflagging would allow the U.S.-owned ships to trade openly with Britain and France. Unlike Standard Oil, United States Lines did not intend to establish a separate, Panamanian corporation to own the ships; instead, the plan was for United States Lines to retain ownership and simply transfer the registry and obtain a new flag. The difference may seem obscure, but it was clear to observers at the time: Esso ships owned by Panama Transport Company were not "U.S.-owned"; United States Lines ships, if registered in Panama, would remain U.S.-owned, and thus, a U.S. company would be using the Panamanian flag to evade the intent of the neutrality law.

Allowing U.S.-owned ships to operate under Panamanian flags would destroy any semblance of genuine neutrality and reduce the effect of the new neutrality law to a symbolic or technical neutrality masking an underlying pro-Allied position. United States Lines decision to ultimately withdraw its transfer request reveals how closely ship registry and the nation's neutrality were tied together, and the debate over the original request illustrates how the issue of an honorable neutrality was navigated by the different parties involved.

United States Lines Ships and the Neutrality Debate

On November 6, 1939, Land's office announced that United States Lines had applied for the transfer of nine ships to the Panama flag.

The announcement listed eight ships (of about 7,500 tons each) that regularly carried freight. Seven ships were named "*American . . .*" followed by "*Trader,*" "*Farmer,*" and so on. The two other nominees for transfer were larger liners named the *President Harding* and the *President Roosevelt*.[14] If the transfer was successful, these two vessels would continue to carry passengers and cargo to Britain as regular liners under U.S. ownership but with foreign crews. American passengers would not be forbidden, under the Pittman Act, from traveling on either these Panamanian-flagged ships or those flying the flag of another neutral. American public attention focused on the issue of Panamanian registry and opinions crystallized.

Four lines of argument emerged during this brief debate: First, transfer was a good idea and perfectly honorable, as it provided a commercial convenience to maintain business as usual. Several representatives of shipping interests took this position. Second, transfer was a good idea because it provided a means to aid the Allies without risking the U.S. flag. Those who favored aid to Britain and France and who rejected isolationism, including Emory Land and (for a short period) Roosevelt himself, argued along these lines. Third, transfer was a bad idea because it was an obvious subterfuge to avoid the strict meaning of neutrality. Secretary of State Cordell Hull and strong isolationists used this line of argument, finding such an obvious evasion of the neutral intent of the law dishonorable. And, fourth, transfer was a bad idea because it represented a business subterfuge in the form of runaway ships that avoided U.S. labor conditions and rates and took employment away from American merchant mariners. Some, but not all, labor union spokesmen and leaders favored this position. Considering the crucial role of U.S. labor in support of the Democratic Party at the time, this issue made it difficult for FDR to continue to support Admiral Land's decision.

Shipowners and representatives of the shipping industry saw the transfer in much the same light as earlier transfers for commercial purposes, designed to keep U.S.-owned ships in the world shipping market. Robert C. Lee, an executive with Moore-McCormack Lines, noted, "We should not allow war hysteria to destroy our business sense. The only question about American ships operating is whether they can involve us in war. These ships, under the Panama flag will not involve us." At the height of the controversy, the editors of the industry trade magazine *Marine Journal* commented, "The transfer is entirely legal and from every practical point of view highly desirable. Moreover, there have been several transfers of oil tankers over which not a word of protest was heard." The editors' position failed to recognize that the first tankers had been transferred to a company, Panama Transport Company, that, although owned by a U.S. parent firm, was a *Panamanian* corporation. They noted that Secretary of State Hull "thought more of consistency than of practical considerations affecting the merchant marine and enthusiastically supported the contentions of the professional pacifist and goozelfixers that the transfer would be a subterfuge to get around the strict letter of the neutrality act." Frank Taylor, president of the American Merchant Marine Institute (another shipping company organization), also emphasized the practical and realistic business view of the matter: "We must insist," he said, "upon the free privilege of sending American products to the nations which normally are our best customers. Facing this situation in a realistic manner, as the American Atlantic Lines [*sic*] have done, permission has been sought to transfer the registry of old vessels to a foreign flag."[15]

When the Maritime Commission members explained their own rationale for the proposed transfers, they demonstrated a slightly different line of thought, based less on business considerations than on the need to aid Britain. The United States, argued Admiral Land, would not violate neutrality in any way by allowing the transfers. Land testified at the Senate Foreign Relations Committee, "I do not understand neutrality; I do not know anybody that does." Land's sarcasm tended to get the better of him; he clearly understood neutrality to mean that the law should keep the United States from getting into shooting conflicts with the belligerents. Speaking to a more receptive audience at the Society of Naval Architects and Marine Engineers, Land commented on the relationship of neutrality to the proposed United States Lines transfers, making clear that he saw the issue as one of keeping the flag and U.S. citizens out of harm's way. "It is my understanding that the [Pittman] Act was passed for two purposes, (a) to protect the American flag, (b) protect the American citizens. In any transfer of registry or in any sale of ships these purposes are accomplished and no claims can be made against the Government in any way—no United States citizens will be on such ships and the ships themselves are no longer United States flag ships."[16] The commission's official press release reflected the idea that the use of the foreign flag would represent a diplomatic convenience: "The proposed transfer to a foreign flag would divorce the ships involved from any and all protection afforded by the United States flag."[17]

Max Orell Truitt, a member of the commission, also took a pragmatic view of the transfers as a way to avoid war: "I don't see any element of a dodge at all; I think it is a completely sound, bona fide solution all around. Congress unquestionably intended to keep the United States flag from going down in the brine and to keep United States seamen from losing their lives. But nowhere in the act does it say an American citizen could not operate a foreign flag vessel with a foreign crew. . . . He is not risking the United States flag or the lives of United States Citizens."[18]

Roosevelt appeared to agree with this interpretation at first, telling reporters that he did not believe the nation's neutral status altered the right of its citizens to sell property to another neutral national. However, the president was usually careful not to get on the wrong side of public opinion, nor did he want to alienate organized labor, so he found himself in a bit of a dilemma.

Labor leaders immediately reacted to the news. Joe Curran, head of the National Maritime Union, stated, "If these ships are manned by alien seamen, the union is going to see to it that the American seamen thrown on the beach as a result are taken down to Washington to maintain a picket line around the commission until those seamen are taken care of." Curran went on to say that he thought United States Lines was "circumventing" the Pittman Act. "The ships should be kept under the American flag and re-routed," he added.[19]

However, it soon became clear that "labor" was not united on the issue. Longshoremen, it appeared, would prefer that the ships stay in business, whatever their flag, so as to keep the ports busy. Joseph P. Ryan of the International Longshoremen's Association (the East Coast longshoremen's union) sent a telegram to FDR and Emory Land, asking them to approve the ship transfer, because otherwise 15,000 longshoremen "would be thrown out of work."[20]

Within two days of the original announcement, FDR announced that he was holding up the transfer, pending investigation. The issue continued to simmer over the next ten days or so, as the administration sought a way through the dilemma and through the conflicting views of Democratic Party constituents.

Roosevelt, with his usual political acumen, saw a chance to defuse Curran's threat. He invited Curran, Ryan, Land, and several shipping firm representatives to the White House, where he announced a plan to direct the Works Progress Administration to set up a project to employ displaced seamen. At the same time, he hinted that he would support the plan to transfer the ships to the Panama flag, as an entirely legal procedure.[21] But opposition went beyond that of the National Maritime Union, as the use of the Panama flag as a way around the neutrality law became more apparent to others. Other elements of Roosevelt's political base besides labor were in revolt as well.

The *New York Times* published a lengthy editorial by noted columnist Arthur Krock on November 10. Krock argued that the measure violated the "spirit" of the Pittman Act. "Search of the Congressional debates on the Pittman act . . . fails to disclose that any of those who voted for the measure expected continued American ownership of vessels trading in the area excluded by Congress." Krock went on to state that reregistry of U.S.-owned ships in Panama was "a clear evasion of the purposes of the Pittman Act's Title II."[22]

Only a few public spokesmen came to the support of Emory Land and Max Truitt. One avowedly pro-British syndicated columnist and radio commentator, Boake Carter, spoke out in favor of the idea. Since Carter was a British national, his pro-Allied position was readily discounted. Union leaders even claimed he was in the pay of the shipping lobby. Senator Tom Connally of Texas and Senator Josiah Bailey of North Carolina agreed with Land's idea that the transfer of United States Lines ships was fully legal and would avoid insults to the flag and the killing of U.S. citizens. "However," Bailey noted, "as the Great Apostle said, 'some things are lawful that are not expedient' and perhaps for the present we have a case of bad timing."[23]

State Department staff members were thrown off by the Maritime Commission announcement of United States Lines' intention to transfer its ships to the Panamanian flag while retaining its corporate ownership. Assistant Secretary of State Adolf Berle had been forewarned by Admiral Land that Panamanian registry might be considered once the neutrality law was amended. "The Maritime Commission," Berle noted in his diary, "on the whole thinks its job is to run ships through hell and high water, which is good naval tradition, but the American people won't stand of it." When Land personally explained the logic of allowing Panamanian registry for U.S.-owned ships, Berle thought the idea a "hypocritical business." Even so, he could understand the merits of the plan. "I suppose," he mused, "if somebody wants to go into the blockade-running business under the Panamanian or Costa Rican flag, there is not [a] great reason why they shouldn't."[24]

Before publicly announcing the proposed transfer, Land had telephoned Secretary of State Hull and informed him that Roosevelt had given prior approval of the transfer. Hull at first indicated he had no objection to the transfer, since it involved no questions of foreign policy. Adolf Berle first agreed with Hull that it was a legal, if disreputable, action. But Berle had reservations. Hull's statement that it had nothing to do with foreign policy, Berle noted, "saved our souls, and accomplishes nothing." Berle went on, "But I have a horrible feeling that it is just the way the American people feel about this. They don't want American ships to go abroad because they might get into trouble. Nevertheless, they do want the commerce and the trade there. So a dirty subterfuge like getting behind the flag of a defenseless neutral will probably fit them."[25]

Berle and others at the State Department informed Hull of their objections, and Hull changed his mind. Hull called Land back to explain his change of heart. "It was now clear to me," he wrote in his memoir, "that the transfer to Panamanian registry of ships . . . was a subterfuge to escape the provisions of the Neutrality Act." Hull then issued a public statement condemning the transfer as a violation of the intent of the neutrality law.[26] Clearly, for Berle and his boss, issues of honor continued to resonate. Although Hull touched base with Land, he failed to clear his position with the president.

With Roosevelt at Hyde Park and Hull in Washington, it briefly appeared that the administration was severely divided over the issue and giving mixed signals. The generally pro-Democrat *New York Times* reported the apparent split in a muted fashion: "In a press conference just before Secretary Hull condemned the proposed transfer to Panama registry as impairing the integrity of the Neutrality Act, the President said the transaction had no bearing on the neutrality of the United States." Roosevelt was quoted as saying, "If there was any danger of the United States becoming involved in the war the Maritime Commission would not have consented to the transaction, but that danger did not exist today." He further argued that the nation's neutral status did not alter the right of U.S. citizens to sell property to a neutral national. However, recognizing the dissent in his own administration as well as the outcry from the National Maritime Union, Roosevelt notified Land to hold up on the final decision.[27] The *New York Times* opined, "While the plan may remain within the letter of the Neutrality Act, it violates the spirit of that measure."[28]

Soon politicians, editorialists, and organization spokesmen started to voice opinions on the transfer. Franz Boas, a noted German-born anthropologist, writer on Latin American history and culture, and honorary chairman of the Council for Pan American Democracy, announced his organization's opposition: "The proposal itself is not only a device to evade the Neutrality Law, but, more than that, its effect is to use the sovereignty of Panama to serve the interests of certain American shipping companies."[29] John T. Flynn, chair of the Keep America Out of War Congress and founder of the isolationist America First Committee, called the proposal "a clear cut evasion of the neutrality act" and "deliberately playing fast and loose with the Congress."[30] Progressive Republican senators, who had sided with Roosevelt on domestic issues but were far more isolationist than the president, strongly opposed the measure, including "Champ" Clark of Missouri, Robert Taft of Ohio, and Borah Johnson of California.[31]

On November 17, 1939, the president gave hints that he was beginning to bow to the surge in public and political opposition to the ship-transfer plan. In a press conference, he said, "Our Government would be reluctant to put a sister Latin American republic in a position different from our own." Furthermore, the *Times* paraphrased remarks by Stephen Early, Roosevelt's press secretary, regarding compliance with the letter of the law while evading its intent: no suggestion of such a proposal had appeared when the president supported the Pittman Act, and hence, the plan "could fairly be regarded both at home and abroad as a too clever move which might remain within the letter of the law but which would certainly violate the spirit of it."[32]

Adolf Berle took credit, in his diary, for finding a way out of the impasse over the proposed United States Lines transfer. Berle had a tendency to inflate his own importance in some crucial decisions, but his account is entirely plausible. "I cruised into the Secretary's office and there we found the whole problem of the transfer of ships to the Panamanian flag fairly boiling. I had had a brain storm and drafted out a statement which I thought settled the matter. The Act permits the transfer of these ships, but the spirit of the Act would indicate a bona fide sale to independent interests. I looked in at the White House with the suggestion that this ought to be introduced in the matter."[33]

A few hours later, Roosevelt called in Berle and told him he hoped United States Lines would withdraw its application and get to work on a bona fide sale. Berle interpreted such remarks by Roosevelt as instructions, and accordingly, the next day, Berle "got to work" on United States Lines to withdraw its application for transfer. Berle put pressure on Basil Harris, a Treasury Department official and the holder of the largest block of United States Lines stock.[34] However, Land had already decided that a sale to a foreign corporation was a perfectly good way through the tangle. He had already explained that point to Roosevelt in a memorandum dated November 8, 1939. In the memo, Land offered a thorough explanation of the logic of the transfer. Under the heading "There is neither subterfuge nor violation of the letter or the spirit of the Neutrality Laws," Land made these points:

1. The vessels would be owned by a foreign corporation. 2. The vessels would not fly the American flag. 3. No American citizens could by law serve on them as officers or crew. 4. The vessels under long-established principles, would lose completely the protection of the United States Government, and would not involve us in disputes with foreign governments. They would not be the basis for claims by the United States. 5. If any of these vessels were sunk, there would be no loss of lives of U.S. citizens. . . . 6. The present owners are merely placing themselves in the position of other American business interests not affected by the Neutrality Act—those which hold stock in foreign corporations which own and operate foreign flag vessels. This has not been, and is not now, illegal under our law.[35]

Land showed that he perfectly understood the intent and purpose of the Neutrality Act; his method around it could not be criticized by either advocates of aid to the Allies or strict isolationists who hoped to keep the American merchant flag from engaging the United States in war.

The controversy subsided as fast as it had arisen, as the planned foreign ownership of the vessels quieted the issue. However, the concept that Panama registry could provide a means around the effect of the Pittman Act had been fully aired in the press. The ships were transferred in December 1939 and January 1940 to a Norwegian company and registered in Belgium with little or no public notice, exactly as Land had argued.[36]

Direct Transfer of Ownership and Flag

Over the next eighteen months (December 1939–July 1941), the Maritime Commission quietly approved the sale and transfer of 267 ships to a variety of nations, including 63 to Panama and 126 directly to Great Britain. The transfers included not only Esso-owned tankers (whose ownership was vested in the Panama Transport Company) but a variety of smaller vessels, including freighters. Brazil received 20, France and Greece 11 each, Belgium 9, and Honduras 7.

The crucial difference between the transfers in 1940 and 1941 and those that had aroused the storm of public, labor, and political outrage in early November 1939 was that the ships transferred during the period of neutrality were no longer directly owned by a U.S. company. The November 1939 protest over the United States Lines ships grew out of the fact that before the company had decided to transfer to Norwegian ownership and the Belgian flag, it had proposed to operate the ships under the Panama flag while retaining U.S. ownership. The Esso tankers and mostly older small freighters were sold to Panamanian or other foreign companies, and the United States Lines ships (after the initial uproar) and others conformed to this model.

Danish, Italian, and Finnish Ships

When Germany invaded Denmark on April 9, 1940, the Maritime Commission interned Danish ships in U.S. ports. Similarly, when Italy officially joined in World War II and participated in the invasion of France on June 10, 1940, the United States interned all Italian ships then in U.S. ports. The numbers of these ships were significant: forty Danish ships and twenty-eight Italian ships. The Danish and (at first) Italian crews remained on board.

On June 6, 1941, the Ship Requisition Act (Pub. L. No. 101) empowered the U.S. government to seize and operate these ships. The Danish ships were then operated with the Danish crews and officers. However, since U.S.-flagged ships had to be crewed by U.S. citizens and the Danish crews could not have stayed on board if the ships were reflagged with the U.S. flag, the ships were renamed (for race horses that had won the Kentucky Derby) and then transferred to Panamanian registry and operated by the Maritime Commission directly or through established U.S. shipping companies, with arrangements made to compensate the Danish owners at the termination of hostilities.

The crews of the Italian ships were removed (some Italian crews had sabotaged their ships) and replaced by mixed crews of stranded Allied seamen, and the Italian ships too were transferred abroad, mostly to Panama. Similarly, seventeen ships under the flag of Finland were impounded, and eight of those were reflagged in Panama. The transfers of the Danish, Italian, and Finnish ships well before the United States entered the war represented an evasion of the Pittman Act, but the actions did not raise the outburst of criticism in mid-1941 that the proposed transfer of the United States Lines ships had raised earlier. In fact, the press explicitly reported that the transfer to Panama of these ships, registered in countries that had come under Axis control, made it possible for the ships to trade with the Allies, trade that would have been impossible under the existing legislation if the ships had been U.S.-flagged. Even though the unneutral policy was clear, no public outrage ensued.

Through 1940 and 1941 public support for administration measures that aided the Allies "short of war" increased. The destroyer-for-bases exchange had been arranged September 1940 and Lend-Lease was enacted in January 1941, both well before the June 1941 enactment of the Ship Requisition Act. Furthermore, the legitimate ownership by foreign firms of the 267 ships transferred abroad fully conformed to the Berle formula—the ships were not U.S.-owned and engaged in a subterfuge, but rather, they were bona fide foreign-owned ships registered abroad. The 85 Finnish, Italian, and Danish ships had never employed U.S. seamen, they had never been U.S.-owned, and thus, they could not be viewed as a dodge or scheme to reflag U.S. ships and throw U.S. seafarers out of work.

Loss of Panamanian and American Merchant Ships to German Subs, 1939–41

The British instituted a convoy system, operating from Halifax, Nova Scotia, in November 1939. Although the United States remained officially neutral, U.S. naval ships and aircraft began participating in

Resigning from the U.S. Navy at the beginning of the Civil War, Raphael Semmes became the most notorious of the Confederate sea captains leading attacks on U.S.-registered merchant ships. *Library of Congress*

The *Kearsage* sank the Confederate raider *Alabama* off Cherbourg, France, on June 12, 1864. The *Alabama* and other Confederate ships had driven many U.S. shipowners to flee the U.S. flag and register under the British flag. *New York Public Library*

In the period 1920–35, the Free City of Danzig registered Esso tankers, the first major twentieth-century use of flags of convenience for U.S.-owned oil tankers. This postcard image of Danzig from the era highlights the city's history as a port. *Library of Congress*

Among the U.S.-flagged ships destroyed by German submarines that precipitated the entry of the United States into World War I was the tanker *Illinois*, destroyed on March 18, 1917, in the English Channel. The *Illinois* is shown here in before and after photographs shot from the deck of the German U-boat for propaganda purposes. One can see the neutrality markings, as well as laundry hanging out to dry, in the top picture. *U.S. Naval Institute Photo Archive*

Robert Lansing was Woodrow Wilson's second secretary of state. As a specialist in international law, Lansing viewed German submarine attacks on U.S.-flagged ships in 1917 as a casus belli. *U.S. State Department*

When American shipowners sought to transfer U.S.-owned and U.S.-registered ships to the Panama registry to get around the 1939 cash-and-carry neutrality legislation, President Franklin Delano Roosevelt at first approved, then disapproved, the arrangement. *New York Public Library*

Adm. Emory Land headed up the War Shipping Administration in World War II and took advantage of Panamanian registry to flag numerous ships that did not meet U.S. standards for safety or crew accommodations. *Library of Congress*

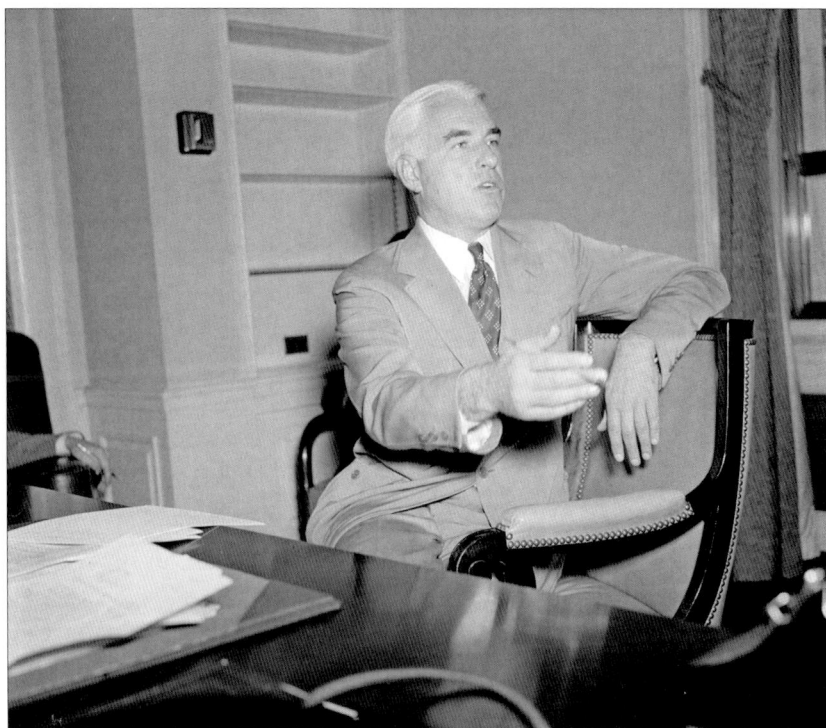

After serving briefly as secretary of state under Franklin Roosevelt, Edward R. Stettinius went on to found Liberian Services, Inc., which established the system of Liberian ship registry in 1948. *Library of Congress*

William V. S. Tubman was president of Liberia from 1944 until 1971, and he cooperated with former U.S. secretary of state Edward R. Stettinius in establishing the
Liberian flag of convenience. *Library of Congress*

protecting the convoys as far as Iceland in September 1941. During the period of official (but clearly pro-Allied) U.S. neutrality, increasing numbers of ships trading to Britain from the Western Hemisphere were torpedoed and sunk by German submarines, either sailing in convoy or on independent voyages. In addition, a few were lost to mines and to Italian submarines. Through 1940 up to December 7, 1941, a total of fifteen Panamanian ships were sunk. Of the fifteen, three were owned in Panama. Twelve were either owned by U.S. parent corporations with a subsidiary in Panama or were former Danish or Italian ships operated for the Maritime Commission by U.S. corporations. Six of the twelve U.S. ships were Esso tankers of the Panama Transport Company fleet, three of them newly added to the fleet. Even though some of the ships were clearly U.S.-owned and some of the seamen who died were U.S. citizens, none of the episodes constituted an attack on the U.S. flag.[37]

Even before the Neutrality Act was modified, the *City of Flint* was seized at sea by the German pocket battleship *Deutschland* on October 9, 1939; the ship carried an admittedly contraband cargo. At first a German prize crew took over the ship, but the *City of Flint* was ultimately returned to its U.S. crew on November 6, 1939, in Norway by the Norwegian navy.

More dangerous for U.S. neutrality, six other U.S.-flagged merchant ships were subject to German attack in the twenty-seven months between September 1, 1939, and December 7, 1941. The MS *City of Rayville* was lost to a German mine off Australia on November 8, 1940. More well-known was the sinking of the steamship *Robin Moor* on May 21, 1941, by the German submarine *U-69* in the South Atlantic, outside the German-declared war zone. All of the seamen from the *Robin Moor* survived after their lifeboats were accidentally located at sea by ships of friendly nations. Germany at first denied responsibility for the ship loss but admitted it in 1943.

The remaining four U.S.-flagged merchant ships were sunk in the two months just before Pearl Harbor: the SS *Lehigh*, carrying cargo from Spain to New York, was sunk off West Africa on October 19, 1941 (by an unidentified submarine); the SS *Steel Seafarer* was bombed off Egypt on November 5, 1941; and the SS *Astral*, a Socony-Vacuum oil tanker, was torpedoed en route to Portugal on December 2, 1941, by *U-43*. The next day, a U.S.-flagged freighter owned by the American–South African Line, the SS *Sagadahoc*, headed for Beira in Mozambique, was torpedoed and sunk by *U-124* in the South Atlantic.[38]

In the first four of the six incidents after the passage of the 1939 Neutrality Act, only one American merchant seaman lost his life when he drowned upon abandoning the *City of Rayville*. However, all eight officers and twenty-nine men (most of whom were U.S. seamen) died when the tanker SS *Astral* went up in flames. Another merchant seaman was killed in the loss of the SS *Sagadahoc*.[39]

Of the six U.S.-flagged ships sunk, one, the *City of Rayville*, was lost to a mine off Australia. One, the *Steel Seafarer*, was carrying Lend-Lease supplies to British forces in Egypt by way of the Red Sea, which Roosevelt had declared open to U.S. shipping. The Lend-Lease program, initiated in March 1941, authorized the "lending" of munitions and other war supplies to the Allies. The goods were mostly sent on board non-U.S. ships in the neutrality period. The first administrator of Lend-Lease was former U.S. Steel executive Edward R. Stettinius Jr.[40]

Four of the ships sunk in 1941 did represent clear-cut acts of war: SS *Robin Moor* and SS *Sagadahoc* had been en route to Mozambique, a Portuguese colony and therefore a neutral, while SS *Astral* had been headed for neutral Portugal itself. SS *Lehigh* was carrying manganese from neutral Spain to the United States. U.S. shipping to and from neutral ports did not constitute violations of the cash-and-carry principle, so these four voyages were legal under U.S. law, and attacks on those ships were acts of war. As noted previously, the Roosevelt administration protested the attack on the *Robin Moor* and closed German consulates in the United States in response on June 16, 1941. However, the losses of *Lehigh*, *Astral*, and *Sagadahoc* were not reported before December 7, 1941, and it appears that the fate of those three ships was not known until after the declaration of war.[41]

Of course, once the United States entered the war, hundreds of U.S.-flagged merchant ships were sunk and thousands of American merchant mariners lost their lives on those ships. Other U.S. seamen lost their lives while sailing on Panamanian ships sunk in the period of neutrality as well as during U.S. participation in the war. The only Axis action against a U.S.-owned and U.S.-flagged merchant ship that had the potential to bring the United States into the war was the destruction of the *Robin Moor*, but as noted, the Nazi government denied responsibility for that sinking until long after Pearl Harbor.

The U.S. Congress amended the Neutrality Act on November 17, 1941, allowing American merchant ships to be armed and to travel through the war zones. The effect of this legislation was to end the "carry" part of the cash-and-carry provision of the 1939 Neutrality Act. Coupled with Panamanian transfers, Lend-Lease, and Roosevelt's opening of the Red Sea to American merchant shipping in April 1941, the November 17 modification of the law meant that U.S. maritime neutrality had been transformed by several steps into a formality rather than a strategic reality. Many other diplomatic and military steps by the United States through 1940 and 1941 had made it clear that while technically neutral, the United States favored the Allies and was preparing for war.

Nevertheless, it was true that for twenty-seven months, from September 1, 1939, to December 7, 1941, American neutrality policy, with the Pittman provision of cash and carry and Panamanian registry of a variety of U.S.-owned and U.S.-controlled ships, had largely succeeded in preventing a replay of the events of February 1, 1917, to April 6, 1917, that had led the United States into war after German attacks on the American merchant flag on the high seas. The successful neutrality policy had changed the status of the Panamanian registry from a sometimes shady cover for smugglers of liquor, transport of refugees, and tax- and cost-haven for U.S. corporations into a semiofficial adjunct of U.S. governmental maritime policy.

Arming Panama Ships and the Arias Overthrow, 1941

The U.S. Maritime Commission had found Panamanian registry a convenient means to allow shipment of U.S. products to the Allies despite the Pittman Act. However, the president of Panama, Arnulfo Arias, inaugurated on October 1, 1940, soon made it clear that he did not intend to allow the practice to lead to a conflict with the Axis powers. Arias had led a coup in 1931 against Panama's liberal president and installed his brother, Hormodio, as president. Arias' Panameñista Party emulated the tactics of oppressive governments around the world (particularly in Nazi Germany and Fascist Italy) by jailing dissidents. Americans and other foreign-born residents of Panama were angered when Arias disfranchised the non-Spanish-speaking population. In many ways, the new president showed sympathy with the Axis powers. He reportedly worked closely with Panama-based undercover agents of Nazi Germany and espoused a racial ideology that closely paralleled the Nazis'.

Just two months before the attack on Pearl Harbor, on October 6, 1941, the United States proposed a policy of providing arms to the

U.S.-owned or U.S.-controlled ships that had been transferred to Panama. President Arias objected and indicated that he would not allow Panamanian merchant ships to be armed.[42] Three days later, Arias was ousted in a coup, and his replacement, Ricardo Adolfo de la Guardia, quickly approved the policy of arming the merchant ships. German spokesmen asserted that the coup was quite engineered by the U.S. government. Although that is entirely possible and it is true that the U.S. State Department was quite satisfied with the change in leadership, evidence of clandestine U.S. support for the coup has not surfaced in the course of research for the present work.[43]

Before the coup, German and Italian liaison officers walked into the Panamanian Seccion de Naviera and obtained lists of newly registered ships. The office stopped supplying the information right after the coup. As early as October 16, 1941, the new foreign minister, Octavio Fabréga, sought U.S. State Department help in preparing legal briefs protesting the sinking of ships, and within a week, the State Department turned the task over to private attorneys in the United States. By the end of 1941, forty-one Panamanian ships had been armed. As noted earlier, during the period of U.S. neutrality, twelve U.S.-owned or U.S.-controlled Panamanian-registered merchant vessels were sunk.

The armed Panamanian-registered ships were operated by a variety of U.S. companies, including Marine Transport Company of New York, United States Lines, Waterman Steamship Company, American President Lines, and Grace Lines. These five large companies operated a total of at least thirty-four Panamanian-flagged former Danish and Italian vessels during the war years.[44]

Effective Control in World War II

On February 2, 1942, by executive order, Roosevelt replaced the Maritime Commission with the WSA. The new agency included many of the same staff and was also headed by Admiral Land. The WSA managed the nation's merchant shipping in support of the war effort and developed several practices during the war to control ships under U.S. registry and under foreign flags. Once the United States entered the war, the Neutrality Act was null, and U.S.-owned ships could again trade with the Allies. Wartime transfers to Panama, like the transfers of the Danish, Finnish, and Italian ships in the neutrality period, were implemented so that ships confiscated or captured that did not meet U.S. shipping standards (in terms of living accommodations or safety features) could be operated in the war effort. Furthermore, since labor was scarce, it was difficult to meet the requirement that U.S.-registered ships be crewed by a majority of U.S. citizens; registry in Panama or another country and operation by the Maritime Commission or a U.S. ship-management firm allowed for employment of foreign seamen and relieved pressure on the limited pool of American merchant seamen.

Vessels registered under the Panamanian flag during World War II provided an adjunct fleet whose details were administered under the direction of Admiral Land. The World War II Panamanian fleet was only one of several such adjunct fleets, and it was clearly designed to serve as a temporary military expedient, not as a long-range system. However, one lasting impact of the arrangements was to give official U.S. government sanction to the operation of foreign-flagged ships by U.S. companies.

The WSA indicated in its reports those vessels sailing directly under the U.S. flag and appended such listings, or included within the lists vessels "under U.S. control" but flying other flags. Thus, for example, a list published by the WSA in January 1945 showed more than 3,800 merchant vessels under U.S. control, including some 3,500 ships under the U.S. flag and 315 vessels under a variety of registries, including the flags of Norway, the Netherlands, Honduras, Venezuela, France, Greece, and Panama. One of the most important methods of effectively controlling U.S., Allied, and foreign shipping in the wide variety of registry arrangements was the ship warrant system. That is, ships could enter U.S.- and Allied-controlled ports only if the WSA had issued them a warrant, and thus, whatever a ship's registry or ownership, its arrival and departure could be regulated by the warrant system.[45]

The designation "U.S. control" simply meant what it said. The ships so designated fell under the WSA's control, either through the ship warrant system or more directly through a time charter agreement, under which the WSA chartered the vessel from the owning company, or through a general agency agreement, in which a WSA-owned ship or a ship requisitioned for use was operated by a company as an agency of the government. U.S. control over the ships under many different foreign flags was exercised through these various systems and not through diplomatic control of another country's foreign policy. That is, effective control was exercised through port control and contractually, not diplomatically.

Postwar Effective Control Doctrine

The U.S. Maritime Commission and WSA practices in using the flags of Panama and other countries first to provide shipping to the Allies during the neutrality period and later to manage captured, requisitioned, and abandoned ships from foreign registries in the war effort set precedents for Cold War era practices. As the flight from the flag continued for economic reasons in the late 1940s and into the 1960s, the Joint Chiefs of Staff (JCS) developed a rather hazy or poorly developed effective control doctrine that became a source of continuing debate in naval and maritime policy circles.

As has been shown, although some U.S.-owned and foreign-registered ships were effectively controlled under agreements and charters during the war, the WSA did not rely on U.S. ownership and registry in a friendly country to constitute control. However, in several staff papers written for the JCS in 1946 and later, military planners overlooked the wartime precedents that developed effective control through the warrant system and through charters and agency agreements. Instead, they relied on the notion that Panama (and later, Liberia) would be politically reliable and that U.S. ownership and registry under a compliant foreign flag would provide a reserve fleet available in periods of national emergency. This doctrine and its reliance on the uncertain political cooperation of Panama and Liberia were discussed in military circles well into the 1980s.[46]

10

Sovereignty for Sale

I n 1948 Arnulfo Arias, who had been deposed in 1941, again ran for president of Panama. Although he lost that election, the nation's legislature ordered a recount and declared him president later in 1949. For the U.S. government and U.S. business, the Arias candidacy and takeover were highly disturbing developments. When Arias returned to power in 1949, he had already shown a willingness to put his definition of Panamanian interests above U.S. interests, especially when it came to ships registered under the Panamanian flag. Any confidence that Panama as a nation could be effectively controlled in postwar maritime matters quickly diminished in U.S. defense circles.

After the Panamanian legislature had installed him in office, Arias suspended the constitution and set up a secret police force. In the United States, Arias was widely perceived to be a fascist, and the United States again supported the results of a coup that ousted him from office two years later, in 1951. However, the emergence of his regime, avowedly hostile to U.S. interests, in 1949–1951 contributed to the original success of the Liberian flag of convenience.

Liberia's registry system was a by-product of an effort by Edward R. Stettinius Jr. to use private capital and public influence to assist the nation of Liberia and, at the same time, to create a strategically reliable but nominally independent flag for American merchant shipping.[1] Stettinius' reasoning for his efforts reflected the lessons of World War II and of the prewar period, when ships were operated much more cheaply under the Panamanian flag: Panamanian and presumably Liberian registry allowed cheaper operation of business, and as long as the semidependent nation remained politically reliable, the United States would have a fleet of ships to support U.S. strategic and diplomatic policies without putting the

Portions of this chapter were presented by the author at an academic conference in 1979, later published as an article in *Business History Review* 54, no. 2 (Summer 1980), and summarized in *Sovereignty for Sale*, chap. 7. Reprinted here with permission.

U.S. flag in harm's way. The maritime community had learned a similar lesson during neutrality and World War II: an honorable course through the dilemmas of U.S. flag exposure to risk abroad was to supplement the U.S.-flagged fleet with a cheaper-to-operate, U.S.-owned, foreign-flagged fleet of commercial ships that would simultaneously avoid putting the flag in harm's way and be available for strategic purposes when needed.

Edward R. Stettinius Jr.

In 1926 Stettinius had headed Welfare Activities at General Motors. In 1934 he moved to U.S. Steel, and by 1938 he had become chairman of the board of that corporation. Franklin Roosevelt recruited Stettinius into government service, appointing him chairman of the War Resources Board in 1939 and placing him in charge of the Lend-Lease program in 1941. In 1943 Secretary of State Cordell Hull brought Stettinius to the State Department as undersecretary. In November 1944 Roosevelt appointed forty-four-year-old Stettinius secretary of state. Some observers thought Stettinius received the appointment for his good looks and charm rather than for any knowledge of international affairs; Roosevelt had grown used to conducting personal diplomacy with Churchill and Stalin in what later journalists dubbed "summit" conferences.[2]

As secretary of state, Stettinius led the U.S. delegation to the Yalta Conference early in 1945. On his return to the United States, he made a brief stopover in Liberia, on the westernmost tip of West Africa, to appear at the opening of the Port of Monrovia, which had been built with U.S. Navy assistance. Both the U.S. Navy and the U.S. Army had chosen to use Liberia for installations during World War II. Liberia had drawn U.S. attention not only because the governing class in Liberia was descended from African American settlers but also because the country had a history of dependency on U.S. charity, used English as its national language, and used the U.S. dollar as its national currency. In addition, and probably most important from a strategic point of view, Liberia was well situated and geographically very attractive. At the westernmost point in Africa, it is a short 1,730-nautical-mile trip from Brazil, making the perilous Atlantic crossing in time of war appreciably shorter than any other route by sea or air. By contrast, New York to Liverpool, Great Britain, is more than 2,800 nautical miles.

Although the Monrovia seaport did not officially open until the war was nearly over, the airport, built with Army funding, had opened some two years earlier and had provided a key route from the Western Hemisphere to the Eastern Hemisphere for important air travelers. Franklin Roosevelt himself had stopped there en route home by air from the Casablanca Conference in February 1943, setting the precedent for Stettinius' later visit on his return from Yalta. Stettinius later recalled the contrast between the people's poverty and the nation's rich resources; as a former executive of U.S. Steel, he took particular note of Liberia's newly discovered high-grade iron deposits.

In 1945 President Harry Truman, Roosevelt's successor, replaced Stettinius with Jimmy Byrnes and then in 1947 appointed the popular and highly effective George Marshall to the post. In 1947 Stettinius, retired from government service, established a corporation to implement plans for Liberian development. Stettinius Associates, starting with $1 million in capital (of which Stettinius personally provided $200,000), formed a profit-sharing arrangement with the Liberian government. Stettinius established the International Trust Company (ITC), with a subsidiary, Liberia Company, that conducted actual operations in Liberia. Sixty-five percent of Liberia Company's profits were returned to the parent corporation, 25 percent went directly to the Liberian government, and 10 percent were given to the Liberia Foundation, a nonprofit organization devoted to Liberian educational, health, and welfare programs.[3] Stettinius hoped that if his economic development plans for Liberia succeeded, they could be emulated elsewhere around the world. Possible locations discussed included Ethiopia, the Netherlands East Indies (later, Indonesia), Morocco, and French West Africa.[4]

Liberia Company's economic development plans included funding for the exploration and start-up of further subsidiaries. Stettinius authorized studies of possible diamond mines, cocoa and coffee plantations, fisheries, and timber operations. He ordered plans for a highway network, electrification of Monrovia, water and sewage systems, and construction of railroads. These long-range plans attracted little outside capital. However, some progress on the ground took place: Liberia Company participated in the management of the Port of Monrovia in a seven-company consortium, helped reorganize the airport, and set up Liberian International Airways.

Stettinius recruited a public relations firm to promote these efforts. As a result, from September 1947 to late 1948, more than five hundred news stories, mostly derived from company press releases, and ten major magazine articles glowingly described the plans. The publicity stressed the three-way split of the profits and the explicit concern with Liberians' welfare.

Observers noted that Stettinius' "progressive capitalism" appeared to coincide with the ideas of Eric Johnson, who, as head of the U.S. Chamber of Commerce, urged U.S. business in a progressive direction. Henry Luce had authored a 1941 editorial in *Life* magazine that dubbed progressive capitalism exported to the underdeveloped world as the "American Century" philosophy.[5] Eric Johnson had popularized the concept: if the United States was to continue to thrive, it would need to develop worldwide markets for its products, which would require the rapid advancement of the underdeveloped colonies and countries of the world. Stettinius, with his capitalist interests in and development plans for Liberia, represented a leading and practical proponent of the concept advanced by Henry Luce and popularized by Eric Johnson.

Seeking U.S. government aid to the Liberian effort, the Stettinius organization played up the growing fear of Soviet influence around the world, stressing policy considerations such as "raw material interests" and the "strategic position of Liberia from the standpoint of U.S. protection of Panama Canal and Brazil." The Cold War, already in its early stages, provided context for reference to Liberia as America's "sole beachhead in Africa." Stettinius warned that if the company failed, "Communism, already at work in Africa, would rejoice."[6]

Shipping Developments, 1947–51

The idea that Liberia might compete with Panama for the growing business of ship registration surfaced in the early months of the Stettinius organization. In January 1948 E. Stanley Klein, an attorney for the corporation, reported "certain shipping interests had indicated a willingness to obtain registration under the Liberian flag."[7] The work of developing the proposed maritime law fell on Klein and James G. Mackey, secretary-treasurer of Stettinius Associates. Both Mackey and Klein also participated in the ownership of another company, American Overseas Tanker Corporation (AOTC), established in September 1947. AOTC, with investments from Stettinius and other members of Stettinius Associates, borrowed additional funds and quietly purchased eight surplus tankers from the U.S. government. Three were transferred to National

Tanker Corporation (a subsidiary of AOTC) and immediately sold to a Chinese-nationalist-financed foundation at a profit of $150,000 per ship. The other five tankers, kept by AOTC, were financed with a loan from Metropolitan Life Insurance Company, operated with assistance from William N. Westerlund, and transferred to Greenwich Marine, a Panama corporation. The tankers were chartered by this Panamanian subsidiary of AOTC to Standard Oil. The operating company was sold to Stavros Niarchos in 1951. This sequence of events led to allegations that the surplus tankers had gone to foreign interests (Greek and Chinese) and prompted a long series of congressional investigations.[8]

One of the tankers, the *Meachum*, continued to attract congressional interest for several years, as government attorneys claimed that the sale of the *Meachum* to foreign investors represented a violation of the Ship Sales Law that gave preference to U.S. owners. The ship had been transferred to United Tanker Corporation, a company in which China International Foundation held a majority interest. The defenders of the transaction argued that China International Foundation was a charitable foundation with a board of directors consisting entirely of U.S. citizens.[9]

While this issue over the *Meachum* and two other tankers simmered through 1949–1951, Stettinius and his key aides actively involved in writing the Liberian maritime code were owners, through AOTC, of oil tankers registered in Panama. Although Aristotle Onassis later claimed that he had first suggested the idea of Liberian ship registry to Stettinius, the idea may have come to him from Westerlund, Stettinius' associate in the Panamanian oil tanker firm. Westerlund asked Stettinius whether Liberia had a ship-registry law, and Stettinius replied that he did not know but that he would look into it.[10]

Writing the Liberian Maritime Code

Several key members of Stettinius' company had served during the war in the State Department or other government agencies. Joseph C. Grew, former ambassador to Japan and later undersecretary of state under Stettinius, joined the corporation and provided considerable help in arranging influential contacts. In March 1948 Grew held what amounted to an informal subcabinet meeting at his home in Washington, D.C. The meeting was attended by the secretaries of the Army and Air Force, the undersecretary of the Navy, an assistant secretary of state, and Brig. Gen. Edwin L. Siebert, deputy director of the newly formed

CIA. At this meeting, Stettinius, Grew, and Gen. Julius Holmes, former assistant secretary of state and another associate in the Stettinius enterprise, detailed the purposes and strategic importance of their planned operations in Liberia. They explained that Liberia Company would be able to provide information and reports and that U.S. strategic interests in Africa would be well served by the corporation. This explicit effort to enlist the endorsement and support of top-level military, diplomatic, and intelligence officers came naturally to Stettinius. The meeting was private, and the record was maintained on a confidential basis.[11]

While staffers prepared the draft Liberian maritime code, Stettinius himself viewed the Liberian ship registration as a minor adjunct to his other Liberian developmental enterprises. He looked into the possibility of transporting iron ore, calculating that a million tons of ore moved from Monrovia to Baltimore could be bought at a rate competitive with the rate offered by foreign-owned ships if the company used "liberty ships manned by officer personnel from some foreign nations such as Dutch, Scotch, etc., with the balance of the crew native Liberian boys, who would receive in the neighborhood of a dollar a day." In this remark, Stettinius reflected his knowledge of the economics that made Panamanian shipping so useful.[12]

Mackey, Klein, and M. D. Franz, who all worked the draft of the Liberian maritime law, viewed the proposed system as designed to lure shipping away from the flag of Panama. Shippers, they noted, were "fed up to the back teeth with Panamanian demands." This perception was prevalent even prior to the reemergence of Arnulfo Arias in leadership in Panama. Since Stettinius' staffers saw the Republic of Panama as a competitor, they maintained some secrecy about their own operations. Mackey quietly investigated the steps that would be required to release a ship from Panamanian registry, requesting the information through his personal part-ownership of the AOTC subsidiary in Panama, Greenwich Marine. Sidney De la Rue, a member of Stettinius Associates and former State Department officer, made quiet inquiries to determine the length of the Panamanian legislative session, using a bank as an intermediary to channel his question anonymously.[13]

By mid-1948 President William V. S. Tubman of Liberia grew anxious to get ship registration under way. The Stettinius organization wanted to show some revenue in order to attract new investment because staff salaries and travel expenses were rapidly consuming the original funding. With both sides eager to get the law under way, Mackey and Klein worked hastily, simply copying comparable elements of the U.S. Maritime Code and quickly printing the resulting patchwork for Liberia.[14]

By July 21, 1948, the code had been drafted, but a further delay was required. Mackey hesitated to send the draft to Liberia until it had been read, amended, and approved by officials of Standard Oil, including the maritime attorney for the firm, Robert P. Nash, and the director of maritime operations and board member, Bushrod B. Howard. Howard had worked for Esso beginning in 1920, in the Marine Transport Department. In 1939 he succeeded Robert L. Hague as director of marine transport. Hague had overseen the Danzig registry of Esso ships and had also arranged the transfer of the twenty-five tankers from Danzig to Panama in 1935. Mackey thought it appropriate to seek input on the Liberian maritime code from the leading experts on Esso tankers since the new code could possibly affect Esso shipping operations in the future.[15]

Given Sullivan and Cromwell's role in the earlier uses of the Danzig and Panama flags, it is noteworthy that the Stettinius group contacted not only Howard and Nash of Standard Oil but also at least one member of the law firm, V. Rodriguez, in January 1949 as the Liberian maritime law was being finalized.[16]

In August 1948 the draft maritime code was further delayed because of additional consultations with shipping company executives. Stettinius personally arranged to send galley proofs of the code to Howard of Standard Oil and Westerlund, president of Marine Transport Lines and a principal in Greenwich Marine. Stettinius noted, "Mr. Westerlund is most anxious as we are, to have Standard Oil committed as far as possible before passage of the legislation." Final approval came August 12, 1948, when Mackey noted, "Bob Nash and Bush Howard of Standard Oil yesterday gave me a green light on the Maritime Code. This previously had been approved by Bill Westerlund and his associates, all of whom had page proofs." Although it is well-known that corporate executives participate in the creation of legislation that has the ostensible purpose of regulating their businesses, finding documentation of executives' review of page proofs before the enactment of a law is rare.[17]

Mackey pointed out that Standard Oil officials felt pleased because they expected Standard to participate in the ownership of the ship-registry company that would provide registration services to the

Liberian government. If Standard Oil had received a portion of its competitors' registration expenses through such an arrangement, it would have resembled the original Rockefeller rebate systems of the 1890s, in which railroad companies paid a rebate to Standard Oil not only on the oil shipped by the company but on oil shipped by competitors. As it turned out, Standard Oil did not participate in the ship-registry firm; the ITC managed Liberia's registration services.

The Liberian president and legislature changed the maritime code slightly, placing direct authority in the Office of the Secretary of the Treasury rather than in the Office of the Secretary of Commerce. Also, the Liberian maritime commissioner, reporting to the secretary of the treasury, was to issue rules and regulations directly, without consultation with the proposed Stettinius-subsidiary company. Aside from these two crucial changes, the draft approved by the legislature kept almost perfect fidelity to the original draft approved by the oil company, even to the amounts of fees and fines. The Liberian legislature passed the code in November 1948, and President Tubman of Liberia signed it into law on December 16, 1948.[18]

The Stettinius organization did not provide the U.S. State Department with copies of the law for editing or approval before sending it to Liberia. Stettinius and other members of the group working on the maritime law were eager to ensure that it did not conflict with official U.S. policy, but they had only secured a general preliminary endorsement of the ideas in principle, at the unofficial meeting at Grew's home. At the State Department, opposition arose in the form of denial that the department had endorsed the Stettinius ideas in detail. Little of the controversy between the Stettinius organization and the State Department was publicized at the time, but the State Department's concerns eventually resulted in a complete review of the Liberian maritime code in early 1949 by a State Department–recruited team of independent experts.[19]

The State Department originally planned to study the proposals and send a report to Liberia before the bills were introduced in the legislature. But the State Department moved too slowly. Although the draft law and related materials were passed to the Americans for study on September 29, 1948, the investigation did not begin until January 1949, and the final report on the draft law was not issued until March 1949, three months after the Liberians had passed the corporation-authored code.

Since many of the Stettinius group were former Roosevelt administration staffers, the company had been able to project the impression that it had a quasi-official character. Even though the State Department denied that the corporation acted in any official capacity, it could not deny that the overall plans did in fact conform to the direction of U.S. foreign policy. The ambivalence came through in instructions to the chargé d'affaires in the U.S. legation in Monrovia. Although Liberia Company had received "no special approval and backing," the instructions pointed out, the department was interested in view of the company's "policy to encourage economic development of underdeveloped countries through private American capital." If the statement was intended as a denial of endorsement, it certainly left a mixed impression.[20]

State Department Review

At the State Department, officials were reluctant to edit legislation for Liberia. An internal statement read, "This Government is not in a position to tell another sovereign government what it should or should not do." On the other hand, a memorandum of a conversation between officials from the Federal Reserve, the Treasury, and the State Department noted that State "should have the privilege of adequately reviewing the various schemes proposed by the company for the purpose of determining whether the proposals are good or bad for Liberia."[21]

While State Department officials seemed ambivalent, caught between a hands-off policy and an obvious concern over the development, the Stettinius group had no such hesitations. Not only did members of the group write the first draft of the legislation, but they also suggested political tactics to spur its passage and even gave Liberian president Tubman tips on dealing with the U.S. State Department. At Sidney De la Rue's suggestion, Tubman asked the State Department to conduct its review in the United States and issue the results to him personally in a confidential report in order to avoid a "political backfire" in Liberia. The Liberian legislators, presumably, did not know of the State Department's review or even of the prior drafting by Stettinius personnel and review by Standard Oil.[22]

Stettinius and his associates were relieved to learn that the State Department review would be conducted by Francis Adams Truslow. A descendant of the presidential Adams family, Truslow had been elected in March 1947 as president of the New York Curb Exchange, the

forerunner of the American Stock Exchange (AMEX). He had earlier
served as president of the government's wartime Rubber Development Corporation. He was personally committed to the same kind of
private-capital assistance to the third world that Stettinius favored and
that had been publicized by Henry Luce and Eric Johnson. Truslow
stated in 1947, "We must finance increased productivity in the rest of
the world or we cannot continue the trend in our export trade which we
have enjoyed for the last fifty years."[23]

As Truslow prepared his report on the Liberian maritime code, he
kept the Stettinius group informed of his criticisms through Sidney De la
Rue, providing a chance for improvements to be worked out informally
before the final issuance of the report. Truslow pointed out to De la Rue
that the aspect so much admired by the officers of Standard Oil, the
collection of initial registration fees by the "Liberian Maritime Bureau
Company," was not properly worked into the code. Truslow further
advised that a bureau, with a commissioner and deputy commissioner,
who might be ITC officers, would represent a better arrangement than a
subsidiary corporation acting as a contracting agency. This change appears
to have been relayed by the Stettinius company directly to Liberia
and implemented during contract negotiations; it was not in the final
Truslow report but was adopted by regulation and later amendment.[24]

Truslow also noted that the maritime code had been hastily drawn
up and that it reflected ignorance of both maritime law and the business of ship operation. Some of the provisions seemed designed to
apply only to U.S. ships operating under U.S. law. He pointed out the
lack of a provision for making or registering ship mortgages. He never
seemed to object to the idea that a Liberian regulatory law could be
written in the United States and reviewed both by the corporations
that it would affect and by his own review group appointed by the U.S.
State Department.[25]

With a combination of suggestions, gently phrased threats, and
harsh criticisms, Truslow won support for his report from both the Stettinius group and the State Department. When he filed the report, he
also submitted an extensive covering letter for the State Department
with explicit comments on the confusion of purpose and technical over-
sights in the maritime code, which confirmed some of the department's
own criticisms. Truslow's report, however, simply spelled out suggested
amendments to the code and the rationales for the changes.[26]

One of his comments in his covering note was quite revelatory of his values. He wrote, "Perhaps the [Stettinius] group was a little ashamed of the idea that it might be seeking profits." Having a good grasp of business principles, Truslow saw profit making as perfectly legitimate, and he believed a profit orientation would benefit both Liberia and the corporation that operated the registry.[27]

Truslow's report suggested four changes of substance in the original 1948 code as passed in Liberia. He proposed that instead of the term "documented," the term "registered" should be used and that the documentation of ships should be clarified by reference to "certificates of registry." This change was not incorporated in the law in 1949. Second, Truslow recommended that the ITC be given a contract only to administer the registration of ships, not to issue rules and regulations. By the time his report was filed, the maritime commissioner in Liberia had already implemented this policy. Third, Truslow recommended a provision for liability protection of passengers on Liberian-registered ships, but again, this specific change was not implemented in Liberia. However, Truslow's fourth major suggestion, that there be a provision for registration and recording of ship mortgages, was put in place by the Liberians in December 1949, a year after the original law was passed. In addition, Truslow pointed out many minor typographical and wording changes, which were also implemented in the December 1949 amended law. On the whole, Truslow's review was conducted in such a friendly and nonthreatening way that any recommendations could be informally handled administratively or formally implemented by amendment, some even before his final report was issued. The whole State Department exercise of asking for an outside review had resulted not in any severe critique of the idea of a Liberian registry but simply in a number of minor adjustments that would make the law more workable and efficient.[28]

While Truslow finished his report in early 1949, the ITC, set up to administer the law, selected George Schaeffer as its first president. A vice president of Chase Manhattan Bank in charge of Caribbean branches, headquartered in Panama and later in New York, Schaeffer had considerable experience with the Panamanian ship-registry system, particularly with ship mortgages and other forms of collateral secured under Panamanian law. He went to Liberia to set up offices and to work out the detailed arrangements between ITC and the

Liberian government under the new maritime code. Schaeffer secured an agreement under which ITC would deduct $0.325 of each $1.20 per ton (27 percent) on new tonnage registered as a fair and legal service charge for acting as a quasi-official agent of the Liberian government. Because of its quasi-official status, ITC would be free of any Liberian taxes. A draft contract indicated that ITC would charge fees for "activities in the solicitation and the procurement of new marine business," a principle reflected in the fact that the company's fees derived only from new, not renewal, business. Schaeffer came to believe that the ship-registration enterprise promised to be the "one visible source of important income" for any of the Stettinius-initiated activities in Liberia. The rate paid to ITC out of new tonnage fees was reduced in 1975, when the rate of return for ITC was reduced to 24 cents per ton of new net registry.[29]

International Trust Company and Liberian Services Inc.

Stettinius faced some stiff economic problems with the overall Liberian venture through late 1948 and early 1949. A small proxy committee was set up to run ITC in December 1948. ITC was not to be a subsidiary of Liberia Company, which split its profits three ways, but instead was to be a separate, U.S.-owned company with E. Stanley Klein as the owner of record.[30] Stettinius carefully provided for Fred T. Lininger, who had served as his personal secretary and aide, by asking Klein to arrange for him to "be dealt with in the Trust Company in a very fair and generous way. . . . We have made a commitment to Fred that he is to have a 'good' place in the Trust Company set-up."[31]

Accordingly, Lininger became a director on the board of ITC and chairman of Liberian Services Inc., which was the U.S.-based firm conducting the U.S. registry office, eventually located in Reston, Virginia. Later, after ITC had been acquired by International Bank of Washington, Lininger served as a senior vice president of that corporation. At first, Lininger deferred some of what he called "important policy questions" to others in the organization, but in effect, he remained the chief executive officer of the registry-service corporation for thirty years.[32]

Although several companies, including the Farrell Lines, Delta Shipping, and the company owned by U.S. shipping magnate Daniel K. Ludwig, National Bulk Carriers, expressed interest in Liberian flag registration in 1948, the first ship officially registered (in 1949) under the

Liberian maritime code was *World Peace*, a tanker owned by the Greek shipping magnate Stavros Niarchos under charter to Gulf Oil. *World Peace* was one of the five tankers owned by Stavros Niarchos that had been transferred to his company by AOTC and registered in Panama; soon Niarchos' other four AOTC tankers joined *World Peace* as the first five ships under the Liberian flag.[33]

By mid-1949 five ships had registered, and in 1950 the total climbed to twenty-two. By 1955 Liberia had surpassed Panama in total tonnage registered and in 1956 in total number of ships, with more than five hundred registered by that year. Liberia earned about $3 million in fees in 1958 and in 1968 about $5 million. In 1977 revenues to Liberia exceed $15 million. ITC was earning more than $2 million in revenue. By 1965 Liberia's ship registry surpassed that of the United Kingdom, rising to first place in total registered tonnage of all flags, a position the country held into the 1990s.[34]

As the Liberian and Panamanian registries came under harsh criticism from labor and later from environmental groups, the question of exactly who had authored the Liberian maritime code became an issue. ITC described the writing of the law as an effort to attract shipowners through a modern system of registration. "Liberia drew on the experience of the world's foremost admiralty law experts and specialists in international law," the company proudly, and correctly, claimed.[35]

A group of U.S.-owned and U.S.-registered shipping and shipbuilding companies opposing the flight of ships from the U.S. flag organized as the U.S. Maritime Committee to Turn the Tide. In 1977 the organization placed an ad in *Newsweek* that said, "The Liberian fleet has little to do with Liberia or Liberians. It is a phantom maritime operation created in 1948 by a handful of Americans who drew up the Liberian maritime law."[36] Although the charge that the law was "created by a handful of Americans" had some validity as shown here, it was not at all true that the registry was a "phantom maritime operation," as it has remained a very real factor in maritime affairs ever since its founding in 1948.

For some opponents, it may have seemed shocking that the registry system had been created by institutions and individuals intimately involved in the shipping industry. Had they been more familiar with the history of regulation, however, they would have realized that it was a common practice for regulatory legislation to be written by (and very often administered by) representatives of or former executives of the businesses regulated.[37] Furthermore, the ship registration systems of Danzig, Panama, and now Liberia, and later such systems, were created precisely to escape the social, labor, or other regulations or taxes of the traditional maritime flag states, not to impose a set of onerous regulations.

The Liberian registry would continue to suffer from charges by critics, some of them fair and some unwarranted. Both the Panamanian and Liberian flags faced increased competition from other flag-registry systems in later decades. The Liberian flag also experienced severe blows from loss of faith in Liberia's stability as the country faced internal crises in the 1980s and 1990s. However, the Liberian registry continued as a major system for international registry of ships into the twenty-first century, and the availability and efficiency of the Liberian ship-registry system accelerated the flight of ships away from the American merchant flag.

11

Challenges Ashore and at Sea, 1955–80

From 1948 to 1963 the fleets registered in Liberia and Panama grew. Honduras also allowed open registry, but that flag attracted few international owners other than United Fruit Company. By 1960 Liberia had some 977 ships registered, while Panama had 607, and both fleets continued to grow.[1] Through these years, labor unions in the United States, particularly the National Maritime Union, which represented seafarers, challenged the system by attempting to organize the crews of U.S.-owned ships registered in Panama, Liberia, and Honduras.

Under the National Labor Relations Act of 1935, workers in U.S. companies can organize and hold elections, and if a majority of those voting in supervised elections approve, a union can win the right to bargain collectively for wages, hours, and work conditions. It is illegal for an employer to harass those advocating a union or to dismiss workers solely for union activity. These rights are protected by the act; elections and enforcement of the law are supervised by the National Labor Relations Board (NLRB).

U.S. owners of ships registered in Panama and Liberia claimed that because their ships were "foreign," the NLRB had no jurisdiction. The shipowners argued that they could dismiss any seafarers attempting to distribute union literature or organize the crews. Through the 1950s, a number of court cases tested whether or not the NLRB had jurisdiction over U.S.-owned, foreign-flagged ships to protect union organizers from dismissal. The outcome of the cases would determine whether the system of overseas registry would succeed; the ability of U.S.-owned ships to evade U.S. labor costs was the biggest attraction of foreign registration in the era.

The legal issue of whether or not the registry of ships in Liberia and Panama was genuine or artificial was debated in both international law settings and the U.S. court system in this period. Both the international and domestic law cases were noted by later writers demonstrating the workability and legitimacy of the flag-of-convenience system.

International Law Cases

The owners of ships registered under the Liberian and Panamanian flags used several principles of international law to defend overseas-registry systems through the 1950s. Since the Muscat dhows decision, the principle that other nations could grant nationality and flags to ships owned elsewhere had become well-established. The practice was strengthened by the operation of twentieth-century friendship, commerce, and navigation (FCN) treaties, in which two nations agreed to recognize each others' vessels and admit them to port. Liberia's FCN treaty with the United States went back to 1862, when the United States first recognized Liberia as an independent state. The United States signed a revised Treaty of Friendship and Cooperation with Panama in 1936. The principles that states could set their own rules and regulations governing the granting of nationality to ships and that these rules could be widely accepted were represented in dozens of similar bilateral treaties. U.S. attorneys representing Panama and Liberia argued that the law of the flag and the recognition of the rights of ships flying Panamanian and Liberian flags, established under the FCN treaties, should take precedence over the law of the port or the law of the owner in determining jurisdiction over those vessels. Cases and treatises on the subject sometimes cited the Muscat dhows decision, as well as other cases in domestic and international law.[2]

A ruling in 1955 by the International Court of Justice (ICJ) had the potential to undermine international legal acceptance of national policies governing the granting of flags. The challenging principle had been developed in a dispute between two minor states, Guatemala and Liechtenstein, in the *Nottebohm* case. In this case, Kurt Nottebohm, a German citizen resident in Guatemala, rapidly changed his citizenship to neutral Liechtenstein at the outbreak of World War II. When Guatemala seized his property as that of an enemy German, Nottebohm obtained a diplomatic protest from Liechtenstein. The ICJ ruled in favor of Guatemala in 1955. The court declared there was no "genuine link" between Nottebohm and Liechtenstein because he had lived there only briefly before the war and did no business there. Nottebohm's naturalization was secured artificially for the purpose of evading the confiscation of property. Because he had no genuine link with his nation of citizenship, Guatemala was correct in viewing Nottebohm as German. In effect, the court ruled against what could have been seen as "citizenship of convenience," thereby offering a precedent that could undermine the practice of off-shoring corporate registry, ship registration, and changes of citizenship for purposes of tax evasion.

From 1956 to 1958, Dutch and British lawyers hoped to extend the genuine-link principle to ships. In 1956 the International Law Commission (ILC), a group of lawyers selected by the UN General Assembly, discussed whether the Nottebohm precedent should apply to ships and whether some international agreement should be reached limiting the powers of states to grant nationality to vessels. The ILC recommended that the issue of whether to require a genuine link between vessel and state of registry be placed on the agenda of the planned Law of the Sea Conference, to be held in Geneva in 1958. The commission recommended to the conference a provision that asserted, "For purposes of recognition of the national character of a ship by other states, there must exist a genuine link between the state and the ship." This provision, if adopted, would represent an international vindication of the view that Panamanian and Liberian registries were subterfuges, since almost all the ships in both registries had never visited their flag state and had nothing to do with Panama or Liberia except for their registrations themselves.[3]

In a hotly contested debate at the Geneva conference, U.S. representatives sided with Panama and Liberia in maneuvering to have the clause "recognition of national character" weakened or removed from the provision. John Foster Dulles was Dwight Eisenhower's secretary of state in 1958, and his department vigorously came to Panama's defense. Dulles' old law firm, Sullivan and Cromwell, still represented Panama's legal interests in the United States.

As adopted, the Law of the Sea Conference provision on the question read, "There must exist a genuine link between the State and the ship; in particular, the State must effectively exercise its jurisdiction and control in administrative, technical and social matters over the ships that fly its flag." Successful U.S. negotiation to remove the recognition clause had taken the teeth out of the provision. The resulting agreement asserted that a ship should be linked but defined the enforcement of regulations as evidence of the link. Since both Panama and Liberia made efforts to enforce their regulations, the resulting formula provided no challenge to the system. Forms of linkage between flag and ship in the traditional maritime states had included requirements that nationals own the ship, that nationals be employed as crew members, that the ship be constructed in the flag nation, or some combination of these. Traditionally, such links went far beyond mere registration or claimed efforts to enforce regulations. The Law of the Sea Conference, with its focus on existence of regulations, had defined linkage in such a way that it could not be used to challenge flag-of-convenience registries. The threat to use the conference to apply the Nottebohm concept of genuine link to ships had been successfully stymied.[4]

Another case before the ICJ showed the 1950s alignment of the United States, Liberia, and Panama against the traditional maritime states in Europe over the flag-of-convenience issue. The Intergovernmental Maritime Consultative Organization (IMCO) was founded under UN auspices in 1958 as a specialized agency. When the organization held its opening meeting, it was to seat representatives of fourteen nations. Under the UN charter for the organization, IMCO members were to be "representatives of governments of those nations having an important interest in maritime safety of which not less than eight shall be the largest ship-owning nations." Since many of the ships registered in Panama and Liberia were nominally owned by corporations established in those countries, both Liberia and Panama were among the top eight maritime nations in the world. In total registry, Liberia ranked as the third-largest ship-registry country in 1959, with more than 10 million tons registered, and Panama ranked eighth, with more than 4 million tons.[5]

When the IMCO general assembly elected members to the Maritime Safety Committee, the assembly pointedly excluded both Panama and Liberia. Arguments presented in favor of excluding the two nations were put forward by representatives of Britain, the Netherlands, Belgium, and Norway. Since the vast majority of ships in both flag-of-convenience countries were beneficially owned in other states, neither Panama nor Liberia could be called "ship-owning countries." The British representative pointed out that the intent of the organization's charter had been to ensure that countries with an interest in maritime safety be seated on the committee, but "neither Panama nor Liberia was at the moment, in a position to make any important contribution to maritime safety." Further, it was argued that automatic selection of certain countries on the basis of the size of their registered fleets did not constitute "election." With support from the United States, this particular dispute was referred to the ICJ. At the ICJ hearing in April and May 1959, representatives from Italy, the Netherlands, Britain, and Norway argued that Panama and Liberia should not be seated. The Europeans asked the ICJ to apply the Nottebohm precedent of genuine link to the IMCO safety committee case. However, the ICJ ruled in favor of Panama and Liberia: "Neither the nationality of stockholders of shipping companies, nor the notion of a genuine link between ships and their country is a relevant test for determining 'ship owning nations.'"[6]

Even though this was a minor organizational disagreement, representatives of Panamanian and Liberian ship-owning companies could tout this particular decision as the kiss of death to the genuine-link challenge to the law of the flag. Since few forums defined international law at the time, the 1905 Muscat dhows ruling at The Hague and the 1959 ruling of the ICJ both appeared to settle the legitimacy of flag-state jurisdiction over ships. Both were cited by legal scholars on the issue as having resolved the matter.

Labor versus Shipowners in U.S. Courts

In the United States, through the 1950s and early 1960s, attorneys for labor unions sought to exert the authority of domestic labor law over U.S.-owned ships registered abroad. At first, they had some success. Several cases reflected the growing body of U.S. domestic law decisions that supported the position of organized labor in district and appellate courts.

In *Lauritzen v. Larsen*, although the court denied U.S. jurisdiction to a foreign seaman seeking damages under U.S. law for an injury on a ship that was both foreign-owned and foreign-registered, it applied a balancing-of-contacts principle, looking at seven factors: the location of the ship, the law of the flag, the allegiance or domicile of the injured party, the allegiance of the shipowners, the place where the contract was issued, the accessibility of the foreign jurisdiction, and the law of the U.S. forum. By opening the discussion to weighing or "balancing" contact, the court suggested that in some cases the factors' combined weight might indicate that a case fell under U.S. jurisdiction. This would be so particularly if the ship was beneficially owned in the United States, the labor contract had been signed in the United States, and the case was brought before a U.S. court by a U.S. citizen. Several cases citing the *Lauritzen v. Larsen* ruling appeared to undermine the flag-of-convenience defense.[7]

The NLRB hoped to further extend jurisdiction in labor versus shipowner cases on Panamanian and Liberian ships through its own rulings, which would later be appealed to the courts. In *Peninsular Occidental*, the NLRB ruled against a U.S.-owned Liberian corporation that operated the cruise ship *Florida*. After the company had fired employees for engaging in union-organizing activity, the NLRB took jurisdiction. The board, using the balancing-of-contacts principle, found that the U.S. company had used unfair labor practices, ordered the reinstatement of the employees, and ordered an election to determine a collective bargaining agent.[8]

Several other cases reflected this NLRB precedent. In *Benz v. Compania Navarra Hidalgo* (1957), the U.S. Supreme Court indicated that it would be appropriate for Congress to rule on the issue of U.S. jurisdiction on flag-of-convenience ships, but Congress took no action. Even so, by 1959–1960, both U.S. courts and the NLRB were using the balancing-of-contacts principle from *Lauritzen v. Larsen* to determine whether a foreign-registered ship came under U.S. jurisdiction. Further, some courts had found that simple foreign incorporation or foreign registry was not enough to preclude U.S. jurisdiction. In individual liability cases, the Jones Act of 1920, which restricted shipping between U.S. ports to ships registered in the United States and held shipowners liable for individual injury, could be applied; in labor union organizing issues, the National Labor Relations Act could be applied.

However, a conflict between U.S. agencies over the issues simmered behind the scenes. At one level, the State Department, under John Foster Dulles, was fighting *against* the genuine-link doctrine. At another level, the courts and the NLRB were applying something like the genuine-link doctrine through the balancing-of-contacts principle. The issue continued to fester. In 1960 the NLRB ruled in *West India Fruit Company Inc.* that it had jurisdiction over the Liberian-registered *Sea Level*. In this case, the FCN treaty between the United States and Liberia guaranteed that Liberian law should prevail over ships registered there, but the NLRB pointed out that its own jurisdiction was based on the commerce clause of the Constitution. NLRB cases dealt not simply with the matters of internal order and discipline referred to in the FCN treaty but involved larger questions of commerce. The board argued that the Supreme Court had ruled that FCN treaties did not restrict jurisdiction to the flag state when events or crimes on board vessels threatened public order in a port. Thus, labor union cases involving both matters of commerce and matters of public order (when strikes or boycotts occurred in port) allowed U.S. jurisdiction.

The NLRB reached a split decision in the *West India Fruit Company Inc.* case in May 1960, ruling 3 to 2 that it had jurisdiction on the basis of these arguments. The majority held that since Congress had not ruled on the issue, agency policies in the Maritime Administration and the Defense Department that might support the notion of jurisdiction by the flag state had no bearing on Labor Department rulings of the NLRB.[9]

The American Committee of Flags of Necessity (ACFN), a group of defenders of flags of convenience, held an emergency meeting. Erling Naess, who had been instrumental in Norway's early uses of the Panama flag, was an active member of ACFN, and he wrote in his memoir about the concerns raised in reaction to the *West India Fruit* decision. ACFN members were concerned that if one or more flag-of-convenience cases reached the U.S. Supreme Court, the court might apply the balancing-of-contacts principle and assert that the NLRB did in fact have jurisdiction over foreign-registered ships. A great deal hinged on which particular case went before the Supreme Court. ACFN members hoped that a case involving a Honduran ship owned by United Fruit would go to the Supreme Court.[10]

Cases involving Honduran ships owned by United Fruit were thought to have "good facts" because they were hardly typical of the ships registered in Liberia and Panama. United Fruit did in fact call at Honduran ports, carry cargoes from Honduras, and employ Honduran crews, which were even represented by a Honduran-based labor union. Using either the Nottebohm genuine-link concept or the U.S. court balancing-of-contacts principle, it would be easy to argue that Honduran-flagged United Fruit ships should not fall under U.S. jurisdiction; there were in fact genuine links and a balancing weight of contacts between Honduras and the United Fruit ships.

Eisenhower Administration Approach

Staffers in the Eisenhower administration sought to produce a coordinated policy from the diametrically opposed viewpoints of the Defense and State Departments, on the one hand, and the Labor Department's NLRB, on the other. David Kendall, special counsel to the president, directed his office to collect materials regarding the interagency disagreement early in January 1959 and turned over the effort to the assistant special counsel, Philip Areeda.

Areeda collected memoranda from the Maritime Administration (MarAd), Navy, State Department, Office of the Attorney General, and NLRB, each explaining the particular agency's positions. MarAd claimed the NLRB should not have jurisdiction. If U.S. labor law applied, MarAd feared that U.S.-owned ships would transfer to North Atlantic Treaty Organization (NATO) countries and thus be available to the United States only in international conflicts in which NATO participated, but not in non-NATO conflicts. The State Department agreed: the law of the flag should govern the ships, and U.S. interests lay with protecting Panamanian and Liberian registry.[11] The Office of the Attorney General tried to avoid giving an opinion, and Assistant Attorney General George Doub wrote in February 1959, "I feel that the ship owners' appeal [from the NLRB position] should be directed to Congress rather than the Executive or the Judiciary."[12] The NLRB responded to Areeda's request, arguing that authority over working conditions on ships beneficially owned in the United States should remain in NLRB hands; according to the NLRB's Stuart Rothman, each case varied and should be decided on its merits.[13]

After he had reviewed the files and opinions of the different agencies and held a White House meeting on the issue in April 1959, President Eisenhower directly ordered the Office of the Attorney General to prepare a brief dismissing NLRB jurisdiction. The brief was prepared and filed with the NLRB on November 18, 1960, just following the victory of John F. Kennedy in the November elections but before Kennedy's inauguration.[14]

However, the NLRB had already ruled on November 15, 1960, in favor of the unions in the United Fruit Company case, *Empresa Hondurena*. The ship was wholly owned by the U.S. company, the NLRB ruled, and "it follows as we emphasized in our West India decision as we reemphasize here, that the particular flag or nationality of the vessels as such, plays no role in our determinations."[15] The issue remained unresolved during the interregnum period before Kennedy's inauguration in January 1961.

Kennedy Administration Approach

The case of the *Empresa Hondurena*, combined with an NLRB ruling on another United Fruit Company ship and a third case about a ship of the Italian-owned Incres Line registered in Liberia (the Incres Line was headquartered in the New York), came before the Supreme Court in 1960 and was still pending during the first months of the Kennedy administration. Archibald Cox, Kennedy's solicitor general, presented the issue at an interdepartmental committee attended by the president and representatives from Commerce, State, Labor, and Defense. At the meeting, all except Willard Wirtz of the Department of Labor agreed that Cox should oppose NLRB jurisdiction in the pending cases, much the same position developed in the previous administration after the interdepartmental review. However, Cox later said that Kennedy had "dropped a bombshell" on the meeting. The president went to a book-shelf and pulled down a collection of his own speeches and communi-cations from his presidential campaign. He read from a memo that he had sent to Joe Curran of the National Maritime Union: "I am especially interested and share your concern with your problems and in particu-lar the 'runaway ship' threat to the high standards which you and your union have fought for and established over the years. The 'runaway ship,' like its counterpart, 'the runaway shop,' is a hit-and-run operation which should be stopped."[16]

After this meeting, Cox met with Secretary of Labor Wirtz to dis-cuss a solution that would be acceptable to everyone and that would avoid embarrassing the president. From this meeting, Cox developed a carefully thought-through position. On the one hand, Cox asked the Supreme Court to reject the National Maritime Union position on the United Fruit and Incres Line ships on the implicit grounds that the balancing of contacts did not favor U.S. jurisdiction. However, he also asked the Supreme Court to leave open the question of possible NLRB jurisdiction over U.S.-owned ships registered under flags of convenience when the ships had no connection with the flag state other than regis-try. Kennedy's Democratic administration would take a slightly more pro-labor position than the Eisenhower administration had planned to do a few months before. As Cox formulated his argument reflecting the contacts principle, he distinguished between ships "with significant links with the flag nation" and "truly flag of convenience vessels, flying the colors of a nation with which they have no substantial connection." By his careful definition of flag-of-convenience vessels, he demon-strated that he understood that the United Fruit vessels represented the "best facts" for the advocates of flags of convenience, and he hoped that the Court would make the distinction between ships with genuine links or a balance of contacts with the flag state and those with no such links or contacts except registration.

Cox made clear that the United Fruit ships were not truly flag-of-convenience ships and that because the Incres Line was Italian-owned, the United States could not claim jurisdiction. He recommended no NLRB jurisdiction in cases with bona fide connections between ship and flag state and no NLRB jurisdiction when both the ownership and the crew were foreign to the United States. Thus, he held that the NLRB should not assert jurisdiction over genuinely foreign-owned, foreign-flagged vessels so as to avoid any affront to foreign nations that would have "disturbing consequences."[17] The position departed from the previous administration's full rejection of any U.S. jurisdiction over ships registered under any foreign flags and clearly recognized Kennedy's campaign statement to Joe Curran. The recommendation, noted Cox, "would postpone the evil day when the Court would have to take a stand one way or the other" on the issue.[18]

Erling Naess and the ACFN noted that Cox was attempting to avoid a decision on the issue and that his position would leave the door open to continued application of the balancing-of-contacts approach and possibly NLRB jurisdiction over some flagged-out ships. The Supreme Court generally gave the solicitor general's opinions serious consideration. However, on February 18, 1963, Justice Tom C. Clark wrote an opinion with seven other concurring justices that simply ruled with regard to the National Labor Relations Act: "The jurisdictional provisions of the Act do not extend to maritime operations of foreign-flag ships employing alien seamen."[19]

The Court opined that since Congress had never indicated a desire to extend jurisdiction over foreign-flag ships, the NLRB should not apply the balancing-of-contacts concept to such ships. The Court ruled that Congress did in fact have the power to extend such jurisdiction if it wished, but since it had not, the NLRB could not take jurisdiction. The ACFN took the decision as an outright vindication of the law of the flag, seeing it as confirmation of the positions taken by the Law of the Sea Conference in 1958 and by ICJ in its 1959 ruling regarding the IMCO.[20]

Despite Kennedy's commitment to Joe Curran, U.S. labor unions had lost a crucial battle; the Kennedy administration could at least claim, for its labor union base, that Cox had made an effort. Even so, the Eisenhower and Kennedy administrations, as demonstrated in the subcabinet meetings under both presidents, had clearly regarded the Liberian and Panamanian registries as appropriate. After all, they assumed, these dependent but nominally independent countries would have no objection to the United States retaining some administrative control over the ships during times of international conflict. The positions of the State Department and the Defense Department outweighed the position of the NLRB and the concerns of the National Maritime Union as expressed by Curran.

The Supreme Court's decision took away any chance U.S. labor had to control the exodus of U.S. ships to Panamanian and Liberian registry by action of the NLRB. Henceforth, U.S. courts upheld injunctions against labor demonstrations and boycotts as illegal attempts to interfere with foreign trade, even when the ship was U.S.-owned, as long as it flew a foreign flag. Although some legal experts disagreed as to the finality of the decision, it seemed that U.S. labor unions could not expect to represent workers on U.S.-owned ships flying foreign flags.

Since the United States chose to treat both Panama and Liberia, nominally independent but in fact very dependent nations, as fully sovereign and equivalent to Britain, Norway, and other maritime nations, attorneys could claim that the Muscat dhows principle of ship registry as a function of sovereignty applied to ministates as well as to any major power. With the court decisions in 1958–1961, the legal status of flags of convenience had been confirmed.

Liberian Tanker Oil Spills

As Liberia became the preferred flag of registry for oil tankers and as the size of oil tankers increased through the 1960s and 1970s, increasingly Liberian registry became front-page news with a number of oil spills from Liberian-registered tankers. By 1978 the total Liberian fleet represented some 19.8 percent of the world tonnage, with more than 2,500 ships.

Of course, tankers and oil platforms registered in other countries, including the United States, Great Britain, and France, also experienced collisions, leakages, and spills. However, many of the major oil companies and independent contract shippers had chosen Liberian registry especially for supertankers ranging over 50,000 tons, for the very large crude carriers (VLCCs, over 100,000 tons) of the 1960s, and for the ultra large crude carriers (ULCCs, over 500,000 tons) of the 1970s. Losses from some of these spectacularly large ships drew the attention of journalists to the growing practice of flag-of-convenience registry. Media attention reached something of a climax in 1976–1978, with newsworthy spills from *Sansinena, Oswego Peace, Argo Merchant,* and *Amoco Cadiz.*[21]

\multicolumn{6}{c}{**TABLE 4.** MAJOR TANKER OIL SPILLS, 1967–79}
Ship	**Type**	**Flag**	**Location**	**Date**	**Note**
Torrey Canyon	VLCC	Liberia	Scilly Isles, UK	March 15, 1967	Wreck, major spill
Ocean Eagle	Tanker	Liberia	San Juan, Puerto Rico	March 3, 1968	Grounded, major spill
Universe Leader	ST	Liberia	Bantry Bay, Ireland	October 22, 1974	Accidental leakage
San-sinena	ST	Liberia	San Pedro, California	December 12, 1976	Exploded
Oswego Peace	ST	Liberia	Connecti-cut	December 24, 1976	Oil spill
Argo Merchant	Tanker	Liberia	Off Nantucket	December 27, 1976	Wreck, major spill
Amoco Cadiz	VLCC	Liberia	Brittany, France	March 16, 1978	Wreck, major spill
Atlantic Express	VLCC	Liberia	Trinidad	July 19, 1979	Collision, major spill

Source: Data from *New York Times* for dates shown and subsequent editions.
Note: Tanker, under 50,000 tons; ST (Supertanker), 50,000–100,000 tons; VLCC (very large crude carrier), 100,000–500,000 tons.

To keep these 1960s and 1970s spills in perspective, recall that later spills dwarfed these events, particularly the loss of the U.S.-flagged VLCC *Exxon Valdez* (1989) and the spill from the Marshall Island–flagged oil platform *Deepwater Horizon* (2010). However, before the massive environmental crises of *Exxon Valdez* and *Deepwater Horizon*, the number and scale of Liberian-flagged losses and resultant oil spills in the 1960s and 1970s were shocking. Reports of the events sought to tie the losses to the fact of Liberian registry, attributing them in part to the failure of Liberia to insist on qualified navigators and officers or experienced crews. This observation tended to overlook the fact that the oil companies had every economic motivation to seek the most qualified officers available at competitive pay scales in the world labor market.

Press reports made it appear that neither the nation of Liberia nor the U.S.-based registry company was effectively regulating the ships under the Liberian flag. These reports also tended not to recognize mitigating factors such as the high proportion of oil on tankers, supertankers, and VLCCS then registered under the Liberian flag, making losses of Liberian ships proportionally more likely; the newness of the larger ships, which meant officers and crews could not have had years of experience with ships of this scale; and the regular occurrence of oil spills from tanker losses since the first introduction of tankers in the 1870s. Public and governmental concern about the more recent events was partly the result of a growing awareness of human impact on the natural environment that characterized the 1960s and 1970s.

The losses made good copy for print and television media. The combination of a dramatic sea story, rich illustration with photographs (and live motion pictures), and the heightened environmental awareness of the era turned each of these major ship losses into a media feeding frenzy for a few days or weeks. Some of the losses, particularly the loss of the *Torrey Canyon*, generated several quickly produced book-length treatments.[22]

Even though public attention faded as soon as these front-page events were superseded by others, the oil spills and the press coverage did have two long-range consequences. One was that public and legislative awareness of flag-of-convenience registry increased. The development of the Panamanian and Liberian flag registries had gone on without much public knowledge, awareness, or concern, and to an extent, the oil spills changed that. A second major consequence was that Liberian Services Inc. made concerted efforts to require inspection and certification of Liberian-registered ships by international inspection agencies. This effort came partly as a result of pressure brought by the Federation of American-Controlled Shipping (FACS), the group that had replaced the ACFN. The FACS representative, Philip Loree, submitted a group of recommendations to the Liberian Marine Board of Investigations, which had examined the circumstances of the *Argo Merchant* disaster. The recommendations included requiring inspection of all new and existing Liberian-registered ships, setting officer standards, conducting investigations of future accidents and of ships with high casualty records, and ratifying the 1974 Convention for the Safety of Life at Sea (SOLAS-74). Liberian Services Inc. and the Liberian

Marine Board implemented all of the recommendations over the next two years.[23]

In later years, executives of the ship-registry firm explicitly recognized that the oil spills served as incentives to improve standards. Clay Maitland, in a speech in 2002, looked back at the experience and said that the registry company "was deeply affected by its investigation into the Liberian-flag *Torrey Canyon* casualty in the late 1960s; and we are also a somewhat bloodied veteran of the *Amoco Cadiz* incident. . . . As a result of these salutary experiences we have aimed at a policy of 'highest quality.'"[24]

The improved Liberian standards had led by the early 1980s to an increased safety and reliability record of Liberian ships, although this achievement received virtually no recognition outside the maritime press. The effort to improve standards on Liberian ships was probably one factor contributing, over the next few years, to the proliferation of new open registries, some of which attracted ships that could not meet the standards of classification and inspection societies such as Bureau Veritas, American Bureau of Shipping, Lloyd's Register, and Det Norske Veritas or the new self-imposed standards of Liberian Services.

In the following decades, many new flags joined the family of flag-issuing nations. The wave of decolonization through the British Empire began with the independence of Ghana on the West Coast of Africa in 1957. Through the 1960s and 1970s, several smaller, insular, but politically more stable and technically more advanced dependences of Britain were among those gaining self-government. They were Cyprus (1960), Singapore (1963), Malta (1964), Bermuda (1968), and the Bahamas (1973). Between 1964 and 1976 each of these newly self-governing states emulated the practice of Liberia and Panama in opening their ship registry as a source of revenue. The fleets of these small states grew slowly at first, attracting British-owned ships and, gradually, ships owned in other nations.

12

The Marshall Islands Register

D uring the late 1940s, the doctrine of effective control had evolved quietly. By 1948 the doctrine required that the JCS certify certain countries as having ship-registry systems appropriate for effective control in case of war. The practical effect of JCS certification was to make U.S.-owned ships registered in the named countries eligible for war-risk insurance that Congress approved. This provision allowed the U.S. government, in the event of war, to charter these ships for transport of matériel into combat areas because the ship-owning companies would not be able to secure insurance from private firms, which insisted on a war-risk exclusion clause in their maritime insurance policies. Of course, another advantage from the perspective of the shipowners was that certification allowed them to operate outside the reach of the Jones Act and the National Labor Relations Act by registering in the approved effective control nations. Some shippers claimed that they would not be able to hire U.S. crews to sail into war zones. The postwar effective control doctrine provided a kind of respectability to U.S. ships registered in Panama, Honduras, and Liberia.[1]

Over the years, the effective U.S. control (EUSC) policy changed slightly, but the Military Sealift Command (MSC) continued to count on a number of foreign-registered ships that would be made available during time of war. Despite the establishment in 1977 of the Ready Reserve Force, which consisted of MarAd-owned cargo ships, the MSC continued to work out voluntary tanker agreements with EUSC ships registered in the listed countries to supplement the fleet in time of emergency. The list of countries varied but included Panama, Liberia, and Honduras, with temporary additions of Costa Rica and the Philippines.

By the 1980s the strategic doctrine of effective control seemed less applicable from the point of view of U.S. defense authorities and some concerned members of Congress owing to signs of potential unreliability in both Panama and Liberia. The Arab oil embargo of 1973 brought on by the Arab-Israeli War of that year raised the possibility that Liberia, as an African nation, might be pressured to join with other members of the Afro-Asian bloc. Liberia had been controlled by a political machine led largely by Americo-Liberians (descendents of the freed slaves resettled there by the American Colonization Society). They were organized in the True Whig Party and ruled through the long-term presidency (1944–1971) of William Tubman. Even this apparently fossil regime faced eventual political change. On the death of Tubman in 1971, William H. R. Tolbert (the father-in-law of Tubman's son) took the presidency, but a coup by a small group of disaffected Army enlisted men under Sgt. Samuel K. Doe in 1980 opened the way to more rapid political change and a chaotic civil war. The political uncertainty in the post–Tubman/Tolbert/True Whig era made Liberia far less dependent and dependable than it had seemed in 1948.[2]

In Panama, anti-American riots in January 1964 set off a chain of events that led to an agreement announced by Henry Kissinger in 1974 that would lead to the eventual turnover of the Panama Canal and the Canal Zone to Panamanian control, scheduled for the year 2000. In 1983–1989 the notorious drug kingpin Manuel Noriega effectively ruled Panama from behind the scenes before his forcible removal from power by U.S. troops. Although the ship registries of both Panama and Liberia continued to attract shipowners with labor-law and tax-law advantages, for purposes of effective control and strategic availability, the United States could not rely on countries with such unstable regimes and possibly anti-American political stances. Although shipowners might consent to contracts with the U.S. government, the fact that the ships were nominally Liberian and Panamanian no longer seemed a reliable assurance of their availability.

Events in Liberia quickly sharpened the debate over EUSC policy in that country. The fragile military leadership under Sergeant Doe that had replaced the Tolbert regime faced two separate armed forces that finally ousted Doe in 1990. The two groups, one headed by Amos Sawyer and the other by Charles Taylor, then fell into a brutal civil war with each other, marked by numerous atrocities.

When former Pacific Trust Territories emerged as semi-independent states in 1986, the MSC decided that the Marshall Islands might represent a more stable and dependable flag-registry state for ships to supply U.S. forces in time of war. The logic of that position was rooted in a good understanding of the historical precedents, which showed that nominal or tacit sovereignty, strategic dependence, and political reliability were essential for ensuring the protection of U.S. strategic interests. EUSC status was extended to the Marshall Islands in 1990.[3]

Capt. Warren G. Leback, MarAd administrator, argued in 1991 that in the wake of Desert Storm the United States should consider establishing a reliable second registry. That registry was established, without much public notice, over the next two years.[4]

Marshall Islands versus Liberia

By 1990 negotiations between International Registries Inc. (IRI), the successor to Liberian Services Inc., and the Republic of the Marshall Islands had established IRI as the agent for the Marshall Islands ship registry. The new nation, under the Compact of Free Association with the United States, was ideally suited for open registry, to get out from under U.S. labor law and tax law and at the same time to be legally bound to U.S. foreign policy. Under the compact, signed in 1986, the Republic of the Marshall Islands had full sovereignty over its domestic affairs, citizenship, and such legislation as its internal maritime and labor codes, but it delegated all defense to the United States, somewhat resembling the dependency status of Panama in the 1920s and 1930s. The newly semi-independent Republic of the Marshall Islands, with about 60,000 citizens, was entirely dependent on an aid package from the United States.[5]

IRI continued to operate the registries of both Liberia and the Marshall Islands from 1990 to 1999. In 1993 International Bank sold the holding company that owned IRI—the ITC—to an IRI management team. IRI continued to grow, trying to build a reputation for good-quality ships and good management of the registry for the Marshall Islands flag through the 1990s, with considerable success reported in the maritime news media. Applying the same standards that had developed for Liberia in the wake of the oil disasters of the 1970s, the Marshall Islands registry was specifically designed to attract responsible, major U.S. shipping companies. The Marshall Islands registry received a boost in 1996, when Overseas Shipholding Group (OSG), a large U.S.-owned shipping firm with open-registry ships in international trade as well as ships in trades restricted to U.S.-flagged carriers, shifted twenty-seven vessels from Liberia to the Marshall Islands. OSG continued to register new vessels, including large tankers, in the Marshall Islands. OSG publicly announced that the political situation in Liberia was behind its decision to shift to the Marshall Islands flag. In the past, OSG had chartered ships to the MSC.[6]

In the effort to attract business, the Republic of the Marshall Islands modeled its corporate and limited liability acts on those of the state of Delaware. Furthermore, IRI modernized its own company systems, allowing for electronic registration and developing representation offices in Singapore, Malaysia, and mainland China. The company retained many of its long-term employees, long familiar with the procedures developed for Liberian registry. IRI president William Gallagher noted that the new Marshall Islands registry placed "great emphasis on quality" and even began to delist ships that did not meet inspection standards. A Dutch maritime commentator noted in January 2000, "The Marshall Islands register is the direct continuation of programmes in place and benefits from the long-term experience and recognized expertise of IRI's staff in privatised management of national vessel registers." Exxon-Mobil, the lineal descendant of Esso, registered a VLCC with the Marshall Islands in 2000. The next year, the Marshall Islands registry grew to more than 11 million tons. By 2002 the Marshall Islands registry included 270 ships over 1,000 gross registered tons. Of those ships, U.S.-based and largely U.S.-owned companies owned 87 ships, German firms owned 70, and Greek companies owned another 54. Expansion of the registry included cruise ships, liquid natural gas transport ships, yachts, and oil-drilling platforms.[7] *Deepwater Horizon*, the oil platform operated for British Petroleum in the Gulf of Mexico that exploded April 20, 2010, was owned by Transocean and registered in the Marshall Islands, drawing some short-lived (and largely inaccurate) media attention to the registry. Transocean is a U.S.-owned company that traces its origins to Louisiana in 1919.[8]

The growth of the Marshall Islands registry was only partially drawn from transfers from the Liberian flag. U.S.-owned ships had only represented a small fraction, about 15 percent, of the Liberian flag registry in 1996. U.S.-owned ships represented only about a third of the total ships registered under the Marshall Islands flag.[9] Some of the registries in the Marshall Islands were new ships, whereas a few were registries drawn from other flags. Nevertheless, over the next decade, the Marshall Islands registry steadily grew, rising in numbers to compete directly with Liberia and Panama. Between 2002 and 2014 the Marshall Islands registry climbed in tonnage, achieving third place in the open registries by 2014, while Liberia fell to second place, after Panama.[10]

Even though the Marshall Islands registry and its reputation among shipping companies grew, IRI at first faced a series of legal battles and public controversies with the nation of Liberia. President Charles Taylor, who had emerged victorious from the seven-year-long civil war by 1997, demanded that IRI stop transferring ships from the Liberian to the Marshall Islands registry. Later, Taylor announced that he would not renew the fifty-year agreement between Liberia and IRI (as successor to Liberian Services) that gave IRI the power to administer the Liberian registry. Finally, when Taylor established a separate U.S.-based company to operate the registry and collect revenues, the new company refused to make claimed payments due to IRI, leading to still further legal challenges and bitter battles, some conducted in the press.

As soon as Charles Taylor emerged as the recognized leader of Liberia in August 1997, he moved quickly to take control of the registry and the revenues it represented, using the registry-generated funds to supplement revenues from a lucrative system of arms and diamond smuggling. Twelve days after his inauguration, Taylor issued Executive Order #1 to the president of ITC, at that time the firm owning IRI. The ITC president was instructed to place 10 percent of the revenues from the ship registry into the personal account of Benoni Urey, commissioner of the Bureau of Maritime Affairs. Although Urey regarded the personal deposits as a perfectly ordinary transaction, critics claimed they were clearly part of a scheme to funnel the registry funds into private hands.[11]

In a suit lodged in Virginia courts in 1998, owing to the Reston, Virginia, domicile of the registry firm, Liberia alleged that IRI had used the civil war in Liberia to convince shipowners to register their vessels in the Marshall Islands. ITC, the parent firm of IRI, responded coolly, stating, "The years of anarchy and horrific violence naturally caused many ship owners to be concerned about the advisability of continuing to register their vessels with a program identified with a nation in chaos." Taylor did not renew the IRI contract to operate the Liberian registry when the contract ended after its term of fifty years, in 1999. A new company, Liberian International Shipping Corporate Registry (LISCR), established by Taylor's associates and attorneys who had represented Liberia in U.S. courts against IRI, took control of the registry January 1,

2000. Legal battles between IRI and LISCR continued to rage over the next year. In May 2001 IRI filed suit against LISCR, alleging the new company had breached its agreement on assuming the registry by failing to make payments of $10 million. The suit further alleged that Taylor himself was a "silent but obsessively controlling partner in LISCR."[12]

IRI claimed that Liberia had not transferred payments due to international maritime organizations but, instead, had illegally retained the funds. IRI officials further noted that they were "dismayed" to discover that the principals in the very law firm (Swidler, Berlin, Sheeff and Friedman) with whom they had hoped to negotiate a settlement with Liberia had become principals in the new LISCR corporation. For its part, LISCR claimed that the audit of IRI books was not transparent and supported claims by the Liberian government that IRI had not paid amounts owing to Liberia.[13]

Critics of the Taylor regime charged that some of the first revenues collected by LISCR were not only channeled to Taylor's inner circle but were used for the purchase of arms, in direct violation of a UN resolution that imposed an arms embargo on Liberia. The International Transport Workers Federation (ITF), long hostile to all flags of convenience, claimed in 2001 that there was a regular flow of income, representing between $15 and $20 million per year, to the Taylor government, and "little evidence of this revenue being used to serve the needs of ordinary Liberians."[14]

The ITF pointed out that in the approximately thirty flag-of-convenience countries, ship-registry funding often did not go to the population of the flag state. However, Liberia was different in that on May 21, 2001, the UN had imposed sanctions on the country for its active efforts to destabilize the regime in neighboring Sierra Leone. In 2001 UN Resolution 1343 listed numerous individuals of the Taylor regime, including Liberian representatives to the International Maritime Organization, to be barred from international travel. Furthermore, UN investigators came to believe that shell companies, supposedly created to own ships in the registry, were being used in the illicit diamond trade to raise funds for arms for Sierra Leone rebel forces.[15]

A specially selected UN Panel of Experts concluded in 2001 that funds from illegal diamond dealings, gun sales, and the ship-registry business were all used to support armed intervention in Sierra Leone and as a source of personal wealth for members of the Taylor regime.

Some experts asserted that there was a Taylor–Al Qaeda linkage after the September 11, 2001, attacks in the United States. In an ironic twist, revenues from the Liberian registry, which had first been established to enhance U.S. security, now appeared to be going to support anti-American terrorism. The charge was leveled not simply by critics of the Liberian registry but by a UN Expert Panel report in October 2001, IRI representatives, and labor advocates.[16]

In the annual report on marine transport issued by the UN Commission on Trade and Development (UNCTAD) in 2002, the shrinkage of the Liberian registry received the following dry comment: "Liberia's fleet contracted by 2.6 percent as a result of the changes in the registration authority and subsequent litigation and findings by a United Nations panel of misuse of funds from the registry to bypass the United Nations arms embargo to the country."[17] The number of ships over 1,000 gross registered tons flagged in Liberia declined from 1,620 in 1996 to 1,478 by 2000.[18] A good part of the decline could be attributed to the deregistration of large U.S.-owned ships, which decreased in number from some 232 to 85 in the same years. Those that left the Liberian registry appeared to account for some of the contemporary increase in the Marshall Islands registry, from 94 ships in 1996 to 212 in 2000. That is, while Liberia dropped 147 ships, the Marshall Islands gained 118 ships.[19]

Despite mounting adverse publicity, many ship companies (especially those with no relationship to the U.S. defense establishment) were slow to change registry from Liberia for other than economic reasons. Meanwhile, LISCR, the new registry firm, engaged in an active campaign to enhance its reputation, to retain ships in the Liberian registry, and to gain further registrations. There continued to be active competition between the Marshall Islands and Liberian registries, with each country lowering its registry rates. This competition was complicated by several other new open-registry countries attempting to simultaneously build up their flag-registry business.

Despite the mounting international outcry (largely muted in the mass media) over Liberia's channeling of registry funds to inappropriate purposes, LISCR continued to treat the issue as a matter of public relations. When the UN Security Council passed Resolution 1408 in 2002 calling for an audit of Liberian revenues from the timber industry and the shipping registry, LISCR responded by appointing the accounting firm of Deloitte & Touche to monitor the way the registry fees were allocated for expenditure by the Liberian government. "We confidently expect," said Yoram Cohen, the chief executive officer of LISCR, "that the appointment of an independent auditor of international repute, will put an end to any uncertainty about the manner in which Liberian ship registry revenues are being used." Cohen went on to say that the company simply wanted to run the "best managed, most efficient, safest" ship register in the world.[20]

By 2007 the Marshall Islands registry was the leading overseas registry for U.S.-owned ships, attracting more than either Liberia or Panama and, in fact, more than both of them combined. By that year, about 26 percent of the tonnage of Marshall Islands–registered ships was U.S.-owned, with about 13 million deadweight tons, due largely to heavy-tonnage tankers.[21] The trend continued so that by 2014 the Marshall Islands registry had climbed to third place in the world after Panama and Liberia, with 152 million deadweight tons and 2,207 ships.[22]

Further Proliferation of Flags

In 1980 the ITF designated only eleven countries as flag-of-convenience countries; by 2002 the labor federation had designated twenty-eight countries as offering a flag of convenience, including land-locked Bolivia. The many ship registries actively and explicitly competed for registrations, some developing reputations for specific illicit trades, such as Belize, which, for a period, registered fishing vessels that operated outside international restrictions on specific species or limitations on fishing areas. By 2002 the ITF had designated nearly thirty country registries as flags of convenience.

U.S. owners accounted for less than 1 percent of all flag-of-convenience vessels. Owning individuals and companies domiciled in Greece, Japan, Hong Kong, Norway, and Korea totaled nearly 60 percent of the registry in the flag-of-convenience countries, with many other countries participating to a lesser extent. British owners, for example, held less than 6 percent of the Liberian registered ships and some 38 percent of the Bermuda-registered ships, while Japanese owners accounted for more than 40 percent of the Panamanian registry. Greeks held about 71 percent of the ships registered in Cyprus. The patterns of relationships between owning state and flag state somewhat reflected historic and strategic ties, like the special relationships that once existed

COUNTRIES DESIGNATED AS FLAG-OF-CONVENIENCE STATES BY ITF, 2002

Antigua and Barbuda	Gibraltar
Bahamas	Honduras
Barbados	Jamaica
Belize	Lebanon
Bermuda	Liberia
Bolivia	Malta
Burma (Myanmar)	Marshall Islands
Cambodia	Mauritius
Cayman Islands	Netherlands Antilles
Comoros	Panama
Cyprus	São Tomé and Principe
Equatorial Guinea	Sri Lanka
German International Registry	St. Vincent and Grenadines

Source: Data from UNCTAD, *Review of Maritime Transport 2007* (New York: United Nations, 2007), 32.

between the United States and Panama and Liberia. However, the choice of flag registry appeared to be driven by business and economic considerations more than by cultural, diplomatic, or strategic concerns in the majority of cases.[23]

13

Second Registers and Port-State Control

The establishment of open-registry systems came in three generations:

First generation: Danzig (1919), Panama (1919), Honduras (1943), Liberia (1948)

Second generation: Cyprus (1964), Singapore (1966), Malta (1973), Bermuda (1974), Bahamas (1976)

Third generation, beginning in the 1990s: some additional twenty-five nations, including such widely dispersed and seemingly unlikely states as Belize, Bolivia, Mongolia, and Vanuatu. The number varied from year to year, as some nations entered the field and others retired.

The proliferation of flags of convenience was part of a larger phenomenon in which corporations and individuals sought the most favorable jurisdictions internationally for hiring staff, obtaining raw materials, and registering for tax purposes. The age of multinational firms with little allegiance to any particular nation was established. With the new registries, ships could be purchased on a competitive, worldwide basis, leading to the growth of shipbuilding industries in Japan, Korea, and Brazil. As colonial empires declined after World War II, many newly independent states sought sources of revenue. If nothing else, those new nations could derive revenue from the mere fact that they had internationally recognized sovereign independence, very useful for the goals of the multinational corporations. Thanks to international recognition of the Muscat dhows decision and the decisions of U.S. and international forums in favor of flags of convenience in the 1950s and early 1960s, new countries like Cyprus, Malta, and Bermuda could market their sovereignty, even if they had little or no prior history of a major merchant marine.

Many of the new countries also set up such convenient facilities as incorporation and banking centers, low or nonexistent corporate and personal income taxes, and other attractive inducements to foreign capital. In these ways, the proliferation of flags of convenience went hand in hand with the proliferation of tax-haven states. In the parlance of international business, off-shoring was under way.

The third-generation open-registry systems were different from those of the first two generations. Some of the newest systems became notorious for their low wage scales and otherwise exploitative labor conditions. By the 1990s the London-headquartered ITF, the confederation of seafarers and longshoremen's unions around the world, would sometimes declare a particular open registry a "flag of convenience." When it did so, it signaled member unions to boycott, if possible, ships registered in those countries. On occasion, unionized longshoremen in various countries would stage such boycotts, usually with limited success since shipowners could often avoid ports notorious for well-organized unions or take other measures. Some open-registry systems that are known for relatively fair labor practices have not been designated "flags of convenience" by the ITF.

Second Registers: Maritime Nations Respond to Open Registry

In response to the development of literally dozens of flags of convenience for ships in international commerce, ten European countries established second registries for ships between 1984 and 2003. This chapter provides a description of the development of these second registries and presents a framework within which to assess their degree of success in offsetting the effect of flags of convenience. The details reveal the latest phase in the flight of shipping from flag to flag; clearly, the flight to foreign flags involved not just U.S. shipping but the merchant marine of most of the traditional European maritime nations as well.

The ten "second registry" systems evaluated here are those of Britain (in the Isle of Man), the Netherlands, Norway, France (in the Antarctic Territory of Kerguelen), Denmark, Belgium (in Luxembourg), Germany, Spain, Portugal, and Italy. As these systems developed, many commentators in the maritime periodical literature included the new Marshall Islands register, discussed in chapter 12, as an eleventh second register especially used by the United States. However, the reasons for the creation of the Marshall Islands registry were largely due to the U.S. defense establishment's dissatisfaction with the reliability of Liberia (and to an extent, Panama) as an effective control registry. The Marshall

Islands registry was created for national security reasons; the European second registers, by contrast, were created for economic reasons.

The European second-register systems were different from the registries of Liberia, Panama, Honduras, Cyprus, Singapore, Malta, Bermuda, and the Bahamas as well as from the registries of many third-generation island states. The second-register systems included some in former overseas colonial territories, like the newly independent states with second- and third-generation registries, but the second registries were created with the full support of the colonizing country to serve its own foreign policy.

In 1984 the Isle of Man opened a second register, and as a quasi-independent state related to Great Britain, it soon began to attract shipowners from not only Britain but also other maritime nations. In 1987 both Norway and the Netherlands adopted systems of second registries, and these were soon followed by others, some based in the home country. The dates of the opening of other second registers were as follows: Danish International Ship Register (DIS), 1989; German International Shipping Register (GIS), 1989; Madeira (Portugal), 1990; Canary Islands (Spain), 1991; and Italian Second Register, 1998. Two second registers lasted only a few years: French Antarctica (Kerguelen), 1989–2003, and Luxembourg (for Belgian ships), also 1989–2003.

All the second registries offered less costly operation than the previous national flag registry. This was especially so because the new second registries allowed the hiring of all or most of the crew on an international basis, often from low-income states like the Philippines or India. As a consequence, the owning firm or individual could operate ships at costs that were competitive in the world market. In some cases, but not all, domestic labor unions as well as the ITF found the creation of second registries a highly antiunion practice. However, in some few cases, organized labor and labor-based political parties actually endorsed the new systems.[1]

The second registries at first seemed capable of offsetting the appeal of flags of convenience, simply by offering a competitive economic structure. But a close examination of the statistics of ship registry in the 1990s and the first years of the twenty-first century reveals a far more complex set of developments. For example, when some of the second registries were opened to owners from several countries, those second registries took on some of the characteristics of open registries, serving not just owners domiciled in the home nation, but others from around the world. As a further complication, the ITF declared several of the second registries as "flags of convenience" because of the labor conditions that had developed on ships in those second registries.[2]

Port-State Control Systems

As the number of flags of convenience and second registries increased, a system of port-state controls evolved. Conformity to various standards on ships at sea had traditionally been enforced by the flag state. But with the development of flags of convenience in various newly independent nations and, later, even in countries with no seaports and no maritime heritage at all, some of the flag states, although signatories to international conventions on safety at sea and environmental pollution, made virtually no effort to enforce the rules. The port states, that is, the countries where the ships loaded and unloaded, rather than the flag states, had to take over inspection and enforcement activities. Countries with major ports at which ships stopped sought to establish some method of placing sanctions on ships that were unsafe, that were ocean polluters, or that had inhumane working conditions on board.

The first successful system of international port-state control was the result of a 1978 agreement known as the Paris Memorandum of Understanding (MOU), in which signatory countries agreed to inspect a standard percentage of vessels calling at their ports. As the number of ships registered in offshore regimes that had little or no facility for ship inspection increased, the MOU took on greater responsibility. In the 1990s, with the development of the Internet, MOU inspection failure rates and rates of ship detentions for ordered improvements were widely and promptly disseminated.

Shipowners and shippers were soon able to anticipate that the registry of a ship under certain flags could result in delays and adverse publicity. A delay in port to address required repairs for safety or environmental protection could be costly, reducing the cost attraction of open registry in states with bad records. By publishing lists of registries ranked according to their detention rates, it was possible to distinguish between white list countries with excellent low records of detention and gray list and blacklist countries with poor records. Thus, the published success or failure rate of port-state inspections itself became a form of sanction discouraging shippers from using ships with poor records or ships registered under the flags of states known to have little regard for the conventions they had signed.[3]

The MOUs represented a strikingly important but little-noted evolution in the field of international law. Previously, international conventions regarding safety and the environment had, like other treaties, relied on the compliance of the sovereign signatory parties, with no international mechanism or institution for enforcement. This lack of enforcement (except by protest, economic sanctions, threats of military action, or use of military force) had always been the core weakness of the concept of international law. With the MOUs, the port states had hit on a method of enforcement that entailed no loss of sovereignty but voluntary cooperation of the port states and the economic power of bad publicity for shipowners whose ships were subject to delays, fines, and forced repairs in remote ports. With the instant dissemination of key information through the Internet, the method fell back on commercial or business motivations, rather than state-on-state applications of threats or force. That is, with bad publicity, responsible shippers would have incentives to shift their business to ships registered under flags that provided better ships.

The evolution of second registries, additional open registries, and MOUs is an intricate and overlapping story captured in the contemporary maritime news media but little noted or understood beyond a narrow circle of specialists in the shipping business. Nevertheless, this evolution is a significant symptom of the globalization of world enterprises. By the first decade of the twenty-first century, well over half of all the shipping in the world was registered either in open-registry states like Panama or in the second registers. The development of second registries in the offshore dependencies of the Isle of Man, the Netherlands Antilles, the Spanish Canary Islands, French Antarctica (Kerguelen), and Portuguese Madeira was a striking phenomenon. The legislatures of the home country found it politically and legally more acceptable to structure a liberalized maritime code for an offshore dependency than to create a wholly new and separate code within the home country. The pattern of using a dependent but quasi-sovereign overseas government as a ship registry, as shown in earlier chapters, characterized the original creation of both the Panamanian and Liberian registries. Although independent nations, their close relationship with the United States had made them informal protectorates with a dependent status similar to the relationship of the later offshore jurisdictions of former European colonies in islands around the world.

In one sense, the original Panamanian and Liberian registries had both been intended as second registries for the United States before they evolved and attracted ships from all over the world. Both nations had special relations with the United States. As already noted, Panama was created by secession from Colombia in 1903 with the blessing of the United States. Even without being invited, the United States intervened in Panama with troops on at least five separate occasions in the 1920s. The right to militarily intervene was formally terminated in the 1930s.[4] Liberia had been formed as a colony in Africa for the resettlement of freed African American slaves in the early nineteenth century and was further aided by the Stettinius organization in the post–World War II era. Although both Panama and Liberia were independent, to varying extents over time, they were dependent on the United States and emulated major U.S. foreign policy positions. Both used the U.S. dollar as the national currency.

As quasi-dependencies of the United States, both countries attracted U.S. shipowners and, as we have seen, owners from Norway, Greece, and other traditional maritime nations. As third-world politics evolved, local political crises arose in both countries, and both registries became flags of convenience for shipowners around the world, the original second-registry status of Panamanian and Liberian maritime flags was almost entirely forgotten. At least one commentator on maritime affairs, Andrew Guest, recognized the U.S. sponsorship and creation of the Liberian flag: Liberia as a second registry, he noted, "was first thought of more than 40 years ago when Edward Stettinius, a former secretary of state, . . . helped set up the Liberian maritime program which evolved into the world's biggest flag of convenience."[5]

Comments, press releases, and public addresses by shipowners, maritime analysts, labor representatives, and registry operators illustrate how the competition of flag states has come to resemble a private-sector marketplace in commercial services. These statements also provide an overview of this development. Some ship-registry services frankly operate as for-profit businesses, rather than as branches of a government, offering services and competing with one another for the registry of ships from around the world. Statistics of ships and tonnage registered shed light on the degree of success or failure of the new systems as they competed with older open registries and even with each other.[6]

Some of the second registries had limited success in achieving the economic goal of supporting the national shipping industry. Others were more successful, preventing the destruction of the home fleet that otherwise would have happened as most of a country's ships transferred to foreign open registries. In several cases, the new second register was so well thought out and so well managed that the new registry itself began to attract the registry of ships owned in other nations. In this way, some second registries acted as efficient open registries for well-operated ships. One such success story was the registry of the Isle of Man.

Isle of Man Second Registry

Created in 1984, the Isle of Man registry had achieved a good level of success by 1996, with 170 vessels registered and a reputation for accepting only good-quality vessels. By adding a section that allowed bareboat charter registry in 1991, the system gained some 20 new ships. The director of the registry frankly attributed its success to the fact that it charged a onetime fee of £375 when the ship was registered, together with the cost of a ship survey. With no income tax or further tonnage taxes in subsequent years, the rate was the very lowest charged for ship registry in the mid-1990s. Although rates increased in later years, the fees remained very competitive well into the twenty-first century. Captain David Ramsbottom, marketing co-coordinator for the Manx flag, said, "I presume that the Isle of Man register must be financially beneficial since owners are leaving other reputable registers for us. But that is only part of it. The safety track record, the quality of service and the British links are all crucially important. . . . We are established as a quality register, and this is becoming more and more important for owners. They are choosing us rather than going for some of the more discredited registers."[7]

In assessing the competition between registries, *Lloyd's List* quoted maritime consultant Stephen Chapman, who had calculated that the least expensive registry in 1993 for large tankers was in the Isle of Man. Despite that, Panama and Liberia, with much more expensive tonnage rates, still had far more tonnage registered. The cost differential, the item noted, "can sometimes give a misleading impression." If cost was the only factor, the Isle of Man would soon have eclipsed the major open registries. But because the registry strictly insisted on safe and correctly maintained ships that conformed to international conventions on environmental conditions, large numbers of international shipowners opted for the much more expensive, but less regulated, flags.[8]

The managers of the Isle of Man registry did not like their system to be considered either as a second register or as a flag of convenience. Colin Douglas, the director of marine administration at the Isle of Man Shipping Register, said, "We are independent from the UK and do not see ourselves as a second register. . . . We are an international British Register and are not in the same league as second registers. They charge annual tonnage taxes and they are there for reasons of getting around crewing costs and to produce an income for themselves." From his point of view, the registry was simply one of several international services provided under the semisovereign status of the island. Even so, the UNCTAD continued to list the Isle of Man registry as the "second register" of the United Kingdom, as did most shipping-law analysts.[9]

Second Registries in the Netherlands Antilles and Luxembourg

Another offshore, insular second registry was that of the Netherlands Antilles. Unlike the Isle of Man registry, the Antilles registry was fraught with difficulties. The Netherlands Antilles became a separate country within the Kingdom of the Netherlands in 1954. As a sovereign state, it was made up of five separate islands: Curaçao, Bonaire, and three smaller islands near the Virgin Islands: Sint Eustasius, Saba, and Sint Maarten. The legislation establishing the ship-registration system was passed in 1987, and the registry office was set up in the port of Curaçao. Despite the competition from other flags, the Netherlands Antilles registry recorded substantial growth in 1993, with forty new entries in the first eight months of the year. Although the flag administration had not worked on marketing, the registry attracted roll-on roll-off vessels, many from Germany. Local administrators hoped to improve the registry further by consolidating services and creating one-stop shopping for shipowners. At this early stage, the Netherlands Antilles offered shipowners a choice of fee structure, either $.22 per ton, with a minimum of $600, or an income tax on profits ranging between 7 percent and 9.6 percent. The registry required a Dutch shipmaster (although that requirement could be waived). Crew and other officers could be of any nationality.[10]

However, through the mid-1990s, interdepartment politics kept the Netherlands Antilles from reaching its potential as a competitive open register. In 1998 administrators complained that discussions of consolidation into a single agency had been going on for at least four years, with little sign of progress.[11] Continuing infighting among maritime agencies in Curaçao led supporters of the registry to hope that various ship services could be combined into one department.[12]

Another political difficulty arose when a series of referenda in 2005 led to a plan to dissolve the Netherlands Antilles into 5 separate states. This dissolution took place in 2010. Curaçao and Sint Maarten became autonomous countries within the Kingdom of the Netherlands, and Bonaire, Sint Eustatius, and Saba became special municipalities of the Netherlands. Although open to owners from around the world, the Netherlands Antilles flag never emerged as a major open registry. After 2010 Curaçao maintained an open registry, but the number of ships registered fell from some 110 under the Netherland Antilles flag to about 100 under the Curaçao flag.

The Belgian second registry in Luxembourg in 1987–2003 was unlike the other second-registry systems in a number of ways, although it was motivated by the same concern for high cost and the flagging-out of vessels. The system was unique in that Luxembourg is landlocked, with no seaports at all. Furthermore, Luxembourg, although closely associated with Belgium in numerous economic and diplomatic agreements, is not an overseas dependency of Belgium. The complex system was worked out in 1987 with agreement from the seamen's unions of Belgium.

Belgian shipping had been transferring out to various foreign flags in order to reduce labor costs. The losses to foreign flags continued despite efforts by the government to offer subsidies and several legal battles to force Belgian companies to remain Belgian-flagged. Under the 1987 agreement, some fifteen ships of Compagnie Maritime Belge (CMB) were flagged in Luxembourg at considerable cost savings. Seamen could be hired in that country at lower wages, but some of the social security benefits extended to Belgian workers would be picked up by the Belgian company, which operated the ships on charter. The ships were actually dual-registered, in both Belgium and Luxembourg. This unique second-registry system was ended in 2003 by Belgian royal decree.[13]

The French Connection

The offshore registry of France also suffered several problems. For one thing, the island of Kerguelen was not a semisovereign dependency of

France, as it had fewer than a hundred year-round residents. In fact, the isolated, semi-Antarctic island cluster may have offered French legislators a convenient fiction—an offshore territory that, unlike the Netherlands Antilles, had no prospect of either dividing into multiple sovereignties or establishing itself as a truly independent sovereign state.

Like other maritime states in the late 1980s and early 1990s, France was suffering a decline of its merchant fleet. In a review of the French shipping industry in 1994, maritime journalist Anthony Dunlop argued that the decline of French shipping "was to some extent shielded" by "internal factors." These included subsidies and close relationships among shippers, brokers, and shipowners. Cabotage too played a part in France's ability to maintain a large coastal fleet. Nevertheless, the recession of the 1980s had a severe impact on the shipping industry. Both Socialist and Conservative governments in France attempted to deal with the problem. The Socialists set up the Kerguelen register by an act passed on June 17, 1989, but reporters believed that the country did not make the same "commitment to the offshore registry" that Norway and Denmark did with their domestic second registries. For example, the French required that 35 percent of the crew of a Kerguelen-registered ship be French nationals. Even so, all of the French oil tanker fleet moved to Kerguelen, where it could operate at half the cost of French registry. Some French shipowners wanted the Kerguelen registry transformed into a true open registry to compete for international shipping.[14]

When the French government considered establishing a third registry in 1999, French unions balked. The seafarers' union of the Confederation Francaise Democratique du Travail reacted with hostility to an announcement from Ministry of Transport Shipping, Ports, and Seaboard director Claude Gressier that the government would consider setting up another international register to replace the Kerguelen register. Delegate general Edouard Berlet of the Central Committee of French Shipowners said, "The Kerguelen register . . . had never put French owners on [a] fully competitive level against counterparts in other countries." Gressier pointed out that because the Kerguelen register was based in waters not covered by European Union law, companies using it had no access to the European cabotage sector. This, he said, could leave French companies in difficulty in the event that a neighboring country such as Italy decided to use its own second register to offer competition on ferry routes between the French mainland

and the island of Corsica. Furthermore, the Kerguelen register was not available to cruise companies, which Gressier suggested was one of the reasons for the virtual absence of French companies in the cruise sector. Although shipowners denied putting pressure on the government to establish a domestic-based register similar to that in Germany, Norway, and Denmark, the arguments in favor of such a registry mounted.[15]

Norwegian and Danish Second Registers

The second registries of Norway and Denmark were both established as domestic, not offshore, registries. Unlike Britain and France, Norway has no overseas semi-independent territories. Although Denmark has two overseas dependencies, Greenland and the Faroe Islands, both have strong local political movements for full independence, which limited the attraction of either one as a possible second register.

Between 1983 and 1987 the Norwegian-flagged fleet declined from 34.5 million deadweight tons to 10.7 million deadweight tons, and the number of Norwegian merchant seamen declined from 18,500 to 9,500. With labor under the national flag representing 25 percent of running costs, the existence of Norway's shipping industry was threatened and flagging-out became common. The Labor government decided to approach the problem with a second register, the Norwegian International Ship Registry (NIS), which allowed foreign seamen to be employed under Norwegian labor terms. Famed shipping magnate Erling Naess had suggested the system in 1984 as a solution to the shipping cost problem. NIS got under way on July 1, 1987, and was credited with preventing a national economic disaster.[16]

Early in the 1990s, shipping analyst Christopher Brown-Humes concluded that both the NIS and the DIS had done rather well in meeting their goals. The NIS was established in 1987 and the DIS was established on August 23, 1988, with "slightly different aims," but both had beneficial impacts on their countries' shipping industries. Even so, Brown-Humes believed that NIS was already "past its heyday," noting a marginal drop in tonnage between the end of 1990 and the end of 1991. He believed that the problem of substandard shipping was already plaguing the NIS.

Brown-Humes also noted that Denmark had not only increased registry with DIS but had increased employment of Danish seamen. He concluded that second registers were no panacea, and to succeed, they would have to guard against substandard ships and be coupled with financial incentives.[17] In 1996 the Danish register added the inducement of no personal income tax.[18] The DIS was not open to ships beneficially owned in either of the two overseas dependencies of Denmark.

In the long run, neither Norway nor Denmark was very successful in stemming the flagging-out process. Figures collected by Lloyds/Fairplay and analyzed by UNCTAD showed that in 1997 shipowners in both Denmark and Norway each flagged about 58 percent of the tonnage of shipping in their home country, counting both the national and second registries as "home." By 2007 both countries had lost tonnage to foreign flags; Danish owners flagged about 45 percent under Danish flags, while Norwegian owners flagged only about 28 percent of the tonnage under both their registries. Neither the Danish nor the Norwegian registries made great efforts to attract foreign owners. By January 1, 2007, 97 percent of DIS by tonnage was owned by Danes; in NIS 61 percent was owned by Norwegians. Both the Norwegian and Danish systems continued to flourish. By 2014 NIS registered 531 ships, and DIS registered 381.[19]

German and Italian Second Registers

The German second register ran into trouble with German organized labor from its beginnings. Germany had lost its overseas colonies at the end of World War I, and thus, if the nation were to establish a second registry, it would have to be a domestic one along the lines of the Norwegian and Danish systems. As soon as the registry was established on April 5, 1989, German unions took the issue of the second registry to court, first to the Bremen Labor Court and then to the European Court of Justice. The second register would allow shipowners to hire crews from other countries at their own prevailing labor rates, which German unions considered a form of discrimination. Of a total German fleet of 276 vessels, 209 had moved to the second registry by 1990.[20]

By 1995 organized labor, both inside Germany and internationally, was still criticizing the GIS. The registry was declared a flag of convenience by the ITF, following a German constitutional court decision in January 1995 that stated that the system did not contravene the German constitution. The ITF blacklisting left the ships open to boycotts by union members in ports around the world, unless the ships met agreements with the ITF-affiliated German union of public service and transportation workers, Öffentliche Dienste, Transport und Verkehr (ÖTV). The

ITF declared the GIS a flag of convenience after a meeting in Geneva in 1994 during which the group urged national-affiliated unions, like ÖTV, to declare their countries' second registries as flags of convenience. Most affiliated unions in countries with second registries did not do so because they had already reached agreements with shipping companies guaranteeing negotiating rights and retaining some union members' employment on ships transferred to the second registries. At that point, only the Spanish Canary Islands register had been similarly blacklisted in 1993 at the urging of Spanish unions.

The hard line by the ITF was attributed to its new general secretary, David Cockroft. The federation claimed that the policy was a result of "continuing victimization and harassment of seafarers by manning agents and certain ship owners" in the second registers. Despite the sentiment at ITF headquarters, the ITF would blacklist the remaining second registers only with the approval of the national unions in the respective countries: Norway, Denmark, and Britain (for the Isle of Man registry). As of 2016, the second registries of Norway, Denmark, and the Isle of Man had not been blacklisted as flag-of-convenience registries by the ITF.[21]

One ship, the *Sea Nordic*, registered in the German second registry, was subject to a boycott by longshoremen in the Danish port of Aarhus. The ship left port only half loaded. The owners later signed an agreement with ÖTV and paid some $100,000 to cover back pay and ITF expenses.[22] Shipping analyst Christopher Brown-Humes noted that the German register was suffering because it had "less clearly defined aims" than the registries of Norway or Denmark. He pointed out the drop in subsidies and the erosion of tax breaks for shipping.[23]

The Italian second registry, like the German registry, encountered labor opposition while earning support from some of the Italian shipowning establishment. However, Italy had more success in attracting shipowners. Italy, like Germany and Norway, has no overseas dependencies, and thus the system created there was a domestic one. When Italy's transport minister, Publio Fiori, announced that he intended to present a bill to the Italian parliament to initiate a second register in late 1994, the announcement was welcomed by the shipowners' association, Confitarma, even before the details of the bill were announced. Confitarma suggested that the new bill be modeled on Norway's, which by that point had some 70 percent of Norwegian beneficially owned ships registered in the NIS. As noted, however, that percentage fell severely in later years.[24]

Aldo Grimaldi, chairman of Confitarma, said in April 1995, "There is no time to lose in creating a second register because the high cost of having to employ all-Italian crews is crippling the country's shipping sector. Italian shipping is in trouble because the costs it has to support do not allow it to be competitive on the international market." Grimaldi said he was "frustrated that other countries have already taken action, created second registers and have a competitive edge over Italian ship owners." He named Norway, Denmark, Britain, and Germany as examples. "With our higher costs, sooner or later Italian shipping will disappear, unless certain drastic measures are taken."[25] With no overseas dependencies, Italy would have to create a domestic second register.

One of the early successes of the Italian second registry was the transfer of the European cruise operator Costa Crociere from Liberia to the Italian second registry. In addition to a new flag ship, the *Costa Atlantica*, due to be handed over from the builder Kvaerner Masa in June 2000, the company would transfer six existing ships, according to Costa Crociere chief executive officer and director Pier Luigi Foschi. Foschi estimated that operating costs would be about the same as under the Liberian flag, but that the Italian flag would add marketing value. Under the new Italian second registry, the profit tax was only 7.4 percent compared to the standard Italian tax of about 50 percent. Furthermore, the ships would only be required to have six EU crew members each.[26]

Without making a concerted effort to attract foreign ships, the Italian register quietly succeeded in increasing its total number and tonnage of ships over the following decade. By 2010 Italy's combined first and second registries amounted to more than 17 million tons, just above the tonnage figures for the registries of the United Kingdom and the United States. Among the countries that had sought to establish a domestic second registry, Italy was the best at stemming the flagging-out process and attracting total tonnage, with one of the highest tonnages of any European country.[27]

Off-Shoring for Portugal and Spain

Portugal and Spain both turned to their relatively ancient offshore possessions in the Atlantic Ocean for the creation of second registries, emulating the British and Netherlands practice of using offshore territories' semisovereign status. Portugal established its second registry, the Madeira Open Shipping Register (MAR), under two laws passed in March 1989, formally opening the registry on January 1, 1990. Under MAR, ships operating outside Portuguese territorial waters would not be liable to income tax on their profits or on the salaries of crew members and officers. By July 1990 four Portuguese ships had registered. Administrators and observers held high hopes for the flag, with its location in the Atlantic off the Strait of Gibraltar, convenient to shipping lanes. Francisco Costa, the director of the Madeira Development Company, stated frankly that the purpose of the registry was to staunch the exodus of ships from the Portuguese flag to open registries. He was confident the registry would continue to flourish.[28]

The Madeira Island registry was open to residents of the European Union and nationals of Portuguese-speaking countries elsewhere around the world (including Brazil, Angola, and Mozambique). In addition, the registry hoped to attract Spanish-owned ships. Spanish shipowners, like those in other European countries, were actively reregistering their ships in open-registry nations through the mid- and late 1980s, and the Madeira flag hoped to compete, especially with a provision exempting all ships registered from income tax until 2011 (later extended to 2020).[29]

Administrators of the Madeira registry were explicit in announcing that the registry's "first object was to stop the flagging out of Portuguese vessels to other flags." However, they also admitted that they sought to establish an open registry that would attract a variety of owners to a flag within the European Union. The number of ships in the registry climbed steadily and by 2004 the flag had twenty-two ships owned by Portuguese, fifty-four by Italians, thirty-five by Spaniards, and twenty-eight by Germans. By 2015 the registry's quality remained high, escaping ITF designation as a flag of convenience, and the flag continued to attract shipowners from several European countries. However, the combined tonnage remained well below that of the major second registries and the competing open registers.[30]

Spain had faced problems similar to those of the other European maritime states. There, as in Germany, shipowners and organized labor took two different views of whether a second registry was a good solution. Registry of ships in Spain had fallen by two-thirds between 1984 and 1993. As measured in gross registered tons, the fall was from about 7.5 million to about 2.5 million. A Spanish second registry was first discussed as a legislative proposal in 1991. The law was passed in October 1992, and the registry opened later that year.[31]

In 1992 the Spanish shipowners' organization, Asociación de Navieros Españoles (ANAVE), had reported that unless a workable second register was implemented, the Spanish-flag fleet could fall from 3.1 million gross tons to only 1 million gross tons by 1996, with the loss of several thousand seafarers' jobs. ANAVE estimated a Canary Islands registry could save six thousand Spanish jobs and prevent the loss of an estimated $1 billion per year in earnings to Spain. It was understood that the master, the first mate, and half the crew on ships in the Canary Islands registry would have to be EU citizens. To bring benefits to the Canaries, it was suggested that an international banking center be established there as well.[32]

While the Spanish law was under consideration, representatives of the shipowners' groups expressed some reservations about the new registry. It was not nearly as "liberal" as the other second registries that had been established, such as the Danish one, according to Fernando Casas Blanco, general director of ANAVE. Under the law as drafted, the corporate income tax would be dropped from 35 to 25 percent and up to half the crew could be hired on an international basis. In light of these provisions, Juan Maria Gomez de Mariaca, chairman of tank shipping operator Repsol Naviera Vizcaina and a prior chairman of ANAVE, disliked the idea that the ship-registry law was part of a package designed for the Canary Islands, rather than an independent piece of legislation. He predicted that tensions between the people of the islands and Madrid would lead to delays and a halfhearted implementation.[33]

Within a year of the system's establishment, Spanish labor unions protested to the ITF. The Canary Islands registry was placed on the ITF blacklist as a flag of convenience, the first of the second registers to be so designated.[34] By 1994, despite a Socialist victory in the Spanish national elections and political promises to address the problems with the Canary register, there were still only 5 ships registered there.[35] Spain offered tax concessions in 1996 that appeared to help.[36] Even so, the reality turned out to be even worse than the earlier dire predictions of ANAVE representatives. By January 1, 1998, more than 88 percent of Spanish-owned ships flew foreign flags. Including the Canary Islands registry, the nationally registered ships dropped to well less than a half million gross registered tons.[37] However, the Canary Islands registry continued to climb; by 2013, 136 ships with over 2.5 million gross registered tons flew the Spanish Canary Islands special registry flag.[38]

Second Registers as Open Registers

As the number of flags of convenience continued to increase in the 1990s, second registers soon became part of the competition. Observers debated whether the second registries would evolve in the direction of elite, high-quality registers with good safety and labor records or whether they would compete with the proliferating open registries that served as flags of convenience for substandard ships. Through the 1990s and into the twenty-first century, both types of developments took place. That is, some of the second registers became more like flags of convenience, becoming known for ships with disreputable labor and safety records. Others maintained high standards on a par with the standards of the traditional maritime nations.

Following protests from local unions, by 1996 the ITF had declared the second registries of Spain, Germany, and the Netherlands flags of convenience because of abusive labor practices. Even so, the ITF found it increasingly difficult to simply criticize all open registries or all second registries as flags of convenience since some open-registry owners had good labor policies. Indeed, some open-registry flags, whether second registers or not, had excellent reputations. ITF leader Cockroft said, "It is becoming harder and harder to just maintain a national flag versus foc [flag of convenience] stance, and therefore we are having to develop a policy which is more sophisticated and which looks firstly at where the ship is trading, and what its competition is." The old distinction between traditional registries and open registries was becoming increasingly blurred.[39] The fact that some second registers, like the Netherlands Antilles, openly sought non-Dutch shipowners also showed there was no clear-cut distinction between second and open registries.

By 2015 only a few of the second registers had partially achieved their goals of preventing the transfer of home-owned ships to flags of convenience. On the other hand, most of them had also succeeded by attracting at least some owners from other countries. In the case of Denmark, more than 90 percent of the tonnage was Danish-owned. In contrast, in the registries of Panama, Liberia, Malta, and Bermuda, nationals of the country owned none of the tonnage. Some of the second registers were quite successful in registering total tonnage, most notably the Marshall Islands. These figures suggest that in the competition for registry against the older flags of convenience, at least some of the second registries were holding their own. The first-generation flags of convenience—Panama and Liberia—outranked the Marshall Islands register, but the newcomers, such as the Madeira register, continued to gain tonnage and compete in the ship-registry marketplace.

However, all of the countries that developed second registries also continued to have large numbers of ships registered under foreign flags of convenience. For example, by 2005 German-owned ships could be found in high percentages in the major open registers, and even the relatively successful Norwegian, Dutch, and Danish second registers did not attract all owners from their home countries. By 2007 almost 85 percent of German-owned ships were registered under foreign flags, about 80 percent of Spanish ships were under foreign flags, and more than 70 percent of Norwegian ships were registered abroad.[40]

Even though the Marshall Islands registry had been created more out of concern for effective control doctrine than for strengthening U.S. maritime industries, many commentators in the 1990s and later came to regard the Marshall Islands register as a second register for the United States. Indeed, the parallels were persuasive. The Marshall Islands were a semi-independent, former dependency of the United States; the registry was operated by a U.S. firm. The Marshall Islands registry was the leading overseas registry for U.S.-owned ships, attracting more than Liberia, Panama, or the Bahamas.[41] That trend remained in place over the next few years. By 2013 the Marshall Islands registered 252 U.S.-owned ships, while Liberia registered 89 and Panama registered 121. The tonnage of U.S.-owned ships registered in the Marshall Islands had also climbed. By 2013 the deadweight tonnage of U.S.-owned ships registered in the Marshall Islands had climbed to 20,666,000, exceeding the combined tonnage of U.S.-owned ships registered in the Bahamas, Liberia, and Panama.[42]

By 2014 it was clear that the phenomenon of flagging-out, whether to traditional open-registry countries or to the newer second registries, had affected all of the major ship-owning countries. Table 5 shows the percentage of foreign-registered ships over 1,000 gross registered tons in eight major ship-owning countries. The UN agency compiling the statistics defined "beneficial ownership" as the location of the primary reference country of the owning individual, partnership, or corporation.

TABLE 5. FOREIGN REGISTRY OF SHIPS OVER 1,000 GROSS REGISTERED TONS IN EIGHT MAJOR SHIP-OWNING COUNTRIES

Beneficial owning nation	Total number of ships over 1,000 GRT	Percentage foreign-registered
China*	5,405	63.0%
Japan	4,022	92.0%
Greece	3,876	73.0%
Germany	3,699	87.0%
United States	1,927	85.0%
Norway	1,864	94.3%
Netherlands	1,234	61.8%
Denmark	955	99.0%

Source: Data from UNCTAD, *Review of Maritime Transport 2014* (New York: United Nations, 2014).
*Not including Hong Kong and Taiwan

UNCTAD staff noted how the distinction between national fleets, open registries, and second registries was becoming difficult to determine. The difficulty arose because national fleets registered foreign-owned ships, and second registries, like those in the Netherlands, Norway, France, Isle of Man, and the Marshall Islands, directly competed for international owners with such countries as Panama, Liberia, Cyprus, and Malta.[43] By 2014 Panama, Liberia, Marshall Islands, Hong Kong, and Singapore had registered 57 percent of the world total tonnage of large ships.[44]

UNCTAD reported in 2014 that U.S. "beneficial owners" of ships had 1,927 ships, with a combined tonnage of 59 million deadweight tons. However, the U.S. flag flew over only 850 ships with a combined tonnage of 11,848,000 deadweight tons. Of that U.S.-flagged tonnage, 28 percent (3,353,000 deadweight tons) was owned by non-American entities. Thus, of the 59 million deadweight tons of large oceangoing ships owned by U.S. owners, less than 9 million deadweight tons were flagged in the United States. These included privately owned ships engaged in carrying government cargo and ships engaged in coastwise trade that remained restricted to U.S. flag registry under cabotage provisions of the 1920 Jones Act because they were engaged in travel between U.S. ports, such as Alaska, Hawaii, or Puerto Rico and the mainland.[45]

Overall Impact

Although the plethora of statistics can be confusing, a few simple observations can be derived from them. By the second decade of the twenty-first century, most U.S.-owned shipping was foreign-registered, and the small fraction of U.S.-owned shipping that remained under the U.S. flag was that protected by provisions of law. Furthermore, the same developments had affected the traditional maritime nations of Europe to varying extents.

After more than thirty years, one can observe several trends and patterns of development in second registries. All of the offshore second registries developed in the direction of open registries, much in the tradition of the original evolution of Panama and Liberia. All were located in insular dependencies of the home country. UNCTAD noted in 2014 that the dissociation between ownership and registry had become even more layered with a new dimension: "Just as today most ships fly a flag that is different from that of the owner's nationality, owners are increasingly locating their companies in third countries/economies, adding a possible third dimension to the nationality of a ship and its owner. A ship's nationality is defined by the nation whose flag it flies, while the owner may have a different nationality and the owner's company that controls the vessel may be based in a third country/economy. These different dimensions render the historical concept of 'national fleets' more blurred and less meaningful."[46]

Two of the offshore registries became high-quality open registers: the Isle of Man and Marshall Islands. While attracting international owners, both of these flags have retained a substantial percentage of the home (UK and U.S.) fleets. Both might be ranked as second-registry success stories.

Three offshore second registries explicitly attempted to become open registries, generating business and revenue for the insular state, but with somewhat less concern for maintaining high quality: the Netherlands Antilles (Curaçao), Madeira, and the Canary Islands. These three all had limited or marginal success, with Madeira showing some growth.

Two of the systems failed or were terminated. The French Kerguelen offshore second registry was discontinued in favor of a domestic second registry. As noted, the Belgian experiment with the Luxembourg registry was also soon abandoned, even though it received endorsement from Belgian labor unions.

Denmark and Italy had notable successes in convincing shipowners to remain under the nation's flag. Germany and Norway had more limited success, with the vast majority of domestically owned ships still flagging-out.

The set of facts presented here shows that the second registers did not halt the problem of flagging-out or the decline of the merchant fleets of the traditional maritime nations. The second registries were attempts to affect the changed dynamics in international shipping that only partially succeeded. Several of them also evolved in the direction of open registries, accepting ships owned in a variety of nations, and this evolution illustrates that the underlying dynamics of internationalization of business are extremely difficult to resist; recall the multiple "dimensions" noted in the 2014 UNCTAD report.

By viewing the U.S. experience in the light of international developments, it is clear that the "flight from the flag" that began in the Civil War and then took off—first with Esso ships in Danzig, then with the Panamanian registries in the 1930s, and later with Liberian registry—was not simply a U.S. phenomenon. Instead, once shipping company executives realized that the Muscat dhows arbitration principles were being accepted around the world, they all sought to find the most favorable economic and legal jurisdiction, regardless of their country of origin, whether Norway or Italy, China or the United States. For unscrupulous owners who were not concerned with ship safety or maintenance or who conducted smuggling operations of one kind or another, registrations with the least effective and least enforced regulations were naturally the most attractive. Even for entirely reputable business operations, the attraction of low-cost labor and tax havens in the competitive world shipping market proved irresistible.

Maritime Nations Fight Back

Two ingenious developments since the 1980s showed that the traditional maritime nations can take somewhat effective steps to offset the negative impact of the flight from flag to flag and the proliferation of open registries. The first development was the proliferation of second registries, some of which succeeded in at least stemming the flight from the traditional maritime flags by setting up ship-registry systems outside the traditional taxation, social legislation, and labor requirements but with a degree of allegiance or alliance with the original maritime nation. The second development was the establishment of MOUs that used information technology to create informal but effective economic pressures on irresponsible ship registries and shipowners. The systems, in the face of no international police force to enforce international law, provided somewhat effective means of pressuring companies and nations that did not play by the rules.

As a consequence of these developments and the forward march of globalization, it was clear by the second decade of the twenty-first century that the close identification between national identity and the merchant flag at sea had almost entirely dissolved. In the U.S. case, one consequence of globalization is that although it is separated from most of the world by oceans and has the third-largest land mass and population in the world, the United States has a disproportionally small fleet of merchant ships under its flag. Another consequence is that it is very rare indeed for a U.S.-flagged ship to encounter hostile forces abroad that would require the engagement of the State Department or the U.S. Navy to protect the flag.

CONCLUSION

For the first decades of the nation's history, the American merchant flag at sea served as an emblem of the nation's honor. Defense of that flag evoked passionate rhetoric and led to the nation's engagement in its first major foreign wars: the Quasi War with France, the Barbary Wars, and the War of 1812. For the next four decades, defense of the flag led to the punitive expedition against Kuala Batu and then to a campaign by some, especially defenders of slavery, to demand an armed response to Great Britain's supposed insult to the flag with the exercise of the right of search U.S.-flagged slave ships.

An Honorable Ruse

During the Civil War, American shipowners transferred registry of their vessels to other nations for protection against Confederate commerce raiders. Some observers noted the similarity of these acts of reflagging to the practice of false flag uses as a *ruse de guerre*. Under the maritime honor code, a warship could legitimately adopt a false flag when it sighted an enemy to avoid being attacked. However, before the crew fired a shot, the genuine flag had to be raised; to fire a gun under a false flag was a perfidious act.

Merchant ships in the same era frequently carried numerous flags, sometimes hoisting a false flag when on the high seas in hopes of avoiding capture, damage, or destruction from enemy warships. However, when armed cruisers overtook merchant ships during time of war, naval officers from the cruiser could and would board a suspect ship and examine the papers and crew to determine if the flag usage was genuine. During the right of search controversies of the 1840s and 1850s, British officers boarded suspected slave ships flying the U.S. flag for just such purposes; the U.S. objection was that Britain was exercising right of search during peacetime. During the Civil War, Confederate cruisers would stop and detain British-flagged ships; if the documentation supported the flag, the ship would be released. No Confederate cruiser was ever accused by the British government of having wrongfully destroyed a genuinely flagged British ship.

When considering twentieth-century open registry, these prec-edents bear on the issue of honor. Sale and transfer abroad to a new flag is similar to the honorable *ruse de guerre* in that the new flag offers protection; it is different in that the transfer is not faked or a deception as in the *ruse de guerre* tradition. The sale and transfer is entirely ethical by the unwritten maritime honor code and fully legal by the standards of international law. That was so in the 1860s and remains so today. Documentation on board the vessel can demonstrate the validity of the reflagging, open to inspection at sea in time of war or upon arrival in coastal waters or port in time of peace.

The reflagging practices of the Civil War and the 1939–1941 neu-trality period were means of protecting either the ship itself (in the Civil War) or the United States from the necessity of defending the ship (in 1939–1941). Significantly, the reflagging offered those protections as in an honorable ruse, but it also did so on a fully legal basis.

The late twentieth-century flight of shipping from the flags of traditional maritime nations continues to anger organized labor leaders and those concerned with the risks to the environment posed by oil tankers registered in nations that fail to enforce safety at sea practices. In Europe, the flight from national flags put sectors of the different national maritime economies at risk. Despite assertions from critics that there was something dishonorable or unethical about the transfers, the systems of open registry were not only "convenient" but also legal by U.S. and international law and completely in accord with the tradi-tions of the unspoken maritime honor code. The practice has become so widespread and so firmly entrenched that the traditional maritime nations have adopted both second registers and port-state control sys-tems to adapt.

While the United States still maintains the largest and most power-ful Navy in the world and carries its flag proudly to waters around the planet, it would be rare indeed to spot a U.S. flag on a merchant ship outside the routes between U.S. ports. The vast majority of U.S.-owned tonnage and ships have completed their flight from flag to flag.

The Survival of the Rhetoric of Honor in Maritime Incidents

Despite all these developments in the late twentieth century and early twenty-first century, the U.S. flag at sea still has the power to bring the United States into conflict with other nations. The following incidents have led either to U.S. military engagements or to extremely strained diplomatic relations with a foreign power:

> USS *Maddox*, approached by North Vietnamese gunboats, August 4, 1964
>
> USS *Liberty*, strafed by Israeli aircraft, June 8, 1967
>
> USS *Pueblo*, seized and crew held by North Korea for eleven months, January 28, 1968
>
> SS *Mayaguez*, seized and crew detained by Cambodian forces, May 12, 1975
>
> USS *Stark*, hit by two Exocet missiles from Iraqi aircraft, May 17, 1987
>
> USS *Samuel B. Roberts*, struck an Iranian mine, April 14, 1988
>
> USS *Cole*, attacked by Al Qaeda suicide bombers, Yemen, October 12, 2000
>
> MV *Maersk Alabama*, seized briefly by Somali pirates, April 2009[1]

In each case, the attack on a U.S.-flagged ship carried echoes of the maritime honor code. The USS *Maddox* episode became part of the Tonkin Gulf incident, which precipitated U.S. expansion of its role in the Vietnam War. In his speech to Congress calling for the Gulf of Tonkin Resolution, President Lyndon Johnson specifically evoked the traditional language of outrage: "The determination of all Americans to carry out our full commitment to the people and to the government of South Vietnam will be redoubled by this outrage."[2] In the other major episodes, some editorialists and government officials also invoked the rhetoric of honor, using the terms "insult," "humiliation," and "honor."

Of these episodes involving U.S.-flagged ships, only two involved merchant ships, reflecting the greatly reduced presence of the American merchant flag on the world's oceans. (The others in the list are U.S. naval ships, designated "USS.") The two merchant ships involved in crises were the steamship *Mayaguez* in 1975 and the motor vessel *Maersk Alabama* in 2009, both engaged in carrying U.S. government cargo. The Cargo Preference Act of 1954 requires that 50 percent of government cargo be carried on board U.S.-flagged vessels to the extent that such ships are available. The act is the primary reason that there is still a U.S.-flagged merchant fleet to be found beyond the trade between U.S. ports. In both the *Mayaguez* and the *Maersk Alabama* incidents, the U.S. government, at the direction of the president, responded with armed force to the attack on the U.S. flag. Many of the commentators on these two merchant ship incidents used language reminiscent of the maritime honor code from the earliest days of the republic.

It is not argued here that the maritime honor code is the cause of armed response to affronts to the merchant flag at sea, but the code has clearly shaped U.S. thinking and rhetoric about attacks on that flag, not only in the nineteenth century but into present times.

One recent book-length analysis of the *Mayaguez* incident recalls that the Gerald Ford administration treated the incident as "piracy," although the Cambodian government forces operated within their territorial waters.[3] At the time, Raoul Berger, a University of California School of Law professor, writing for the *New York Times*, opposed the action ordered by President Ford on the grounds that he exceeded the constitutional limits on the president's war-making powers. Berger accused congressional supporters of the action as reflecting a "rally round the flag" mentality.[4] Rod MacLeish, a nationally known news commentator, quoted Secretary of State Henry Kissinger as saying that the "United States should not be pushed around."[5] A writer for the *Chicago Defender* regarded the *Mayaguez* seizure as a "threat to U.S. prestige."[6] Rowland Evans Jr. and Robert Novak, famous for their nationally syndicated political column, suggested that the United States should "avoid repeating the humiliation of *Pueblo*."[7] Defending Gerald Ford, James Reston argued that to have acquiesced in piracy would have "added humiliation to embarrassment."[8] The terms used all echoed the sentiment and language that had described similar circumstances in the nineteenth century. Both supporters and opponents of Gerald Ford's action cast their arguments in rhetoric reflecting the maritime code of honor, especially the aspect that required a stern response to outrages or affronts from low-caste opponents.

The outcome of the MV *Maersk Alabama* episode in 2009 was far less controversial, as the attempt to seize the ship was clearly an act of piracy, and the successful suppression of the Somali pirates by the ship's crew and the rescue of the shipmaster by the U.S. Navy received widespread public support. Nevertheless, the published accounts of the episode and its aftermath showed that elements of the vocabulary and rhetoric of the maritime honor code were very much alive in the twenty-first century. Leaders of the Marine Engineers Beneficial Association (MEBA) published a comment at the conclusion of the MV *Maersk Alabama* episode that captured the fundamental notion that the U.S. flag on board a merchant ship represented U.S. sovereignty at sea: "When a vessel flies the U.S. flag, it becomes an extension of the United States itself, regardless of where in the world the vessel is operating."[9]

In general, the news coverage of the *Maersk Alabama* incident, and reviews of the Tom Hanks film that later presented a Hollywood version of the events, tended to focus on the heroism of the crew and the U.S. Navy SEALs involved in rescuing the master. The crew resisted the pirates, prevented their control of the ship, and then regained control of the ship—a series of events unique among the more than two hundred cases of Somali pirate attacks on shipping that had preceded the *Maersk Alabama* attack.

Debates over the film treatment focused on whether Capt. Richard Phillips deserved as much attention as the crew members. Some complained that the real heroes of the action were the less-celebrated crew members who immobilized the ship and forced the hijackers off the ship. In point of fact, the actions of the crew members in resisting the pirates did show considerable presence of mind, courage, and heroism, as did the actions of the Navy SEALs involved in the rescue of Captain Phillips. The point here is that the episode was discussed and viewed in terms traditionally associated with the sea.[10]

A Final Word

After the extensive development of off-shoring of ship registration since the Civil War, the Muscat dhows decision, experiments in Danzig and Panama, and official support from the U.S. government and courts through the 1940s and 1950s, the U.S. fleet is now extremely small in proportion to the economy, population, and geographic extent of the nation. The U.S.-flagged merchant marine has shrunk, sustained by virtue of two legal provisions: traditional cabotage incorporated in the Jones Act of 1920, which restricts shipping between U.S. ports to ships registered in the United States, and the 1954 Cargo Preference Act, which requires a proportion of U.S. ships to be so registered.

Despite the flight from flag to flag, the remaining small fleet of U.S.-flagged ships almost inevitably will encounter aggression around the world from terrorists, pirates, rebel groups, or the maritime forces of small, poorly governed or hostile nations. When these incidents occur, it is inevitable that the maritime code of honor will be invoked, both by supporters and opponents of a forceful response. After all, any attack on the American merchant flag at sea is still today an attack on the symbol of the nation itself.

Notes

Introduction

1. United Nations Conference on Trade and Development (UNCTAD), *Review of Maritime Transport 2014* (New York: United Nations, 2014), 44. This study, dated January 1, 2014, ranked countries by registered tonnage of oceangoing ships over 1,000 deadweight tons. In recent years, the U.S. rank in size measured by registered tonnage has varied from sixth to twenty-second.
2. A perceptive analysis of the topic of honor in several societies is Frank Henderson Stewart, *Honor* (Chicago: University of Chicago Press, 1994), especially chap. 2, "The Nature of Honor." Grotius' work is the subject of an extensive literature. David Armitage's concise introduction to a recent edition of the English translation of *Mare Liberum* is a good introduction to the work: Hugo Grotius, *The Free Sea*, ed. David Armitage (Indianapolis: Liberty Fund, 2004).

Chapter 1. The Maritime *Code Duello*

1. David Hackett Fischer, *Albion's Seed: Four British Folkways in America* (New York: Oxford University Press, 1989), 383, 384, 396–97. See also Bertram Wyatt-Brown, *Southern Honor: Ethics and Behavior in the Old South* (New York: Oxford University Press, 1982), for the influence of the code in the South. See his *A Warring Nation: Honor, Race, and Humiliation in America and Abroad* (Charlottesville: University of Virginia Press, 2014), especially 62–79, for the influence of the honor code in U.S. foreign policy and wars in 1776–1848.
2. Joanne Freeman, *Affairs of Honor: National Politics in the New Republic* (New Haven, CT: Yale University Press, 2001), xv, xviii.
3. Paul A. Gilje, *Free Trade and Sailors' Rights in the War of 1812* (New York: Cambridge University Press, 2013), especially 190–96. Throughout the book, Gilje demonstrates that the code of national honor lay behind the motto Free Trade and Sailors' Rights.
4. For a full discussion of the Cilley affair, see William Oliver Stevens, *Pistols at Ten Paces: The Story of the Code of Honor in America* (Boston: Houghton Mifflin, 1940), 220–26.
5. Freeman, *Affairs of Honor*, 168–69.
6. John K. Mahon, *The War of 1812* (Cambridge, MA: Da Capo Press, 1991), 250.
7. The variety of designs of the U.S. flag in this period is discussed extensively in George Henry Preble, *History of the Flag of the United States of America* (Boston: A. Williams, 1880), 345–47. The author is indebted to Harold Langley for the observation regarding the ability to recognize the general pattern of the different flags at sea. See Harold Langley, *So Proudly We Hail: The History of the United States Flag* (Washington, DC: Smithsonian Institution Press, 1981).
8. The series of historical novels by Patrick O'Brian featuring the fictional Capt. Jack Aubrey reflects both the internationally understood honor code and many accurate specifics of how the maritime *code duello* worked out in the conduct of warfare.

9. Just such a direct challenge was issued by Captain B. V. Broke, Royal Navy, of HMS *Shannon* to U.S. Navy captain James Laurence of the USS *Chesapeake* on May 31, 1813. In the battle on June 1, 1813, Laurence was killed. William S. Dudley, ed., *The Naval War of 1812: A Documentary History* (Washington, DC: Naval Historical Center, 1992), 126. Paul Gilje makes note of a challenge to a ship duel at the opening of his study, when Sir James Yeo of HMS *Alert* issued a challenge to Capt. David Porter of U.S. frigate *Essex* on July 12, 1812. Gilje, *Free Trade and Sailors' Rights*, 1–2.

10. Capt. James Laurence of USS *Chesapeake* went to some lengths in his dispatch describing the defeat of HMS *Peacock* on March 19, 1813, to show the equivalence of the two ships: "*Peacock* about the tonnage of the *Hornet*. . . . Her beam was greater by 5 inches, but her extreme length not so great by four feet." Dudley, *Naval War of 1812*, 71.

11. Ibid., 183.

12. Such a court-martial for cowardice was filed against a U.S. seaman on board *Enterprise* who hid behind a mast during a gun battle. Ibid., 241. The parallels between standing to receive fire on board a ship and the usual position of gentlemen engaged in a personal duel—who were expected to stand and receive fire—are notable.

13. Charles Oscar Paullin, *Dueling in the Old Navy* (Annapolis, MD: Naval Institute Press, 1909), 5.

14. Martha Elena Rojas, "'Insults Unpunished': Barbary Captives, American Slaves, and the Negotiation of Liberty," *Early American Studies* 1, no. 2 (Fall 2003), as cited in Wyatt-Brown, *Warring Nation*, 71. It was a feature of the personal honor code that gentlemen did not engage in duels with people of inferior social status, who were instead punished by caning or thrashing. Freeman, *Affairs of Honor*, 177: "Caning displayed the victim's inferior status."

15. Dudley, *Naval War of 1812*, 355. A torpedo was a type of shellfish for which mines were originally named. In the 1890s, when self-propelled mines (known first as "automobile torpedoes") were developed, the distinction was made between a mine, which was either tethered or free-floating, and a torpedo, which moved through the water with its own engine. Mines continued to be perceived by some naval officers and others as dishonorable well into the twentieth century.

16. Much of the Canadian-U.S. boundary was by lake and river. An exception was the relatively short land boundary with the British colonies of Canada, which ran from the St. Lawrence River east across the northern border of New York and Vermont. In this period, the Maine–New Brunswick border was not defined, and there was no significant overland trade to Spanish holdings to the west or south to Spanish Florida. Thus, the United States was virtually an island nation when it came to foreign trade.

17. In the twenty-first century, such treaties have been replaced by bilateral investment treaties designed to facilitate trade between independent states.

18. Clashes on the Spanish frontier in West Florida, the Patriot War filibustering expedition into East Florida, and the Battle of Tippecanoe, growing out of the rebellion of Native Americans against U.S. control, all represent land-based conflicts of the era not reflective of maritime honor code issues; however, the major international conflicts all centered around shipping, both merchant and naval, and the rhetoric of honor surrounded all such conflicts.

19. Petition dated September 16, 1786, published in the *New Haven Gazette and Connecticut Magazine*, January 11, 1787, 1, 47, quoting from the *Providence Gazette*.

20. Craig Symonds, *Navalists and AntiNavalists: The Naval Policy Debate 1785–1827* (Newark: University Press of Delaware, 1980).

21. Jonathan Elliott, ed., *The Debates in the Several State Conventions on the Adoption of the Federal Constitution* (Philadelphia: Lippincott, 1861), 2:526.

22. James Madison, June 12, 1788, in ibid., 3:309.

23. Alexander Hamilton, Federalist No. 11, in *The Federalist Papers*, ed. Clinton Rossiter (New York: New American Library, 1961), 85.

24. Nancy Isenberg, *Fallen Founder: The Life of Aaron Burr* (London: Penguin, 2007), 164. The original study noting the eleven affairs is Freeman, *Affairs of Honor*. Freeman gives details of Hamilton's ten affairs of honor before the duel with Burr in note 13, on pp. 326–27.

25. John Jay, Federalist No. 4, in Rossiter, *Federalist Papers*, 44.

26. Jefferson to Adams, July 11, 1786, in *The Letters of Thomas Jefferson, 1743–1826*, www.let.rug.nl/usa/presidents/thomas-jefferson/letters-of-thomas-jefferson/jefl46.php, accessed September 1, 2014.

27. George Washington, Speech of President Washington, December 7, 1796, *American State Papers: Foreign Relations*, 1:30–34.

28. Gilje, *Free Trade and Sailors' Rights*, 59.

29. Marshall Smelser, *The Congress Founds the Navy, 1787–1798* (Notre Dame, IN: University of Notre Dame Press, 1959).

30. Charles Pinckney reputedly said, when asked for the bribe, "Not a sixpence." Robert Goodloe Harper, one of the commissioners asked to pay the bribe, stated at an 1808 dinner that the response had been, "Millions for defense, but not one cent for tribute." For a discussion of the famous quip, see Burton Stevenson, ed. *The Home Book of Quotations*, 10th ed. (New York: Dodd, Mead, 1967), 63; and "Notes and Queries," *South Carolina Historical and Genealogical Magazine* 1 (1901): 100–103, 178–79. Wyatt-Brown, *Warring Nation*, 68, noted the "insult to American honor" represented by the XYZ affair.

31. Thomas Jefferson, State of the Union address, *Philadelphia Repository and Weekly Register*, October 29, 1803, 3, 44.

32. Pinckney to Don Pedro Cevallos, June 22, 1804, *American State Papers: Foreign Relations*, 2:618–19.

33. Patriotic piece by "F," "The Visitor," *Literary Magazine and American Register*, March 1805, 3, 18.

34. Report filed September 13, 1805, *American State Papers: Foreign Relations*, 2:678.

35. *National Intelligencer and Washington Advertiser*, July 13, 1807.

36. *National Intelligencer and Washington Advertiser*, July 27, 1807.

37. Wm. Smock, "At a Meeting of the Citizens of Fredericksburg and Its Vicinity, Convened at the Town Hall," *National Intelligencer and Washington Advertiser*, July 15, 1807, col. D; *National Intelligencer and Washington Advertiser*, July 20, 1807.

38. *National Intelligencer and Washington Advertiser*, July 20, 1807.

39. *National Intelligencer and Washington Advertiser*, December 1, 1810.

40. As noted in the following chapter, Roger H. Brown argues in *The Republic in Peril: 1812* (New York: Columbia University Press, 1964) that the division was partisan, not regional; *all* Federalist members of Congress, North and South, opposed the war. Fischer, in *Albion's Seed*, however, demonstrates that

the cultural orientation of southerners—from the Scotch-Irish borderlands of Britain—helps account for the heightened sensitivity to affront and to more bellicose values and attitudes.

41. James Madison, Message of President Madison, November 5, 1811, *American State Papers: Foreign Relations*, 1:78–80.

42. The observations on the rhetoric of honor are shared by other historians. For example, Bradford Perkins, in his classic discussion of the events leading up to the War of 1812, *Prologue to War* (Berkeley: University of California Press, 1961), points out how the *Chesapeake* affair and other clashes were discussed with the rhetoric of honor: "to disentangle honor and self-interest is often difficult, and editors and congressmen frequently cloaked material appeals in the rhetoric of honor, sovereignty, and independence" (p. 291). The role of honor values in U.S. politics, especially in the early nineteenth century, has been the subject of several recent studies, including Gilje, *Free Trade and Sailors' Rights*.

Chapter 2. Right of Search, 1812–58

1. Reginald Horsman, *The Causes of the War of 1812* (Philadelphia: University of Pennsylvania Press, 1962); and Perkins, *Prologue to War*. Hacker made the point that desire for more territory, particularly British-controlled Canada, drove the war hawks in Louis M. Hacker, "Western Land Hunger and the War of 1812: A Conjecture," *Mississippi Valley Historical Review* 10, no. 4 (March 1924): 365–95. The "Hacker thesis" has been the subject of criticism by other historians over the decades, but all agree that maritime New England was far less enthusiastic about a war at sea than other regions of the nation. As shown in the previous chapter, the rhetoric of honor was widely used in discussion of British (and French) treatment of U.S. shipping in the period. See also Mark Zuehlke, *For Honour's Sake: The War of 1812 and the Brokering of an Uneasy Peace* (New York: Random House, 2007).

2. Brown, *Republic in Peril*, 47, 58, 65, 72. Further discussion of the point, throughout Brown's chap. 4, 47–74. Brown shows Republicans feared not only that the nation was in peril but also that the principle of a republican form of government was at stake; many others coming to the defense of the republic quoted by Brown reflect the same rhetoric of national honor. Brown disputes the Hacker thesis and others who identify the pro-war sentiment as southern and western, demonstrating that the division in Congress over the war was between Federalists, who *all* opposed the war, and Republicans, most of whom supported the war.

3. Symonds, *Navalists and AntiNavalists*.

4. Edgar Stanton Maclay, *A History of the United States Navy from 1775 to 1883* (New York: Appleton, 1898), 434.

5. Mahon, *War of 1812*, 250.

6. Roy Adkins and Lesley Adkins, *The War for All the Oceans* (New York: Viking, 2007), 363, cites *New York Herald*, June 3, 1811, in B. J. Lossing, *The Pictorial Field Book of the War of 1812* (New York, 1868), 186. The work by Roy and Lesley Adkins, which incorporates many direct quotes, is only one of many such modern sources that could be used to demonstrate the point.

7. Adkins and Adkins, *War for All the Oceans*, 363, citing Donald Henchy Obrien, *My Adventures during the Late War: Comprising a Narrative of Shipwreck, Captivity, Escapes from French Prisons, etc. from 1897 to 1824* (London: H. Colburn, 1839), 2:210.

8. Adkins and Adkins, *War for All the Oceans*, 388, 389, 392, 394, 422, 434, 442, 445. Nearly all literature on the naval engagements of the War of 1812, including fictional treatments, reflects similar aspects of the maritime *code duello*. The Aubrey-Maturin novels of Patrick O'Brian, set in the 1790s–1810s, are redolent with such references.

9. In *Republic in Peril*, Brown convincingly argues that those who favored the war with Britain were concerned that the concept of republican government itself was at stake; when the United States survived the War of 1812, the concern that the republican experiment might fail diminished. See 177–91.

10. Freeman, *Affairs of Honor*, 283–84.

11. Because members of Congress (in most states) represented areas by population and the seaports dominated in population New York, New Jersey, Pennsylvania, Massachusetts, and North and South Carolina, the interior counties of those states, while larger geographically than the coastal areas, were lightly represented in Congress. Consulting a congressional district map for 1838 yields an *estimate* of seacoast and inland members of Congress in 1838, putting the inland members at about 90, versus 140 coastal; by 1858 the tally was probably just about even between coastal and inland representatives with about 115 members from coastal constituencies and 115 from interior constituencies; by then the senatorial division was 38 coastal, 24 inland (counting Texas as "inland"). Thus, seaport interests had a working, although diminishing, majority in both houses of Congress through this period. See Kenneth C. Martis, *Historical Atlas of United States Congressional Districts: Seventeen Hundred and Eighty-Nine thru Nineteen Hundred and Eighty-Three* (New York: Simon & Schuster, 1994).

12. Preble, *History of the Flag*, 351ff., 360ff., 368ff., 373, 385, 387, 389.

13. The Kuala Batu raids are discussed at Sabri Zain, "The United States Attack on Kuala Batu," *Sejarah Melayu*, http://www.sabrizain.org/malaya/potomac.htm, accessed June 2, 2014.

14. John H. Schroeder, *Shaping a Maritime Empire: The Commercial and Diplomatic Role of the American Navy, 1829–1861* (Westport, CT: Greenwood Press, 1985), 26–28.

15. Ibid., 44–45.

16. Ibid., 29–30.

17. Ibid., 73–74.

18. Brian Rouleau, *With Sails Whitening Every Sea: Mariners and the Making of an American Maritime Empire* (Ithaca, NY: Cornell University Press, 2014), especially 102–32.

19. Howard Jones, *To the Webster-Ashburton Treaty: A Study in Anglo-American Relations, 1783–1843* (Chapel Hill: University of North Carolina Press, 1977), 69.

20. *New York Times*, December 8, 1860.

21. On the Aroostook flag episode, see Preble, *History of the Flag*, 353. There is an interesting and growing literature on the Aroostook War controversy. See Francis Carroll, "The Passionate Canadians: The Historical Debate about the Eastern Canadian-American Boundary," *New England Quarterly* 70 (March 1997): 83–101. It is quite likely that the map produced by Jared Sparks from the French archives was fraudulent, designed to allay the concerns of the Maine legislature. A secret federal fund designed for international intelligence operations was used to ensure that antiwar editorials were published in Maine newspapers.

22. On the *Douglass*, see *New York Herald*, November 10, 1841; *Penn. Inquirer & Daily Courier*, December 16, 1841; *Niles' National Register*, December 18,1841; *Weekly Herald* (New York), November 13, 1841. On the *Susan* and *Mary*, see *Niles' National Register*, December 18, 1841. On the *Iago* and *Hero*, see *Boston Courier*, December 16, 1841.

23. Full text of Lewis Cass' pamphlet was published in several U.S. newspapers at the time, including as "The Right of Search" in *Niles' National Register*, March 26, 1842.

24. In addition to the antislavery press, the avowedly pro-British press also supported the exercise of the right of search on suspected slave ships. During the 1850s, the Anglophile *Albion* favored the British practice; the *New York Times*, although maintaining an objective tone, tended to show the logic of the British position, while also showing that from the American point of view, the question of national honor was at stake.

25. Jones, *To the Webster-Ashburton Treaty*, 115, 176–77.

26. Ibid., 167.

27. Colin Matthew, *The Nineteenth Century: The British Isles, 1815–1900* (New York: Oxford University Press, 2000), 48.

28. Eric Hobsbawm, *The Age of Capital 1848–1875* (New York: Scribner, 1975), 15–16.

29. The U.S. census of 1840 showed more than 17 million; although Canada did not have an equivalent census in that year, provincial census for 1841 totaled less than 2 million.

30. Christine Kinealy, "The Liberator: Daniel O'Connell and Anti-Slavery," *History Today* 57, no. 12 (2007): 51–57. Kinealy erred by claiming that Stevenson was not a slave owner. See also the more detailed Howard Temperly "The O'Connell-Stevenson Contretemps: A Reflection on the Anglo-American Slavery Issue," *Journal of Negro History* 47 (1962): 217–33.

31. Lewis Cass' pamphlet was titled "An Examination of the Questions Now in Discussion between the American and British Governments Concerning the Right of Search." The pamphlet was widely circulated in Britain and France and reprinted in U.S. newspapers. See also William Carl Kluger, *Lewis Cass and the Politics of Moderation* (Kent, OH: Kent State University Press, 1996), 106–7. The pamphlet is reprinted in William L. G. Smith, "The Appeal of General Cass to the People of France," in *Fifty Years of Public Life: The Life and Times of Lewis Cass* (New York: Derby and Jackson, 1856), 403–27.

32. W. E. B. DuBois, *The Suppression of the African Slave Trade to the United States of America, 1638–1870* (New York: Longmans, Green, 1896), chap. 9, n. 62.

33. William Beach Lawrence, *Visitation and Search; or, An Historical Sketch of the British Claim to Exercise a Maritime Police over the Vessels of All Nations* (Boston: Little, Brown, 1858), 41; Jones, *To the Webster-Ashburton Treaty*, 76–77.

34. *Pennsylvania Inquirer and National Gazette*, February 23, 1843; Jones, *To the Webster-Ashburton Treaty*, 162–63.

35. *Fayetteville Observer*, April 12, 1843.

36. See Donald L. Canney, *Africa Squadron: The U.S. Navy and the Slave Trade, 1842–1861* (Washington, DC: Potomac Books, 2006), 233–34, which provides a detailed list of thirty-six ships captured by the Africa Squadron in 1842–1861, along with another six by the U.S. Brazil Squadron in 1845–1849 and nine by the Home Squadron off Cuba in 1858–1860.

37. DuBois, *Suppression of the African Slave Trade*, 162n35, citing *Papers Relative to the Suppression of the Slave Trade on the Coast of Africa*, 13.
38. Ibid., 166n60, citing Senate Exec Doc, 31 Congress, 1 session XIV, no 66.
39. Canney, *Africa Squadron*, 138–39.
40. Howard Hazen Wilson, "Some Principal Aspects of the British Efforts to Crush the African Slave Trade, 1808–1929," *American Journal of International Law* 44, no. 3 (1950): 505–26.
41. "The British Aggressions," *New York Times*, June 4, 1858.
42. "The Question of Search," *New York Times*, May 17, 1858.
43. "The Right of Visit," *New York Times*, August 11, 1858.
44. DuBois, *Suppression of the African Slave Trade*, makes the points about increased prices in Cuba and the United States stimulating the trade; Canney, in *Africa Squadron*, 201–3, notes that the U.S. Navy made twenty-two captures of slavers between September 1859 and June 1861, largely because the squadron saw the addition of four steamers.
45. DuBois, *Suppression of the African Slave Trade*, 179–80n41, citing "The African Slave Trade," *New York Herald*, April 1, 1857. One estimate showed 15,000 slaves imported directly to the United States in 1859. DuBois, *Suppression of the African Slave Trade*, 182. Later analysts suspect that these figures were greatly exaggerated.
46. The pro-slavery vice president John C. Breckinridge saw the exercise of searches in the West Indies as particularly offensive—it was an "American sea." Noted in "Political Review: The Administration Defended: Speech of Vice-President Breckinridge, at Florence Ky," *New York Times*, July 29, 1858. British antislavery patrols in the West Indies stimulated American naval efforts off Cuba beginning in 1858, as noted by Canney, *Africa Squadron*, 220–21.
47. The last two factors as noted in *New York Times*, July 1, 1858; also DuBois, *Suppression of the African Slave Trade*, chap. 11, especially 172–76.
48. *New York Times*, April 22, May 14, May 17, and June 4, 1858.
49. *New York Times*, July 1 and July 3, 1858.
50. "Right of Search—The Present State of the Question," *New York Times*, July 21, 1858.
51. "The Last British Outrage—The Right of Search Again," *New York Times*, February 10, 1859.
52. Wilson, "Some Principal Aspects."
53. DuBois, *Suppression of the African Slave Trade*, 187; Canney, *Africa Squadron*, 234.
54. "Another 'British Outrage,'" *New York Times*, February 9, 1859. By putting the term "Outrage" in quotation marks, the *Times* editors were probably indicating a degree of disdain for the concept that the search under the new understandings constituted a true offense that would rise to the level of "outrage."

Chapter 3. Flagging-Out in the U.S. Civil War

1. Chester G. Hearn, *Gray Raiders of the Sea: How Eight Confederate Warships Destroyed the Unions High Seas Commerce* (Camden, ME: International Marine Publishing, 1992).
2. An exception, of course, was the method irregulars or bushwhackers used during the war. Not wearing uniforms, and often not taking prisoners but

executing captured enemies, irregular units were treated as criminals when they were captured. There were more such units on the Confederate side than on the Union side, although some bands of Union loyalists operated in the South. However, Confederate naval ships, despite being described as "pirates" in the Northern press, operated within the traditional practices of international law.

3. George W. Dalzell, *The Flight from the Flag: The Continuing Effect of the Civil War upon the American Carrying Trade* (Chapel Hill: University of North Carolina Press, 1940).

4. Hearn, *Gray Raiders of the Sea*.

5. "American Ships under the British Flag," *Philadelphia North American and United States Gazette*, March 5, 1861. Use of British consuls for registry is reported in "Piracy and Marine Insurance," *New York Times*, April 28, 1861.

6. "Statistics of Trade and Commerce," *Merchants' Magazine and Commercial Review*, August 1, 1863, quoting from the *Journal of Commerce*.

7. "American Ships under the British Flag." The term "denization," apparently derived from the term "denizen," appeared to be a neologism, possibly unique to this piece of legislation.

8. Ibid.

9. On humiliation, see, for example, Kenneth S. Greenberg, *Honor and Slavery* (Princeton, NJ: Princeton University Press, 1996), 3–23.

10. "Piracy and Marine Insurance."

11. "The Rebel-Anglo Pirates," *Daily Cleveland Herald*, June 3, 1863.

12. "European News," *New York Times*, February 28, 1864, subhead: "Foreign Vessels Sailing under the British Flag," from the *European Times*, February 6, 1864.

13. "From Europe," *New York Times*, January 29, 1864. The alliteration of the names of the three countries suggests that the reporter may have been indulging in a fanciful turn of phrase; to date, research has uncovered no records of transfers of U.S. ships in this period to Peru, Portugal, or Prussia.

14. Moses Jesuron to W. H. Seward, August 26, 1861, "Operations of the Cruisers," in *Official Records of the Union and Confederate Navies in the War of the Rebellion* (Washington, DC: Government Printing Office, 1897), ser. 1, 1:89.

15. "Statistics of Trade and Commerce."

16. "The Rebel Privateers and American Commerce, an Appeal to the Secretary of the Navy," *New York Times*, November 18, 1863.

17. James P. Baughman, *Charles Morgan and the Development of Southern Transportation* (Nashville: Vanderbilt University Press, 1968).

18. "Affairs in New Orleans," *New York Times*, May 25, 1862. The French flag may have been a ruse rather than a case of re-registry in France.

19. George H. Preble to Benjamin Butler, May 16, 1862, Papers of West Gulf Squadron, in *Official Records*, ser. 1, 18:498.

20. R. B. Lowry to H. W. Morris, September 10, 1862, Papers of West Gulf Squadron, in *Official Records*, ser. 1, 19:188–89.

21. E. W. Henry to H. H. Bell, July 11, 1863, Papers of West Gulf Squadron, in *Official Records*, ser. 1, 20:382–83; "European News."

22. Hugh McCulloch to Schuyler Colfax, "Ineligibility for Reregistration," HR Exec. Doc. 25 (January 17, 1866).

23. "Statistics of Trade and Commerce."
24. Andrew Johnson, "First Annual Message," December 4, 1865, in *The American Presidency Project*, ed. Gerhard Peters and John T. Woolley, www.presidency.ucsb.edu/ws/index.php?pid=29506&st=&st1=, accessed June 2, 2014. Johnson probably intended his observations to carry some weight in the negotiations over the *Alabama* claims, by stressing the vast costs that could be attributed to the depredations of the Confederate cruisers.
25. *Boston Daily Advertiser*, February 23, 1869.
26. McCulloch to Colfax, "Ineligibility for Reregistration." The author is indebted to historian Paul Fontenoy for drawing his attention to this legislation.
27. Ibid.
28. "Decline of Our Mercantile Marine," *Frank Leslie's Illustrated Newspaper*, January 26, 1867.
29. "Decay of American Shipping," *Daily Evening Bulletin* (San Francisco), January 23, 1867. Among such reports was "American Shipping," *Boston Daily Advertiser*, June 15, 1866, quoting from the *Journal of Commerce*.
30. A. Cook, *The* Alabama *Claims* (Ithaca, NY: Cornell University Press, 1975).
31. H. P. Willmott, *The Last Century of Sea Power* (Bloomington: Indiana University Press, 2009), 1:10.
32. John Lynch, *Causes of the Reduction of American Tonnage and the Decline of Navigation Interests* (Washington, DC: Government Printing Office, 1870).
33. "The Decline in American Ship-Building," *Albion*, April 23, 1870, 264.
34. *Banker's Magazine and Statistical Register*, August 1875, 117.
35. *International Review*, May 1879, 532.
36. Hamilton Andrews Hill, *American Shipping: Its Decline and the Remedies, 1827–1895* (Boston: J. H. Eastburn, 1869); Henry Hall, *American Navigation, with Some Account of the Cause of Its Former Prosperity and Present Decline* (New York: D. Appleton, 1878); Charles H. Marshall, *The Decline of American Shipping, and the True Methods for Its Restoration* (n.p., 1878); Henry W. Peabody, *Some Facts in Regard to the American Merchant Marine and Pending Legislation for Its Re-Creation: A Reprint of Four Letters Published by the* Boston Herald *and the* New York Journal of Commerce and Commercial Bulletin (Boston: Press of Samuel Usher, 1901).
37. The following is a partial selection of such essays and articles: C. J. Brockway, "A Defense of American Shipping," *International Review*, January 1883; Joseph Hutchinson, "American Shipping", *Overland Monthly*, May 1883; Nelson Dingley, "The Decline of American Shipping," *North American Review*, April 1884; E. P. North, "American Shipping, the Disease and the Remedy," *North American Review*, May 1888; John Hall, "The Decline of Our Merchant Marine," *Overland Monthly and Out West Magazine*, December 1888; Percy Thompson, "Our Merchant Marine—The Causes of Its Depression," *Belford's Monthly and Democratic Review*, March 1892. Numerous unsigned editorials through the period reiterated the same issue, for example: "The Merchant Marine," *New York Times*, June 27, 1868, and "Our Shipping Interests," *New York Times*, September 2, 1872. All of these treatises and articles tended to focus on present economic conditions and issues of government policy rather than on historical Civil War issues.
38. Semmes later claimed that the use of chains as armor, concealed under exterior planking, was inappropriate on the grounds that in personal pistol duels, it was always regarded as a dastardly act to conceal metal objects that might deflect

shots in a duelist's pockets. At the time and later, Semmes explicitly regarded the *Kearsage-Alabama* encounter as a duel. For details of this encounter, see Spencer C. Tucker, *Raphael Semmes and the* Alabama (Fort Worth, TX: Ryan Place Publishers, 1996), especially 82–83; see also Stevens, *Pistols at Ten Paces*, 248–49.

Chapter 4. The Flag Insulted, 1865–95

1. Marc Leepson, *Flag: An American Biography* (New York: St. Martin's Griffin Press, 2005).
2. Ibid., 105.
3. Leepson devotes a chapter to this topic and demonstrates convincingly that the firing on Sumter unified the North in support of armed suppression of the Confederacy and that the emotional outburst of patriotism focused on the insult to the flag represented by the firing on Sumter. Ibid., 105ff.
4. Ibid., 100.
5. National anger, feigned or genuine, over insults to the flag was not unique to the United States. The incident that sparked Britain's second Opium War with China in 1856 sprang from an insult to the flag on board the ship *Arrow*, which had been engaged in piracy under an expired British registry. Julia Lovell, *The Opium War: Drugs, Dreams and the Making of China* (London: Picador, 2011). A thorough exploration of the argument of the parallel between the primitive totem rituals and the cult of the flag can be found in Carolyn Marvin and David Ingle, *Blood Sacrifice and the Nation: Totem Rituals and the American Flag* (New York: Cambridge University Press, 1999).
6. Erik Larson, *The Devil in the White City* (New York: Vintage, 2004), 332. It was notable that the pledge stressed "one nation indivisible," an explicit rejection of the Confederate view of the constitutionality of secession.
7. An extensive literature regarding blue-water imperialism has been developed by U.S. historians, including Ernest May, Philip Foner, and Victor Perlo. Walter LaFeber, in *The New Empire: An Interpretation of American Expansion, 1860–1898* (Ithaca, NY: Cornell University Press, 1998), traces the rise of U.S. overseas imperialist ambitions in the period under discussion in this chapter.
8. These episodes are identified by name in Carlisle, "Flag Insulted," 267–82. Since both *Foreign Relations of the United States* (*FRUS*) and the *New York Times* are computer searchable, the numerous reports were identified by a Boolean search for "ship" and "insult" or "outrage" in those files.
9. Mark Russell Shulman, *Navalism and the Emergence of American Sea Power, 1882–1893* (Annapolis, MD: Naval Institute Press, 1995), 49, and more generally, chap. 3, "Selling the Navy: Popularization of the Service," 46–57.
10. Ibid., 57.
11. Coverage of the nautical art in the period is captured in J. Welles Henderson and Rodney Carlisle, *Jack Tar: A Sailor's Life, 1750–1910* (Woodbridge, UK: Antique Collector's Press, 1999).
12. Shulman, *Navalism and the Emergence*, 57.
13. Some of the coastal states had senators who represented agricultural and inland interests more than the seaport interests of their states, resulting in a definite minority position for maritime interests. Representation in the House tended to even more strongly favor inland interests by the 1890s. The isolationism of the interior states would become politically significant in 1914–1941.

14. See John Kenneth Galbraith, *American Capitalism: The Concept of Countervailing Power* (Boston: Houghton Mifflin, 1952).

15. U.S. Congress, *Biographical Directory of the American Congress, 1774–1961* (Washington, DC: Government Printing Office, 1961).

16. Professor Josh Smith of the U.S. Merchant Marine Academy identified this ship for me; the vessel had a long life and was preserved as a school ship and then as a museum ship. Professor Smith serves as the caretaker of the ship's engine, which is preserved at the academy.

17. The *Puritan* was built in response to the *Virginius* affair. See Richard H. Bradford, *The* Virginius *Affair* (Boulder: Colorado Associated University Press, 1980). The *Puritan* saw action in the Spanish-American War in the bombardment of Matanzas, Cuba, April 27, 1898. See *Dictionary of U.S. Naval Fighting Ships*, www.history.navy.mil/research/histories/ship-histories/danfs/p/puritan-i.html, accessed July 2, 2015.

18. Boleslaw Szczesniak, "Letters of Homer Crane Blake Concerning His Naval Expedition to China, Japan, and Korea, 1869–1872," *Monumenta Nipponica* 13 (1957): 313–28; Frederick C. Drake, *Empire of the Seas: A Biography of Rear Admiral Robert Wilson Shufeldt, USN* (Honolulu: University of Hawaii Press, 1984).

19. Records for the episodes can be found in *FRUS* and the *New York Times*.

20. The retaliatory expedition in response to the original incident is reported in "The Pirates of Formosa: Official Reports of the Engagement of United States Naval Forces with the Savages of the Island," *New York Times*, August 24, 1867. See also *New York Times*, August 14 and 15, 1867.

21. Spanish-U.S. arbitration discussed by Hamilton Fish, in U.S. Department of State, *The Executive Documents Printed by Order of the House of Representatives during the Second Session of the Forty-Second Congress: 1871–'72* (*FRUS* 1871–1872), 744ff.

22. "The Florida Case: Affidavit of Her Officers Touching the Spanish Outrage, What the Spanish Officers Really Did—Two Vessels Board the Florida," *New York Times*, January 13, 1873.

23. Bradford, Virginius *Affair*, 1.

24. Ibid., 16, 25–26. Bradford used *FRUS* 1874, 1001–2, 1048.

25. Ibid., 26, 28.

26. Ibid., 26–27, 29–31.

27. Ibid., 39–41, 43.

28. Ibid., 107. The precise number executed and the number of survivors varied slightly with reports. According to U.S. Department of State, *Executive Documents Printed by Order of the House of Representatives: 1875–'76* (*FRUS* 1875–1876), 2:1213–15, a total of 102 survivors of the original 155 complement on board the *Virginius* were delivered to the U.S. Navy. The 53 executed included captain and crew totaling 37 plus 16 rebel officers.

29. "Congressional Opinion," *New York Times*, November 21, 1873.

30. Bradford, Virginius *Affair*, 64, 65, 66, 72–73.

31. Ibid., 69.

32. Ibid., 63. The three men mentioned in the quotation are Thomas H. Parne, U.S. consul in Kingston, Jamaica; Henry C. Hall, U.S. consul general in Havana; and Spanish ambassador José Polo de Barnabé.

33. Memorandum, November 27, 1873, in U.S. Department of State, *Executive Documents Printed by Order of the House of Representatives: 1873–'74 (FRUS 1873–1874)*, 986–87.
34. Bradford, *Virginius Affair*, 93, noting the resolution as the "The Thanksgiving Protocol."
35. Ibid., 102.
36. Hamilton Fish to son, December 24, 1873, in Allen Nevins, *Hamilton Fish: The Inner History of the Grant Administration* (New York: Dodd, Mead, 1936), 694.
37. "The American Flag, How It Is Regarded by the Government of Santo Domingo," *New York Times*, July 8, 1876.
38. See Herbert Millington, *American Diplomacy and the War of the Pacific* (New York: Columbia University Press, 1948).
39. Kenneth Hagan, *American Gunboat Diplomacy and the Old Navy, 1877–1889* (Westport, CT: Greenwood, 1972). Hagan covers the Grace Line ships in 1879 on p. 132. On the *Rising Sun*, see *New York Times*, July 12, 1877; on the *Eva*, see *New York Times*, January 8, 1878; on the ships off Cuba in 1880, see *New York Times*, July 20 and August 5, 1880; on the *Diana*, see *New York Times*, December 26, 1881.
40. For the influences on Mahan, see Robert Seager, *Alfred Thayer Mahan: The Man and His Letters* (Annapolis, MD: Naval Institute Press, 1977).
41. These minor cases were all reported in the *New York Times* and in *FRUS*, as well as in other newspapers.
42. "Subsidies for American Ships," *Scientific American*, July 26, 1890.
43. Shulman, *Navalism and the Emergence*, 57.
44. Marcus Wilkerson, *Public Opinion and the Spanish-American War: A Study in War Propaganda* (New York: Russell & Russell, 1932; repr., 1967), 17.
45. Ibid., 17–20.
46. "It Was a Willful Insult," *New York Times*, March 19, 1895, quoting from William C. Whitney, Cleveland's Secretary of the Navy.
47. *Sun*, March 14, 1895; *Tribune*, March 16, 1895; *Sentinel*, March 16, 1895; *Chronicle*, March 14, 1895; *Times*, March 13, 1895, all cited in Wilkerson, *Public Opinion*, 18.
48. "The Allianca Incident," *New York Observer and Chronicle*, March 21, 1895.
49. *Herald*, March 16, 1895, cited in Wilkerson, *Public Opinion*, 20.
50. Wilkerson, *Public Opinion*, 24.
51. Ibid., 27.
52. Other U.S.-flagged filibuster ships that drew press attention through 1897 included the *Three Friends*, the tugboat *George W. Childs*, the *Commodore*, the *Dauntless*, and the *Silver Heels* as noted in ibid., 27–28.

Chapter 5. The New American Empire and the Muscat Dhows Decision

1. A treatment of the early history of the Liberian colony and republic and its influence on African American thinkers can be found in Rodney Carlisle, *The Roots of Black Nationalism* (Port Washington, NY: Kennikat Press, 1975), chaps. 5 and 11.
2. Guano Act of 1856, 164 Stat., 1856; Jimmy M. Skaggs, *The Great Guano Rush: Entrepreneurs and American Overseas Expansion* (New York: Palgrave/Macmillan, 1994).
3. Louis A. Perez Jr., *Cuba under the Platt Amendment, 1902–1934* (Pittsburgh: University of Pittsburgh Press, 1991).

4. Naval ship figures from Tim Colton, Shipbuilding History, http://shipbuilding history.com, accessed June 2, 2014.

5. James R. Reckner, *Teddy Roosevelt's Great White Fleet: The World Cruise of the American Battlefleet, 1907–1909* (Annapolis, MD: Naval Institute Press, 2001); Kenneth Wimmel, *Theodore Roosevelt and the Great White Fleet: American Sea Power Comes of Age* (London: Brassey's Ltd., 1998).

6. Merchant tonnage is from *Nautical Gazette*, January 22, 1921. U.S.-flagged ships carried only 9 percent of the nation's international (as distinct from lake, river, coastal, and territorial) commerce in 1914, as noted in Highbeam Business, "Ship Building and Repairing," http://business.highbeam.com/industry-reports/equipment/ship-building-repairing, accessed June 2, 2014.

7. Eric Paul Roorda, *Cuba and the Sea: The Story of the Immigrant Boat* Analuisa *and 500 Years of History between Cuba and America* (Mystic, CT: Mystic Seaport Museum, 2005), 66, 75.

8. For Standard Oil, see "Esso International Tankers, 1910–1919," Auke Visser's International Esso Tankers site, www.aukevisser.nl/inter/id29.htm, accessed June 2, 2014; "Esso International Tankers, 1900–1909," Auke Visser's International Esso Tankers site, www.aukevisser.nl/inter/id570.htm, accessed June 2, 2014.

9. On Texaco, see Robert Greenhalgh Albion and Jennie Barnes Pope, *Sea Lanes in Wartime: The American Experience* (New York: Norton, 1942), 314. Works on the topic of merchant fleets in the period include Jonathan Kinghorn, *The Atlantic Transport Line, 1881–1931: A History with Details on All Ships* (Jefferson, NC: McFarland, 2012); James P. Baughman, *The Mallorys of Mystic: Six Generations in American Maritime Enterprise* (Mystic, CT: Wesleyan/Marine Historical Association, 1972); Rene de la Pedraja, *The Rise and Decline of Merchant Shipping in the Twentieth Century* (New York: Twayne, 1992); Mark H. Goldberg, *Going Bananas: One Hundred Years of American Fruit Ships in the Caribbean* (Kings Point, NY: North American Maritime Books, 1992).

10. See Boleslaw Adam Boczek, *Flags of Convenience: An International Legal Study* (Cambridge, MA: Harvard University Press, 1969). Boczek and other international law citations never presented the historical context of the decision.

11. Depending on the exact sailing route, the trip could have been much longer, especially if cruising relatively close to the coasts of what are now Iran, Pakistan, and India, rather than a more direct route from Djibouti to the southern tip of Ceylon, now Sri Lanka.

12. H. J. Whigham, *The Persian Problem: An Examination of the Rival Positions of Russia and Great Britain in Persia with Some Account of the Persian Gulf* (London: Isbistor, 1903), 21.

13. George Lydiard Sulivan, *Dhow Chasing in Zanzibar Waters and on the Eastern Coast of Africa: Narrative of Five Years' Experiences in the Suppression of the Slave Trade* (London: S. Low, Marston, Low & Searle, 1873), http://archive.org /details/dhowchasinginzan00sulirich, accessed June 2, 2014.

14. The original conference members and signatories were Great Britain, Germany, Belgium, Spain, the Congo, France, Italy, the Netherlands, Portugal, Sweden, Norway, and Turkey. In 1900 Austria-Hungary, the United States, Liberia, and Persia also signed.

15. Great Britain, *Muscat Dhows Arbitration: In the Permanent Court of Arbitration at The Hague: Grant of the French Flag to Muscat Dhows* (London: Foreign Office,

1905), vol. 1, http://babel.hathitrust.org/cgi/pt?id=coo.31924007461209;page=root;view=image;size=100;seq=20;num=14, accessed June 2, 2014.

16. Acceded to in January 1892; see especially articles 30–35 dealing with granting of flag; must actually be residents, etc. Great Britain, *Muscat Dhows Arbitration*, 180.

17. James Brown Scott, *The Hague Court Reports* (New York: Oxford University Press, 1916), 94. Although the French signed the Quintuple Treaty in 1841, they did not ratify it, and they explicitly abrogated prior search conventions in 1845. The British agreed and "expressly abjured any 'right' of visitation," as noted in Wilson, "Some Principal Aspects," 516.

18. Great Britain, *Muscat Dhows Arbitration*, app. 7, 47ff.

19. "Faisal ibn Turki, 1888–1913," GlobalSecurity.org, www.globalsecurity.org/military/world/gulf/oman-faisal.htm, accessed June 2, 2014. This version of events is supported by *New York Times* reports from 1899.

20. In May 1897 another thirty-eight dhows had registered through the French consul at Zanzibar, as reported by the captain of HMS *Blonde*. Great Britain, *Muscat Dhows Arbitration*.

21. *Sydney Morning Herald*, February 15, 1899.

22. Great Britain, *Muscat Dhows Arbitration*, app. 14, 56.

23. *New York Times*, March 7 and 8, 1899.

24. P. J. V. Rolo, *Entente Cordiale: The Origins and Negotiation of the Anglo-French Agreements of 8 April 1904* (New York: Macmillan, 1969).

25. Scott, *Hague Court Reports*, 93, 102.

26. The first "modern" arbitration was initiated in Jay's Treaty of 1794, in which U.S. and British disputes over claims were referred to arbiters for a decision. Numerous arbitrations in the nineteenth century successfully resolved disputes. The largest was the *Alabama* claims discussed in chapter 4.

27. Great Britain, *Muscat Dhows Arbitration*, app. 12, 55

28. "Muscat Dhows Case: Award," August 8, 1905, The Hague Justice Portal, http://www.haguejusticeportal.net/index.php?id=6926, accessed June 2, 2014. In 1897 Fuller had served on the Venezuelan–British Guiana border arbitration commission, which had produced a decision favorable to Britain, so he was known to the British as acceptable. He continued to serve on The Hague permanent court panel until his death in 1910.

29. February 17, 1905, Box 13, Muscat Dhows folder, Fuller Papers, Library of Congress Manuscript Division, Washington, DC (hereafter LCMD).

30. Fuller to Ruyssenaers, cable draft, February 23, 1905, Box 13, Muscat Dhows folder, Fuller Papers, LCMD.

31. Ruyssenaers to Miller, February 25, 1905, Box 13, Muscat Dhows folder, Fuller Papers, LCMD.

32. Numerous press reports in May–July 1888 remarked on Fuller's background as an attorney, rather than as a judge. See "Melville Fuller," *American Law Review*, May/June 1888, 448ff.

33. Undated typed carbon copy of the draft decision, edited in Fuller's own hand, Box 13, Muscat Dhows folder, Fuller Papers, LCMD. The printed page proofs appear in the folder Permanent Court of Arbitration, Box 13, Fuller Papers, LCMD.

34. Scott, *Hague Court Reports*, 93ff. The text of the final decision showing that the status of protégé had to be granted before 1863 can also be found in "Muscat Dhows Case: Award."

35. A review of Fuller's opinions in other cases shows that he was committed to a rather formal "equality under the law" concept that is reflected today in the modern technical equivalence between the maritime flag of Panama or Liberia (and some even smaller nations) and that of Britain or the United States.

36. See Scott, *Hague Court Reports*, 93–109; Boczek, *Flags of Convenience*.

Chapter 6. Attacks on the American Merchant Flag as Casus Belli in World War I

1. Most Anglo-American treatments of the origins of World War I do not mention the legitimacy of the Austro-Hungarian grievance against Serbia since both Britain and the United States eventually fought on the Serbian side of the conflict. See the author's treatment in *World War One: An Eyewitness History* (New York: Facts on File, 2007).

2. The practice of calling torpedoes and submarines "infernal" dated back to the U.S. Civil War. The *New York Times*, quoting the *Boston Herald*, referred to the Confederate submarine *Hunley*, which on February 17, 1864, sank the Union ship *Housatonic*, as an "infernal torpedo machine." *New York Times*, March 2, 1864.

3. Sources vary regarding the precise number, but the most reliable estimates tend to agree on the number of deaths shown here.

4. Robert Lansing was an uncle (by marriage) of John Foster Dulles. Lansing's wife, Ellen Foster, was a daughter of John W. Foster, who had served as secretary of state under William Henry Harrison; Ellen's sister, Edith, was John Foster Dulles' mother.

5. There were in fact at least eighteen episodes in the period, but most of them were quite minor, consisting of U-boats hailing or stopping a U.S. ship and perhaps also some slight damage to the merchant ship. The seven cases mentioned here were more serious, resulting in major damage to, capture of, or destruction of ships and led to the exchange of diplomatic notes. These cases were widely regarded in the anti-German press as evidence of German aggression.

6. Detailed descriptions of each of these incidents and some of the more minor encounters are in Carlisle, *Sovereignty at Sea*, especially 31–120. To the extent possible, that work identifies the individual casualties on the U.S. merchant ships as well.

7. Blaine Pardoe, *The Cruise of the* Sea Eagle*: The Amazing True Story of Germany's Gentleman Pirate* (Guilford, CT: Lyons Press, 2005).

8. Following the acquisition of Hawaii and Puerto Rico, ships owned in those territories were admitted to the U.S. registry and cabotage rules applied, but that "coastwise restriction" was not applied to the Philippines. Under an act of April 15, 1904, the territorial government of the Philippines was authorized to regulate Philippine shipping, and Philippine-registered ships did not fly the U.S. merchant flag. See Emory Richard Johnson et al., *History of Domestic and Foreign Commerce of the United States* (Washington, DC: Carnegie Institution, 1915), 303.

9. "American Ship *Columbian* Sunk by U-Boat: Crew Saved, London and Washington Hear," *New York Times*, November 12, 1916; "American Skipper U-Boat's Prisoner: Captain Curtis of the *Columbian* Held for Six Days in Submarine's Brig," *New York Times*, November 14, 1916; "U.S. Ship Captain U-Boat Prisoner," *Chicago Tribune*, November 14, 1916.

10. Britain blockaded those neutrals on the grounds of a "continuous voyage doctrine," claiming that food was being imported to the neutrals and then shipped overland into Germany. The continuous voyage doctrine had been declared improper in the Declaration of London, but Wilson chose not to protest this technical violation of international law despite German requests that he do so.

11. Whereas in English "ruthless" conveys an overtone of cruelty, in German the term simply suggests "without restraint." Such differences in nuance probably helped contribute to Anglo-American horror at the German announcement.

12. "Comment of This Morning's Newspapers on the German Note," *New York Times*, February 1, 1917.

13. "War with Germany," *Outlook*, March 7, 1917, 402.

14. A close examination of the events surrounding the Zimmermann telegram shows that it was not the overt act that prompted Wilson to ask for a declaration of war. Barbara Tuchman, in *The Zimmermann Telegram* (New York: Macmillan, 1958), 150, exaggerates when she suggests that it was the overt act. See also Patrick Beesly, *Room 40: British Naval Intelligence* (London: Hamish Hamilton, 1982), 204–36; David Kahn, *The Codebreakers* (New York: Signet, New American Library, 1973), 129–53. Although Wilson was shocked at the telegram, he did not ask the cabinet about a declaration of war until after the loss of the *Vigilancia*, *Illinois*, and *City of Memphis*, more than a month after the February 17 revelation of the telegram.

15. "Sharp Words by Wilson," *New York Times*, March 5, 1917; "'Willful Men' Deny Aiding Filibuster," *New York Times*, March 7, 1917.

16. An exploration of Woodrow Wilson's idealistic and moralistic viewpoint is beyond the scope of the present work. A fuller treatment of his thinking process can be found in Carlisle, *Sovereignty at Sea*, 122–49, especially 138–40.

17. Wilson's support for self-determination was moderated with regard to non-European peoples, including the residents of the Middle East, Africa, and Oceana who had formerly been under Turkish or German rule. In those cases, the resolution was to establish "mandates" or "protectorates" in which a European power (or Japan or Australia in the case of Pacific islands) would administer the region with a vague promise of eventual local sovereignty. The mandates included the former Turkish territories of Syria, Lebanon, and Iraq and the former German colonies of the Cameroons, German East Africa, and German Southwest Africa. As noted earlier, Japan was given a mandate to many of the German-held islands in the Pacific. In retrospect, the racial overtones of the different treatment of non-European peoples compared with the immediate creation of Czechoslovakia and other nations out of the European parts of the former empires are obvious.

18. Lansing to E. N. Smith, February 28, 1917, Container 24, Robert Lansing Papers, LCMD.

19. *Outlook Magazine*, September 20, 1916, 117.

20. Josephus Daniels, *The Wilson Era: Years of Peace—1910–1917* (Chapel Hill: University of North Carolina Press, 1946), 594.

21. "Uncertainty in Washington," *New York Times*, March 29, 1917.

22. Lansing to Wilson, March 19, 1917, quoted in Robert Lansing, *War Memoirs of Robert Lansing* (Indianapolis: Bobbs-Merrill, 1935), 235–37.

23. "House Will Pass Resolution Today," *New York Times*, April 5, 1917. Shackleford's report appears in Congressional Report 1 at 12–14 (1917). See also Carlisle, *Sovereignty at Sea*, 154–55.

Chapter 7. Danzig, the Missing Link in Flags of Convenience

1. Other anomalous outcomes of Wilson's principle, which continued to create crises through the 1920s and 1930s, included Latvian sovereignty over ethnically German Memel, administered as the Klaipeda Region; the assignment of ethnically German regions of the Sudetenland to Czechoslovakia; and Italian control over Slovenian-speaking Trieste.
2. Henrietta M. Larson, Evelyn H. Knowlton, and Charles S. Popple, *History of Standard Oil Company (New Jersey): New Horizons, 1927–1950* (New York: Harper & Row, 1974), 305.
3. The first four ships, the *Vistula*, *Baltic*, *Gedania*, and *Zoppot*, have been confirmed from Lloyd's; the *Niobe*, previously owned by DAPG, was transferred first to the United States and then in 1927 to Danzig.
4. The firm had played a leading role in the founding of the Republic of Panama. For further detail, see Gustavo A. Mellander, *The United States in Panamanian Politics: The Intriguing Formative Years* (Danville, IL: Interstate Publishers, 1971); Peter Grose, *Gentleman Spy* (New York: Houghton Mifflin, 1991). There is quite a New Left literature denouncing the role of Sullivan and Cromwell in regime change in several countries, summarized and cited in Stephen Kinzer, *Overthrow: America's Century of Regime Change from Hawaii to Iraq* (New York: Times Books, 2007). The firm is still renowned for its expertise in Delaware incorporation law.
5. John Foster Dulles Papers, Diaries and Journals, July 29,1919, Box 278, Seeley Mudd Library, Princeton, NJ.
6. Lujo Brentano, *What Germany Has Paid under the Treaty of Versailles*, Berlin: Walter de Gruyter, 1923.
7. Auke Visser's German Esso Tanker's website, www.aukevisser.nl/german/, accessed June 2, 2014. Bedford, supervisor of Esso sales abroad; Riedemann, head of Riedemann shipping; Seidel, director of the Esso-Farben Company; Mowinckel, director of Esso's European Operations; Senior, CEO of Esso's largest Latin American company; Hurll, director of the Esso-Farben Company; Wolfe, manager of the Montreal office of Imperial Oil; Harden, director of Esso, New Jersey; Ross, president of Imperial Oil; McKnight, very early vice president of Standard Oil. Biographical notes compiled from the *New York Times*.
8. In 1929 three new ships of the Bapico fleet did not quite fit the pattern described here. Before the ships were named for Standard Oil executives in 1930, *Hanseat* was named for the port of Danzig affiliations of the first period, *Stanasfalt* was named for a Standard Oil brand of asphalt, and *Svithoid* retained its original Swedish name after transfer from that flag. In addition, one ship, transferred from the United States in 1924, retained its U.S. name in honor of one of the founding incorporators of Standard Oil, the *Josiah Macy*. Otherwise, the periodization of ship naming was quite consistent.

9. S. Swiggum and M. Kohli, "Artus Danziger Reederei & Handels-Aktien-gesellschaft: 1919–1927 Danzig," The ShipsList, November 20, 2006, www.theshipslist.com/ships/lines/stinnes.shtml, accessed June 2, 2014. Stinnes also started a line in Hamburg at the same time. Apparently, he did not fear confiscation of new ships. However, his choice of Danzig may have addition-ally reflected concerns over the German economy and social programs. Recent research has revealed that the Stinnes line, like the Bapico line, was actually owned in Germany. As far as can be determined, all other Danzig-registered ships in 1920–1939 were locally owned. Most of the biographies of Stinnes tend to be rather laudatory.

10. A complete and detailed listing of the locally owned Danzig ships that have been identified can be found in Carlisle, "Danzig," 142–43.

11. Larson, Knowlton, and Popple, *History of Standard Oil*, 216–17. The authors here offer the classic economic defense of flags of convenience. The assertion of contemporary concern over the Nazi regime is difficult to document, as discussed later. Larson, Knowlton, and Popple may very well have made such an assertion out of hindsight and concern to clear Esso of any taint of pro-Nazi sympathy.

12. Neale Rosanoski, "Baltisch-Amerikanische Petroleum-Import-Gesellschaft," Flags of the World, February 13, 2008, http://www.crwflags.com/fotw/flags/de~dapg.html#bapig, accessed June 2, 2014. Waried continued to operate the fleet in Panama until 1937–1938.

13. "Finland Breaks Up Rum-Running Group," *New York Times*, August 19, 1936; "Control of Liquor in Sweden," *New York Times*, August 21, 1932; statistics are from "Finland Ends Rum Running off Her Coast," *New York Times*, June 23, 1934; "The Cat and Rat Game in the Baltic," *New York Times*, June 10, 1932.

14. John Brown Mason, *The Danzig Dilemma: A Study of Peacemaking by Compromise* (Palo Alto, CA: Stanford University Press, 1946). As discussed in chapter 14, "The Status of the Free City of Danzig under International Law," 228–48.

15. Grose, *Gentleman Spy*, 90.

16. Since Larson, Knowlton, and Popple produced a volume that was accurate but also quite positive in its descriptions of Esso policies, they may have had a motivation to emphasize Esso concerns with Nazi policies and possible war. Certainly in 1935 the prevailing attitude toward the Nazi regime in the United States was not one that anticipated war, so an assertion that Esso feared for the plight of its tankers in a war with Germany appears the result of hindsight.

17. Grose, *Gentleman Spy*, 134.

18. Ibid., 135.

19. "The sources ordinarily used to produce local histories are largely unavailable for Danzig. The community itself was destroyed in 1945." Herbert S. Levine, *Hitler's Free City: A History of the Nazi Party in Danzig, 1925–1930* (Chicago: University of Chicago Press, 1973), 5. The destruction of local records, combined with the unavailability of the records of Sullivan and Cromwell and Standard Oil to independent researchers, helps account for the lack of prior historical treatment of this development.

Chapter 8. Panama, 1919–39

1. A more detailed account of the ship's career is presented in Carlisle, *Sovereignty for Sale*, 6–9.
2. The former names of some have been determined: *Isonomia* ex *Nassovia*, *Casco* ex *Elmshorn*, and *Pequot* ex *Ockenfels*. *Arcadia* was *Arcadia* in German service.
3. *New York Herald*, October 1, 1923.
4. "Ships Furl U.S. Flag to Sell Rum at Sea: The *Resolute* and the *Reliance* to Be Transferred to Panama," *New York Times*, November 10, 1922. Daugherty actually cited Daniel Webster's communication with Lord Ashburton regarding the right of search in 1842. "Text of Daugherty's Opinion on Liquor on Ships," *New York Times*, October 7, 1922.
5. The statement of reasons is found in *Proceedings of the United States Shipping Board*, November 1, 1922, 1091–5555, RG 32, NA.
6. *Cunard et al. v. Mellon et al.*, 262 U.S. 100 (1923).
7. Orr Report, Orr to Carr, December 15, 1923, Central Decimal Files (1920–1929), 819.801/2, 819.801/3, RG 59, NA. It is also possible that attorneys for the shipping lines, including Sullivan and Cromwell, may have sought such a clarification.
8. The 1958 maritime academy's successor, the Universidad Marítima Internacional de Panama, was set up in 2005.
9. Gunsaulus to State, June 1, 1923, Central Decimal Files (1920–1929), 819.864/ orig., RG 59, NA. Gunsaulus served as consul in several posts around the world, and in 1920–1923 he was consul general in Halifax, Nova Scotia.
10. The top speed of Coast Guard vessels in the era rarely exceeded fifteen knots, so depending on the ships involved, the coastal configuration, and the route taken, the jurisdiction in a specific instance under the convention could have been as low as fourteen nautical miles from shore.
11. For a more detailed treatment of these cases, see Carlisle, *Sovereignty for Sale*, 22–31.
12. Morris also served as honorary consul of Chile: José del Pozo, "Relations between Chile and Canada during the Second World War: The First Experiences of Chilean Diplomats," *Historia* 1 (2006). Morris was a "Chilean" of North American birth.
13. Central Decimal Files (1920–1929), 811.114/4641, RG 59, NA.
14. The practice continued until at least September 1937, when three more ships were added. "Panama Gets More Ships," *New York Times*, September 29, 1937. The Basque region of Spain sought autonomy in this period; shipping there was in a slump owing to the worldwide Great Depression and to Spanish regulations. Fernando Aguada, who owned three of the ships, the *Pilar*, *Santa Marta*, and *Ignacia Aguada*, in the coal trade to Italy, went bankrupt by 1933. Rafael González Echegaray, *50 Años de Vapares Santanderinos* (Santander, Spain: Editorial Cantabria, 1951), 161. The U.S. State Department later learned that the Panamanian consul in Bilbao was dismissed for pocketing registration fees. In 1933 the local Basque government adopted a separate flag for the region known as the "*ikurriña*," suggesting the larger symbolic importance of a flag to Basques at the time and perhaps one reason why a flag other than that of Spain was preferred. Report on Corruption of Panamanian Consul in Bilbao, George F. Summerlin to Secretary of State, January 4, 1938, Central Decimal Files (1930–1939), 819.85/2, enclosing clipping, RG 59, NA.

15. Information on the three tankers can be found at Auke Visser's International Esso Tankers site, www.aukevisser.nl/inter/id31.htm, accessed June 2, 2014.
16. Erling Naess, *Autobiography of a Shipping Man* (Colchester, UK: Seatrade Publications, 1977), 34–38.
17. Scattered reports indicated that the British monitors ignored Italian violations of the agreement, allowing shipments of weapons from Italy to the Falangist insurgents. "Loyalists Still Get Arms Abroad: Ships in Traffic Use French Ports," *New York Times*, February 5, 1939.
18. Since smugglers by definition do not keep records, the actual count of such ships may be impossible to determine. From press reports and correspondence of U.S. consul general Harold Shantz in Athens, it appeared they may have numbered as many as ten or more. Harold Shantz to State, correspondence, 1939, Central Decimal Files (1930–1939), 819.861/29–59, RG 59, NA. Greek seamen received hazard pay to engage in the trade, attracting many unemployed from Marseille and other ports. The Shantz correspondence is particularly rich in details regarding the gunrunning operations.
19. For Onassis and Kulukundis claims to priority in using Panamanian registry, see Carlisle, *Sovereignty for Sale*, 59.
20. Again, as smugglers, the ships were difficult to identify, but some thirteen have been documented. Because the illegal immigration later became a point of historic pride among Israelis, there are several sources on the ship-lift of Jewish refugees to Palestine in the 1930s besides the famous Leon Uris novel. One website among several with some details of the ships is Yehuda Lapidot, "The Illegal Immigration of the Irgun," trans. Chaya Galai, www.etzel.org.il/english /ac04.htm, accessed June 2, 2014. Other ships were identified in contemporary news reports.
21. The *New York Times* reported one transfer from Germany in 1931: "German Ship Transferred," February 9, 1939. For the transfers from China, see "Panama Stops Registry Transfer," *New York Times*, October 29, 1937. Several Chinese owners transferred ships to Panama after the Japanese had launched attacks in July 1937 and set up a blockade of Chinese ports. See also "Japanese Praise British Proposal," *New York Times*, September 21, 1937.
22. The transfers were done in two batches: December 5, 1935, and August 13, 1936. Orders of Transfers of Vessels to Foreign Registry, vol. 11, nos. 2530, 2531, and 2570, RG 32, NA.
23. According to records at the U.S. Maritime Commission, the number of ships over 1,000 gross registered tons flagged in Panama as of November 15, 1938, was 96. Division of Research (Maritime Commission) Report #2843, Central Decimal Files (1930–1939), 819.851/29 1/2, RG 59, NA.
24. Research by the author has identified more than 120 of the 145 ships registered in Panama in 1939 and more than half of the tonnage of ships registered there in the period, including the Greek, Norwegian, and Basque vessels and the tankers of Esso and Standard Oil of California. Information about all of these transfers is of course scattered across several countries. Furthermore, smugglers tended not to document or publicize their activities. For such reasons, not all Panamanian-flagged ships in these different categories have been identified.
25. In later years, concerns over smuggling, illegal immigration, and use of flags of convenience by terrorists demonstrated that these early uses of the Panamanian flag had set some dangerous precedents. See, for example, Tina Shaughnessy

and Ellen Tobin, "Flags of Inconvenience: Freedom and Insecurity on the High Seas," *Journal of International Law and Policy* 5 (2006–2007), www.law .upenn.edu/journals/jil/jilp/articles/1-1_Shaughnessy_Tina.pdf, accessed June 2, 2014.

Chapter 9. Neutrality and War

1. Kennedy had previously served as head of the Securities and Exchange Commission and later was appointed as U.S. minister to Great Britain.
2. Herbert Feis, "The American Merchant Marine and Neutrality," September 25, 1937, Central Decimal Files (1930–1939), 195/1851, RG 59, NA.
3. Herbert Feis to Joseph Kennedy, September 27, 1937, Central Decimal Files (1930–1939), 195/1851, RG 59, NA.
4. Some of the material that follows in this chapter previously appeared in Carlisle, *Sovereignty for Sale*, chap. 5.
5. Neutrality Act of 1935, 49 Stat. 1081 (1935); Neutrality Act of 1937, 50 Stat. 121 (1937).
6. Cash and Carry Act, 54 Stat. 4 (1939).
7. William Langer and S. Everett Gleason, *The Challenge to Isolation* (New York: Harper, 1952), 235.
8. The Propeller Club (a shipowners' organization) and the National Foreign Trade Conference opposed the Pittman Act: *Marine Journal*, October 15, 1939, 8, 16. Shipowners had argued that they were singled out as scapegoats in response to earlier neutrality legislation: *Marine Journal*, January 15, 1936, 9.
9. The totals transferred are recorded in Standard Oil Company of New Jersey, *Ships of the Esso Fleet in World War II* (Wilmington, DE, 1946).
10. Ibid., 63.
11. Embassy to State, September 2, 1939, Central Decimal Files (1930–1939), 819.851/39, RG 59, NA; Under Secretary (Sumner Welles) to Berle, August 28, 1939 (re "caught in a jam" about the crews on *George McKnight* and *Clio*), Central Decimal Files (1930–1939), 819.664/4, RG 59, NA. In later years, the issue of the dismissing of German crews became a major concern regarding the reliability of Panamanian ships during times of war. See U.S. Senate Committee on Interstate and Foreign Commerce, Subcommittee on Merchant Marine and Fisheries, *Hearings on Ship Transfers*, 85th Cong. 79 (1957); Ainsworth to Areeda, February 20, 1959, Areeda Papers, DDEPL. See discussion of the issue of reliability in case of war in chapter 12.
12. Central Decimal Files (1930–1939), 819.8591/25, /29, /49, RG 59, NA; Larson, Knowlton, and Popple, *History of Standard Oil*, 394–95.
13. Hackworth to State, March 10, 1937, Central Decimal Files (1930–1939), 195.2/3488, RG 59, NA.
14. "US Lines Seeking New Flag to Stay in European Trade," *New York Times*, November 6, 1939.
15. *New York Times*, November 9, 1939; *Marine Journal*, November 15, 1939, 7, 9–10; *New York Times*, November 29, 1939.
16. Emory Land, "Off the Cuff" (speech, Society of Naval Architects and Marine Engineers, November 17, 1939), in Speeches, 23, Emory Land Papers, LCMD.
17. *New York Times*, November 7, 1939.
18. *New York Times*, November 8, 1939.

19. "Labor Is Incensed by Ship Line Move—Curran Threatens Picket Line in Washington If American Seamen Are Displaced," *New York Times*, November 7, 1939.
20. "Labor Is Divided on Ship Transfers," *New York Times*, November 8, 1939.
21. "Roosevelt Shapes Relief for Seamen: Union Leaders, After Talk, Are 'Convinced' He Will Allow Ship Transfers to Panama. Relief Program Outlined," *New York Times*, November 11, 1939.
22. Arthur Krock, "In the Nation—the Law and Spirit of the Panama Transfers," *New York Times*, November 10, 1939.
23. Boake Carter, National Maritime Union Minutes, January 16, 1940, Baarslag Collection, Herbert Hoover Presidential Library (HHPL), West Branch, IA; Tom Connally, *New York Times*, November 7, 1939; Bailey to Roosevelt, November 10, 1939, Emory Land Papers, LCMD.
24. Berle Diary, Roll 1, Frames 1155–56, October 3, 1939, Franklin D. Roosevelt Presidential Library (FDRPL), Hyde Park, NY.
25. Ibid., Frame 1232, November 6, 1939, FDRPL.
26. Cordell Hull and Andrew Thomas Hull Berding, *The Memoirs of Cordell Hull* (New York: Macmillan, 1948), 1:698.
27. "Roosevelt Halts Transfer of Ships to Panama's Flag," *New York Times*, November 8, 1939.
28. *New York Times*, November 8, November 9, November 10, November 12, 1939.
29. "Franz Boas Opposes," *New York Times*, November 13, 1939. Boas was German born and educated but had lived in the United States since 1896; he was active in the isolationist movement. He was probably fully aware that Panamanian sovereignty had been used by shipping interests for some twenty years when he made this comment.
30. "Labor Is Divided on Ship Transfers," *New York Times*, November 8, 1939. Flynn kept a close watch on Roosevelt's pro-Allied positions and consistently opposed any measures designed to aid the Allies or to impair U.S. neutrality in the period. Flynn later went on to write several popular works severely critical of Roosevelt's failure to maintain neutrality in 1939–1941.
31. "Senators Condemn Transfer of Ships," *New York Times*, November 8, 1939.
32. "No Ship Transfer," *New York Times*, November 17, 1939.
33. Berle Diary, Roll 2, Frame 49, November 11, 1939, FDRPL.
34. Ibid., Frame 50–51, November 12, 1939, FDRPL.
35. Memo Land-Roosevelt, November 8, 1939, Miscellaneous files of Adm. E. S. Land, Chairman WSA, Entry 5a, Box 2, RG 178, NA.
36. Transfer of Registry Orders, 10/25/1936–05/24/1950, transfer numbers C 2923, 2923a, 2924, 2924a, 2925, all dated December 29, 1939, and 2925a dated January 4, 1940, RG 178, NA.
37. The dates and ship names of the fifteen Panamanian ships lost through 1940 and up until December 7, 1941 are as follows: July 2,1940: *Santa Margarita*; July 7, 1940: *Beme*; December 21, 1940: *Charles Pratt*; April 25,1941: *Joseph Seep* (lost to a mine); May 31, 1941: *James McGee* (lost to a mine); August 17,1941: *Longtaker*; September 5, 1941: *Trinidad*; September 11, 1941: *Montana;* September 19, 1941: *Pink Star*; September 20, 1941: *T . J. Williams*; September 27, 1941: *I. C. White*; October 16, 1941: *Bold Venture*; October 18, 1941: *W. C. Teagle*; November 11, 1941: *Meridian*; November 14, 1941: *Crusader*. Data compiled from the *New York Times*.

38. The losses of U.S.-flagged ships during the neutrality period were brought to the author's attention by Professor Josh Smith of the U.S. Merchant Marine Academy. Some 1,554 U.S.-flagged merchant ships were lost during U.S. participation in the war ("U.S. Merchant Ships Sunk or Damaged in World War II," American Merchant Marine at War, January 21, 2004, www.usmm.org /shipsunkdamaged.html, accessed June 2, 2014), and 9,521 merchant mariners lost their lives ("U.S. Merchant Marine Casualties during World War II," American Merchant Marine at War, February 12, 2007, www.usmm.org/casualty .html, accessed June 2, 2014). The percentage of merchant mariners who lost their lives while in service exceeded even the percentage of Marines who were killed during the war.

39. On the SS *Astral*, see "SS Astral (2) The Loss," Auke Visser's Mobil Tankers and Tugs Site, www.aukevisser.nl/mobil/id1136.htm, accessed February 17, 2016. On the SS *Sagadahoc*, see "Ships Hit by U-Boats: *Sagadahoc*," http:// uboat.net/allies/merchants/1213.html, accessed February 17, 2016.

40. "Sunken Seafarer Had Arms Cargo," *New York Times*, September 10, 1941. Another U.S. ship was damaged during the German attack on the *Seafarer*: the *Arkansan*, which was also carrying Lend-Lease supplies. *New York Times*, September 14, 1941. As far as can be determined, no other German or Italian attacks on U.S. merchant ships carrying Lend-Lease supplies occurred between the beginning of the Lend-Lease program on March 11, 1941, and December 7, 1941. Lend-Lease, although clearly an unneutral policy, did not engage the United States in war because the war matériel was sent on board non-U.S.-flagged ships through the war zone. On April 11, 1941, FDR declared the Red Sea and Gulf of Aden to no longer be combat areas and open to U.S. shipping, allowing U.S.-flagged ships carrying Lend-Lease supplies to reach British forces in Egypt by way of the Indian Ocean and Red Sea.

41. On the SS *City of Flint*, see "Ships Hit by U-Boats: *City of Flint*," http://uboat .net/allies/merchants/2603.html, accessed February 17, 2016. On the MS *City of Rayville*, see Peter Dunn, "MS City of Rayville Sunk by a German Mine off Cape Otway, VIC, on 8 November 1940," Peter Dunn's Australia at War, 2006, www.ozatwar.com/german/cityofrayville.htm, accessed February 17, 2016. On the SS *Robin Moor*, see Steve Terjeson, "SS Robin Moor," *World War II History* (blog), May 21, 2008, http://wwarii.com/blog/archives/ss-robin-moor/, accessed February 17, 2016. On the SS *Steel Seafarer*, see Skip Lewis, "S.S. Steel Seafarer," Isthmian Lines, 2003, isthmianlines.com/ships/sa_steel_seafarer.htm, accessed February 17, 2016. On the SS *Lehigh*, see Sam Hakam, "Sinking of the SS Lehigh, October 19, 1941," American Merchant Marine at War, June 5, 2000, www.usmm.org/lehigh.html, accessed February 17, 2016.

There was no public outcry over the loss of the *Lehigh*, *Astral*, or *Sagadahoc* and no public announcement of diplomatic protest on these events apparently because of the lack of details about the fate of the ships. The news of the loss of SS *Sagadahoc* on December 3 was not public knowledge until December 31, 1941. "U.S. Freighter Sunk in Atlantic on Dec. 3," *New York Times*, December 31, 1941. There was no report at all in the contemporary U.S. press of the loss of *Lehigh* or *Astral* that modern research into newspaper archives uncovers. On the morning of December 7, 1941, just before the attack on Pearl Harbor, the Japanese sank another U.S. merchant ship, the SS *Cynthia Olson*; none of the thirty-three crew members survived. That event was reported nineteen days after the event. "Enemy Caught on Surface," *New York Times*, December 26, 1941.

42. "Panama Forbids Arming of Ships: Loss of Registry Is Ordered for Owners Who Fail to Comply with Edict," *New York Times*, October 7, 1941.

43. If the coup was engineered by U.S. operatives, of course the fact was classified information and may indeed remain classified as secret. However, the coup was widely reported as having U.S. "blessing."

44. Some forty-eight of the former Danish, Italian, and Finnish ships under the Panamanian flag were damaged or sunk during the war. "Foreign Passenger and Cargo Ships Taken Over by U.S. Maritime Commission during World War II," American Merchant Marine at War, last modified March 21, 2011, www .usmm.org/foreign.html, accessed June 2, 2014.

45. Draft of December 17, 1941; John W. Mann to Director, May 19, 1942; and memo of November 11, 1944, Records of WSA Office of Assistant Deputy Administration for Ship Operations Division of Foreign Charters and Ship Warrants, Box 6 (and further information in Box 7), RG 248, NA.

46. A fuller discussion of the evolution of the effective control doctrine in 1946–1947 is found in Carlisle, *Sovereignty for Sale*, 198–201.

Chapter 10. Sovereignty for Sale

1. The creation of the Liberian maritime code can be fully documented because Edward R. Stettinius Jr. left his personal papers to the library of the University of Virginia in Charlottesville. Stettinius Manuscript Collection, Alderman Library, University of Virginia (UVAL).

2. Walter Johnson, "Edward R. Stettinius, Jr.," in *An Uncertain Tradition: American Secretaries of State in the Twentieth Century*, ed. Norman Graebner (New York: McGraw-Hill, 1961), 210–22.

3. By the mid-1970s, when the author visited Liberia, it was rumored that the local office of the Liberia Foundation provided cover for the CIA station chief.

4. Dr. Sulzberger to M. J. Chancerelle, June 4, 1948, Box 790; Blackwell Smith to Haile Selassie, July 19, 1948, Box 789; Sidney De la Rue to E. R. Stettinius, July 7, 1948, Box 789; Sidney De la Rue to E. R. Stettinius, July 14, 1948, Box 789, all in Stettinius Papers, UVAL.

5. Articles appeared in *Time, Life, National Geographic, Ebony*, and *Reader's Digest*, among others. Henry Luce's "American Century" appeared in the February 17, 1941, issue of *Life*. The concept was widely promoted by others. See, for example, Allen Dulles, then of Sullivan and Cromwell (he was appointed to head the CIA in 1953), promoting a Marshall plan by the U.S. business community: "Marshall Plan Aid Urged on Business," *New York Times*, January 7, 1948. In the article, Dulles specifically mentioned assisting Europe in helping to develop Africa.

6. "Original Press Release," September 22, 1947, Box 767; Report on Meeting, April 21, 1948, Box 791, Stettinius Papers, UVAL.

7. Stettinius to Blackwell Smith, December 31, 1947, Box 767, Stettinius Papers, UVAL, referring to a conversation with E. Stanley Klein. The "certain shipping interests" were undoubtedly those involved in the AOTC transactions.

8. *Hearings Before the Permanent Subcommittee of Investigation of the Senate Committee on Government Operations: Sale of Government Owned Vessels*, 82nd Cong. 1, 24–26,

40, 135–36 (1952). The intricacies of the ship transactions apparently baffled investigators who sought to find out if U.S. surplus tankers had been improperly sold to foreigners. However, because the ships were registered in Panama by a U.S. corporation before they were sold to the China Foundation, they were apparently insulated from the effect of the law prohibiting sales of U.S.-registered ships to foreign owners at that time. "The Olga Boat Song," *Life*, March 17, 1952. Numerous articles in the *New York Times* through the period, authored by C. P. Trussel, traced the intricacies of the "Casey Group." One such account reports Stettinius' interest in AOTC and Panamanian registry in 1947: "Officials Dispute Casey on Tankers," *New York Times*, March 14, 1952.

9. "Chinese Alien Rule of Tanker Is Denied," *New York Times*, July 8, 1952. The foundation's ostensible purpose was to assist Chinese engineering students studying in the United States.

10. For the claim by Onassis, see Nicholas Fraser, *Aristotle Onassis* (Philadelphia: Lippincott, 1977), 101–2. On the Westerlund question, Fred Lininger, interview with author, February 5, 1979. Lininger, recalling the exchange about thirty years after the event, could not be precise as to exactly when the question was asked.

11. Joseph Grew resigned from the State Department in August 1945, as did Gen. Julius Holmes, who had been appointed by Stettinius as assistant secretary of state. Another officer, Blackwell Smith, president and general counsel of Liberia Company, had served as an officer of the Foreign Economic Administration during the war. *New York Times*, August 18, 1945, September 27, 1947. On the memo of meeting at the home of Grew, see March 13, 1948, Box 790, Stettinius Papers, UVAL.

12. Report by Stettinius, April 21, 1948; Stettinius to Blackwell Smith, August 5, 1948, both in Box 791, Stettinius Papers, UVAL.

13. Sidney De la Rue to F. T. Lininger, January 24, 1949, Box 797; J. G. Mackey to M. D. Franz, November 30, 1948, Box 793; De la Rue to H. L. Green et al., with copy to Stettinius, December 16, 1948, Box 793, Stettinius Papers, UVAL.

14. W. K. Trimble to B. Smith, June 24, 1948, Box 789, Stettinius Papers, UVAL; Francis Adams Truslow, *Report on the Corporation Code of Liberia, the Maritime Code of Liberia and the Act Establishing the International Trust Company of Liberia*, March 10, 1949, 80, Central Decimal Files (1940–1949), 882.516/3–1049, RG 59, NA.

15. B. Smith to G. Dennis, June 10, 1948, Box 790; Joseph Loucheim to Stettinius, July 21, 1948, Box 789; J. G. Mackey to B. Smith, July 29, 1948, Box 791, Stettinius Papers, UVAL. On Howard's background, see *New York Times*, September 1, 1945, January 17, 1948.

16. Mackey to V. Rodriguez of Sullivan and Cromwell, January 7, 1949, Box 797, Stettinius Papers, UVAL.

17. Stettinius, memorandum of conversation, August 3, 1948, Box 791; J. G. Mackey to B. Smith, August 14, 1948, Box 796, Stettinius Papers, UVAL.

18. J. G. Mackey to B. Smith, November 29, 1948; Trimble to Smith and Stettinius, December 16, 1948, Box 793, Stettinius Papers, UVAL. The company draft of the law in print is in Box 791, titled "Draft of an Act Repealing 'Part 19, Sections 916 to 928, Inclusive, of the Revised Statutes of the Republic of Liberia' and Establishing a Maritime Code of Law for the Republic of Liberia." The legislative-approved version signed into law in December, titled "Draft—

Maritime Code as Accepted by Government" on the cover sheet and "Draft of an Act to Establish a Maritime Code" on the first page, is in mimeographed form. Box 793, Stettinius Papers, UVAL. The crucial variations appear in Title I, sections 3 and 4 of both versions.

19. S. B. Adams to Palmer, December 31, 1947, 882.5034, RG 59, NA; J. C. Holmes to D. Zulzberger, May 11, 1948, Box 790, Stettinius Papers, UVAL; Meetings summarized in State Department Office Memorandum, Satterthwaite to Nitze, October 12, 1948, 882.5034, RG 59, NA; Stettinius to B. Smith, August 2,1948, Box 793, Stettinius Papers, UVAL; Memo of Conversation re Operations of Liberia Company, p. 4, August 8, 1948, Central Decimal Files (1940–1949), 882.5034, RG 59, NA.

20. Satterthwaite to Nitze, October 12, 1948, as sited above in Central Decimal Files (1940–1949), 882.5034, RG 59, NA.

21. Memo of Conversation, August 8, 1948, Central Decimal Files (1940–1949), 882.5034, RG 59, NA.

22. It is altogether possible that word of the U.S. role circulated orally, but at least the Liberian legislators did not need to take official notice that they were rubber-stamping a U.S.-authored document.

23. De la Rue to B. Smith, December 14, 1948; B. Smith to Trimble, December 17, 1948, Box 793, Stettinius Papers, UVAL.

24. De la Rue to F. T. Lininger, January 18, and 21, 1949, Box 797, Stettinius Papers, UVAL.

25. De la Rue to Stettinius, February 11 and 18, 1949, Box 797, Stettinius Papers, UVAL.

26. Sims to Satterthwaite, March 7, 1949, Central Decimal Files (1940–1949), 882.5034, RG 59, NA.

27. Truslow to Thorp, p. 5, March 10, 1949, Central Decimal Files (1940–1949), 882.516, RG 59, NA.

28. Truslow, *Report*, 36, 38, 47, 57. Comparison of Truslow's suggestions with the 1956 republication of the Liberian maritime code shows only the filing of liens incorporated: Republic of Liberia, *Liberian Code of Laws of 1956 Adopted by the Legislature of the Republic of Liberia, March 22, 1956* (Ithaca, NY, 1957), 2:811–12, art. 22, sec. 106. This 1956 annotated version shows minor typographical corrections incorporated in June and December 1949.

29. Blackwell Smith to E. W. Klein, December 1948, Box 793; J. G. Mackey to Schaeffer, December 22, 1948, Box 793; Mackey to Trimble, January 6, 1848, Box 797; Mackey to V. Rodriquez of Sullivan and Cromwell, January 7, 1949, Box 797; Schaeffer to Lininger, January 17, 1949, Box 797; Mackey to Schaeffer, no date, Box 797; Mackey to Franz, January 5, 1949, enclosing contract, Box 797; Mackey to Schaeffer, December 22, 1949, Box 793; Schaeffer to Lininger, January 17, 1949, Box 797, Stettinius Papers, UVAL.

30. Stettinius to Grew, December 18, 1948, Box 793, Stettinius Papers, UVAL.

31. Stettinius to Klein, December 24, 1948, Box 793, Stettinius Papers, UVAL.

32. Mackey to Franz, January 5, 1949, Box 797, Stettinius Papers, UVAL; "Liberia: A Phantom Maritime Power Whose Fleet Is Steered by Big Business," *New York Times*, February 14, 1977; Republic of Liberia, *Liberia—25 Years as a Maritime Nation* (Monrovia: International Trust Company of Liberia, 1975), 19; Lininger to Green, January 24, 1949, Box 797, Stettinius Papers, UVAL.

33. Republic of Liberia, *Liberia—25 Years*, 5.
34. "OECD Study of Flags of Convenience," *Journal of Maritime Law and Commerce* 4 (January 1973): 231–54.
35. Republic of Liberia, *Liberia—25 Years*, 6.
36. Advertisement, *Newsweek*, May 30, 1977. "U.S. Maritime Committee to Turn the Tide" defined itself as "a management coalition of ship-builders, ship operators and marine supportive industries."
37. See, for example, Alfred Dupont Chandler, *Strategy and Structure: Chapters in the History of the American Industrial Enterprise* (Cambridge: Massachusetts Institute of Technology Press, 1969).

Chapter 11. Challenges Ashore and at Sea, 1955–80

1. Economist Intelligence Unit, *Open Registry Shipping: Some Economic Considerations* (London: Economist, 1979), 13–14, 17.
2. Boczek, *Flags of Convenience*, 95.
3. Ibid., 215–42, 246–65.
4. Ibid., 272–74.
5. Constitution of the Maritime Safety Committee of the Intergovernmental Maritime Consultative Organization: Advisory Opinion, June 8, 1960, ICJ Reports (1960), 150–78.
6. Ibid.
7. Cases included *Sielinski v. Empresa Hondurena de vapores* (113 F.Supp. 93, SDNY [1953]), in which the court ruled that U.S. ownership outweighed registry and flag; and *Bobalkais v. Compania Panamena Maritima San Gerassimo* (168 F.Supp. 236 SDNY [1958]), in which the judge ruled, "An American owner might escape his statutory liability merely by interposing a foreign corporation between himself and the vessel, both of which, for all practical purposes, he owns. I do not believe that the law can be so easily baffled." These and other cases cited *Lauritzen v. Larsen*, 145 U.S. 571 (1953).
8. *Peninsular Occidental Steamship Company and Green Trading Company and Seafarers International Union of North America* (Case 12-CA-235), 132 NLRB 10 (1958).
9. *West India Fruit*, 130 NLRB 143 (1960).
10. Erling Naess, *The Great PanLibHon Controversy* (Epping, UK: Gower Press, 1972), 120–25. At the time, advocates of the use of flags of convenience, like the ACFN, commonly used the term "PanLibHon" to refer to Panamanian, Liberian, and Honduran ships.
11. Gardner Ainsworth to Areeda, February 11, 1959; Clarence Morse to Areeda, February 9, 1959; Chief of Naval Operations Office to Areeda, February 7, 1959, Areeda Papers, Dwight D. Eisenhower Presidential Library (DDEPL), Abilene, KS.
12. George Daub to David Kendall, February 23, 1959, Areeda Papers, DDEPL.
13. Stuart Rothman to Kendall, August 25, 1959, Morgan Papers, DDEPL.
14. Areeda to Daub, December 4, 1959, Areeda Papers, DDEPL; Brief of the United States, Intervenor, as Amicus, NLRB Cases 15-CA-1454, 12-CA255, 21-RC-415, 2-RC-10379, NLRB jurisdiction, Suitland Records Center.
15. *United Fruit Company and National Maritime Union of America AFL-CIO*, 134 NLRB 287 (1961).

16. Archibald Cox, telephone interview by the author, November 1979. Kennedy had consulted U.S. Senate Committee on Commerce, Subcommittee on Communications, *The Speeches of Senator John F. Kennedy, Presidential Campaign, 1960*, Final Report Pursuant to 395, at 1075 (1961). The telegram, dated October 3, 1960, was read at the National Maritime Union convention and therefore also reported in *National Maritime Union Proceedings, 12th National Convention* (1960), 53.

17. Solicitor general's brief, Supreme Court Briefs, 372 U.S. 10 (1963).

18. Cox interview.

19. Incres-Hondurena cases, 372 U.S. 10 (1963).

20. Erling Naess took the case as a vindication: Naess, *Great PanLibHon Controversy*, 110. A review of Boczek's *Flags of Convenience* by L. F. E. Goldie indicated that the victory of the flag-of-convenience shippers should not have been interpreted as so unqualified. See L. F. E. Goldie, review of *Flags of Convenience: An International Legal Study*, by Boleslaw Adam Boczek, *International Law and Comparative Law Quarterly* 12 (1963): 989–1004.

21. The details of these ship losses and others are presented in Carlisle, *Sovereignty for Sale*, 176–84. It was this flurry of media attention to Liberia that first engaged the author of this work in the subject.

22. Works included Edward Cowan, *Oil and Water: The Torrey Canyon Disaster* (New York: Lippincott, 1968) and two different works titled *In the Wake of the Torrey Canyon*, one by Richard Petrow (New York: McKay, 1968) and one by L. Oudet (London: Royal Institute of Navigation, 1972). Newspaper and magazine reports were extensive.

23. FACS publication, March 31, 1977; Frank Wiswall, interview by the author, May 13, 1980.

24. Clay Maitland, "Flag State Responsibility Paramount in Ship Safety Improvement" (speech delivered to London press conference, May 25, 2001), www.register-iri.com/index.cfm?action=page&page=277.

Chapter 12. The Marshall Islands Register

1. Carlisle, *Sovereignty for Sale*, 193–216.

2. "Liberia, Blood on the Flag," *Transport International*, December 2001.

3. In 1983 the author of the present work was asked by MarAd to submit a study of the comparative value of the various trust territories as potential effective control registries to replace Liberia and Panama. That study suggested that the Marshall Islands were potentially the most favorable jurisdiction; it is altogether probable that MarAd intended to advocate the Marshall Islands registry regardless of the result of the study. Rodney Carlisle, *Effective United States Control—Risks and Opportunities*, Report #N00033-83-M-4574 (Washington, DC: U.S. Military Sealift Command, April 4, 1983).

4. Andrew Guest, "U.S. Furor over Talk of Second Register," *Lloyd's List*, September 13, 1991, 8; Warren Leback, conversation with the author, June 8, 2009. Leback advocated that position at the time and by 2009 regarded the development of the Marshall Islands registry as a good development from the perspective of U.S. national security.

5. Compact of Free Association, Pub. L. No. 99-239 (1986); Dirk H. R. Spennemann, ed., Digital Micronesia, http://marshall.csu.edu.au, accessed June 2, 2014.

6. "DOCs in the News," *MEBA Telex Times*, n.d., ca. November 1996. Reference to OSG charters to the MSC are found in OSG form 10K filed in 2001 and 2002.

7. "Variety, Diversity Mark Recent RMI Registrations," *Marshall Islands Report* 12, no. 3 (May 2003); Gallagher quoted in David Young, "Marshall Islands Proves Quality Attracts Quantity," *Shipping and Trade News*, April 19, 2001, 1; International Registries, "Marshall Islands Tonnage Now at 11 Million," press release, May 25, 2001; Dutch commentator in "IRI Moves into Its Second Half-Century," *Maritime Advocate*, no. 10 (February 2000); International Registries, "Marshall Islands Achieves 15 Million Gross Tons," press release, December 11, 2002; CIA, "Liberia," in *The World Factbook* (Washington, DC, 2002); William Gallagher, "The Progress and Goals of the Marshall Islands Ship Registry" (speech delivered to a London press conference, May 25, 2001), www.register-iri.com/index.cfm?action=page&page=277, accessed June 2, 2014.

8. Transocean, "Our History," www.deepwater.com/fw/main/Our-History-3.html, accessed June 2, 2014.

9. UNCTAD, *Review of Maritime Transport 1997* (New York: United Nations, 1997), 32.

10. UNCTAD, *Review of Maritime Transport 2004* (New York: United Nations, 2004), 37; UNCTAD, *Review of Maritime Transport 2014* (New York: United Nations, 2014), 44.

11. "Liberia's 'Flag' Pays for Sanction Busting," *The Perspective*, October 25, 2001. *The Perspective* was published online from Atlanta, Georgia, and represented the viewpoint of some Liberians resident in the United States.

12. David Hughes, "Row over Who Should Run Liberian Register Rages On," *Informore*, January 11, 1999. Suit claiming Taylor's obsessive control quoted in "Suit Alleges Taylor Controls Liberian-Flag Franchisee," *Marine Log*, May 17, 2002. ITC representative quoted in Tim Shorrock, "Lawsuit Reawakens Hostility to Flags of Convenience," *Global Policy Forum*, April 17, 1998.

13. Hughes, "Row over Who Should Run."

14. ITF comment quoted from "Liberia, Blood on the Flag."

15. UN Security Council, "Expert Panel on Liberia Presents Report to Security Council," press release, November 5, 2001.

16. "Suit Alleges Taylor Controls"; "Liberia, Blood on the Flag"; "Liberia's 'Flag' Pays"; UN Security Council, "Expert Panel on Liberia"; Hughes, "Row over Who Should Run."

17. UNCTAD, *Review of Maritime Transport 2002* (New York: United Nations, 2002), 30.

18. CIA, "Liberia," in *The World Factbook* (Washington, DC, 1996, 2000).

19. Figures compiled from UNCTAD, *Review of Maritime Transport 1996* (New York: United Nations, 1996); and UNCTAD, *Review of Maritime Transport 2000* (New York: United Nations, 2000).

20. Yoram Cohen, quoted in *Flagship: News for the Liberian Registry*, no. 8 (October 2002).

21. The figures for U.S.-owned tonnage in deadweight tons were Liberia, 3,610,000; Panama, 2,278,000; Bahamas, 10,352,000; Marshall Islands, 12,889,000. UNCTAD, *Review of Maritime Transport 2007* (New York: United Nations, 2007), 38–39.

22. UNCTAD, *Review of Maritime Transport 2014*, 44.

23. Percentages from UNCTAD, *Review of Maritime Transport 1997*, 32. Although this UNCTAD review was quite thorough, it did not include Marshall Islands registrations in its analysis.

Chapter 13. Second Registers and Port-State Control

1. Labor or Socialist governments supported second registries in several countries, and labor unions specifically endorsed the second-registry system established by Belgium in Luxembourg (discussed later). Furthermore, in a system not reviewed here, labor in Brazil supported the establishment of a special registry in the tax-free zone of Manaus to allow payment of wages in U.S. dollars to avoid the inflation in Brazilian currency. Brazil established a second registry in 1997, the Registro Especial Brasileiro.

2. In some cases, the legislation creating the registry was passed in the year before the first ships were registered. Systems not discussed here include those of Brazil (1997), Turkey (1999), and Hong Kong, which is sometimes regarded as a second-registry system for the People's Republic of China. South Korea also considered, but did not adopt, a second-registry system in 1998. Since 1979 China has employed almost 4 million tons of its merchant fleet through wholly owned and controlled shipping companies registered and flagged in Hong Kong. Still other Chinese-owned ships have been registered in Singapore. For these reasons, some analysts consider both Hong Kong and Singapore as second registers for China. Michael Clark, "Shipping: An Overview," in *Oxford Encyclopedia Maritime History*, ed. John Hattendorf (New York: Oxford University Press, 2007), vol. 3. Martin Stopford also considers Hong Kong to be a second register of China. He includes it along with Singapore, NIS, Marshall Islands, and Isle of Man as among the largest second registers. Martin Stopford, *Maritime Economics* (New York: Routledge, 2007).

3. The operation of this and other MOU systems and their impact has been analyzed in Elizabeth DeSombre, *Flagging Standards: Globalization and Environmental, Safety, and Labor Regulations at Sea* (Cambridge: Massachusetts Institute of Technology, 2006), 87–134.

4. Ralph Miner, "Panama, the Canal Zone, and Titular Sovereignty," *Western Political Quarterly* 14 (1961): 544–54; Walter LaFeber, *The Panama Canal: The Crisis in Historical Perspective* (New York: Oxford University Press, 1978), 66n8.

5. Guest, "U.S. Furor over Talk," 8. Full details of these developments are covered in the earlier study by the author, *Sovereignty for Sale*, 1–18, 110–33.

6. An excellent source for running commentary on contemporary competitive developments in ship registry is the British maritime news journal *Lloyd's List*. Other periodicals consulted include *Asia Times* and *Business Times* (Singapore), as well as the *New York Times* and *Financial Times*. Specific issues cited are among hundreds of other issues of these periodicals reviewed for this chapter. An excellent source of ship registry statistics is the annual report of UNCTAD, the *Review of Maritime Transport*. All of these sources document the competitive nature of the open-registry systems. The commercial and competitive nature of open-registry systems is obvious from an examination of the more than twenty registry websites readily found on the Internet.

7. Robert Ward and Julian Bray, "Manx Register Claims Success," *Lloyd's List*, June 20, 1996, 3.

8. "Open Registers: Isle of Man Tops Low-Cost League," *Lloyd's List*, November 26, 1993, 8.

9. Robert Ward, "Special Report on World Ship Registers: Distinctions Becoming More Blurred," *Lloyd's List*, February 11, 1997; Ademuni-Odeke, *Bareboat Charter Registration* (Alphen aan den Rijn, The Netherlands: Kluwer Law International, 1997), 34, also regarded the Isle of Man as a second register. UNCTAD's Reviews of Maritime Transport for the years 2003–2007 also explicitly categorize the Isle of Man register as a second register.

10. Tony Gray, "Special Report on Netherlands Antilles: Registry Set for Growth as Marketing Moves Take Off," *Lloyd's List*, September 1, 1993, 6.

11. John MacLaughlin, "Special Report on Dutch Caribbean: Netherlands Antilles Edges Closer to Ship Registry Structure," *Lloyd's List*, September 22, 1998, 9.

12. Bruce McMichael, "Special Report on Ship Registers: Newcomers Seek Share of the Spoils," *Lloyd's List*, September 8, 1998, 6.

13. Greta Devos and Guy Elewaut, *CMB 100: A Century of Commitment to Shipping, 1895–1995* (Tielt, Belgium: Lannoo, 1995), 251–53. The author thanks Michael Clark for bringing this source to his attention.

14. Ademuni-Odeke, *Bareboat Charter Registration*, 33; Anthony Dunlop, "Long Haul to Stem the Exodus from Gaul," *Lloyd's List*, April 4, 1994, 2.

15. Andrew Spurrier, "French Seamen in Register Warning: Union Says State Proposal Must Not Threaten Jobs," *Lloyd's List*, January 27, 1999, 12.

16. Dag Bakka, *Hoegh: Shipping through Cycles* (Oslo: Leif Hoegh, 1997), 174. The author is indebted to Michael Clark for bringing this source to his attention. Erling Naess authored *The Great PanLibHon Controversy*.

17. Christopher Brown-Humes, "Special Report on World Ship Registers: Striking a Balance on Quality and Cost—Christopher Brown-Humes Looks on the Progress of 'Second Registers,'" *Lloyd's List*, April 1, 1992, 11.

18. McMichael, "Special Report on Ship Registers," 6.

19. UNCTAD, *Review of Maritime Transport 2007*, 36; *Review of Maritime Transport 2014*, 44.

20. Edelgard Simon, "EC Court to Rule on German Register," *Lloyd's List*, October 20, 1990, 5.

21. See ITF Seafarers, "Defining FOCs and the Problems They Pose," http://www.itfseafarers.org/defining-focs.cfm, accessed June 8, 2016.

22. Andrew Guest, "ITF Blacks GIS-Flag Vessels: German Owners Face Union Boycotts," *Lloyd's List*, March 13, 1995, 1.

23. Brown-Humes, "Special Report on World Ship Registers," 11.

24. Sarah Cunningham, "Italy May Start Second International Ship Register," *Lloyd's List*, December 16, 1994, 3.

25. Sarah Cunningham, "Competitive Spirit Vital for Italian Shipping's Survival," *Lloyd's List*, April 7, 1995, 5.

26. Giovanni Paci, "Costa Crociere Re-flags to Italian Second Register," *Lloyd's List*, December 28, 1999, 1.

27. UNCTAD, *Review of Maritime Transport 2007*, 36. For 2010 figures, see International Maritime Organization, *International Shipping Facts and Figures—Information Resources on Trade, Safety, Security, Environment* (London: Maritime Knowledge Center, March 6, 2012), Table 4, www.imo.org/KnowledgeCentre/ShipsAndShippingFactsAndFigures/TheRoleandImportanceof

InternationalShipping/Documents/International%20Shipping%20-%20
Facts%20and%20Figures.pdf, accessed May 17, 2015. In Europe, Italy was
third after Greece and Malta.

28. David Rudnick, "The Register Gets Shipshape," *Times* (London), July 20,
1990.

29. The details of the Madeira ship registry were found at www.eco-madeira
.com/DocumentLibrary/OperationalInfoGuidesAndProcedures/shipregist
guide, accessed August 8, 2008.

30. "A Very European Register That Flies the Flag for Madeira," *Lloyd's List*, March
12, 2004, 11.

31. Andrew Guest, "Canaries Register Blacklisted," *Lloyd's List*, February 11, 1993, 1.

32. Fiona Gibson, "Special Report on the Canary Islands: Second Register May Be
Too Little, Too Late," *Lloyd's List*, December 2, 1992, 9.

33. Herbert Fromme, "Special Report on Spanish Maritime Industries: Owners
Welcome State Plans for Second Register," *Lloyd's List*, May 7, 1992, 9.

34. Guest, "Canaries Register Blacklisted," 1.

35. John Tavner, "Special Report on Spanish Maritime: Size of Fleet Faces Critical
Decline," *Lloyd's List*, May 11, 1994, 11.

36. McMichael, "Special Report on Ship Registers," 6.

37. UNCTAD, *Review of Maritime Transport 1998* (New York: United Nations,
1998), 30.

38. See Anave, *Merchant Marine and Maritime Transport in Spain 2012–2013*
(Madrid, 2013), www.academia.edu/4285313/Merchant_Marine_and_Maritime
_Transport_in_Spain_2012-2013, accessed May 17, 2015.

39. Ward, "Special Report on World Ship Registers."

40. UNCTAD, *Review of Maritime Transport 2005* (New York: United Nations,
2005), 38; *Review of Maritime Transport 2007*, 32. In these figures, registry in the
country's overseas or domestic second registry is treated as part of the national
registry. That is, percentage for "foreign" registry does not include registrations
in the nation's second registry.

41. The figures for U.S.-owned tonnage in deadweight tons in 2007 were Liberia,
3,610,000; Panama, 2,278,000; Bahamas, 10,352,000; Marshall Islands,
12,889,000. UNCTAD, *Review of Maritime Transport 2007*, 38–39.

42. UNCTAD, *Review of Maritime Transport 2013* (New York: United Nations,
2013), 173, 175, 176, in annex 3. In 2013 UNCTAD reported that the registry
of U.S.-owned ships in the Bahamas was 3,284,000; Liberia, 5,582,000; Panama,
4,500,000. The 2014 report did not include this breakdown of information.

43. UNCTAD, *Review of Maritime Transport 2007*, 37.

44. UNCTAD, *Review of Maritime Transport 2014*, 43.

45. Ibid., 37, 44.

46. Ibid., 32.

Conclusion

1. Details of each of the episodes involving U.S. naval ships have been covered
extensively by other researchers. Among such sources are Edward J. Marolda,
The United States Navy and the Vietnam Conflict. Vol. 2, *From Military Assistance
to Combat 1959–1965* (Washington, DC: Naval Historical Center, 1986); A. J.
Cristol, *The* Liberty *Incident: The 1967 Israeli Attack on the U.S. Navy Spy Ship*

(Washington, DC: Brassey's, 2002); Mitchell B. Lerner, *The* Pueblo *Incident: A Spy Ship and the Failure of American Foreign Policy* (Lawrence: University Press of Kansas, 2002); Jeffrey L. Levinson, *Missile Inbound: The Attack on the* Stark *in the Persian Gulf* (Annapolis, MD: Naval Institute Press, 1997).

2. "The President's Address," *New York Times*, August 5, 1964.

3. Gerald Reminick, *An Act of Piracy: The Seizure of the American-Flag Merchant Ship* Mayaguez *in 1975* (Palo Alto, CA: Glencannon Press, 2009). See also Robert J. Mahoney, *The* Mayaguez *Incident: Testing America's Resolve in the Post-Vietnam Era* (Lubbock: Texas Tech University Press, 2011).

4. Raoul Berger, "The *Mayaguez* Incident and the Constitution," *New York Times*, May 23, 1975.

5. Rod MacLeish, "The *Mayaguez* Ordeal," *Washington Post*, May 20, 1975.

6. "*Mayaguez*, Its Implications," *Chicago Defender*, May 21, 1975.

7. Rowland Evans and Robert Novak, "Retrieving the *Mayaguez*: 'It Was Pure Ford,'" *Washington Post*, May 19, 1975.

8. James Reston, "'Twas a Famous Victory," *New York Times*, May 16, 1975.

9. "Don't Give Up the Ship! Quick Thinking and a Boatload of Know-How Saves the *Maersk Alabama*," *Marine Officer*, Summer 2009, 18, quoting a letter signed by MEBA union officials.

10. Another, unsuccessful 2009 attack on a U.S. government cargo ship, the *Liberty Sun*, received little press attention, as the pirates did not board the ship. *New York Daily News*, April 15, 2009; "Pirates Attack U.S. Ship off Somalia," *New York Times*, April 15, 2009.

Bibliography

Archival Collections

Dwight D. Eisenhower Presidential Library, Abilene, KS.
    Areeda Papers
Franklin D. Roosevelt Presidential Library, Hyde Park, NY.
    Berle Diary
Herbert Hoover Presidential Library, West Branch, IA.
    Baarslag Collection
Manuscript Division, Library of Congress, Washington, DC.
    Papers of Melville Fuller
    Papers of Robert Lansing
Seeley G. Mudd Library, Princeton University, Princeton, NJ.
    Woodrow Wilson Papers
University of Virginia Alderman Library, Charlottesville, VA.
    Edward R. Stettinius Manuscript Collection
U.S. National Archives, Washington, DC.
    RG 32 Records of the U.S. Shipping Board
    RG 59 Records of the Department of State
    RG 178 Records of the U.S. Maritime Commission
    RG 248 Records of the War Shipping Administration

Published Primary Document Collections

American State Papers: Foreign Relations
Foreign Relations of the United States (*FRUS*). Washington, DC: Government Printing Office, various dates.
Great Britain. *Muscat Dhows Arbitration: In the Permanent Court of Arbitration at The Hague: Grant of the French Flag to Muscat Dhows*. London: Foreign Office, 1905. http://babel.hathitrust.org/cgi/pt?id=coo.31924007461209. Accessed June 2, 2014.
Lloyd's Register of International Shipping. London: Lloyd's Register, 1920–1939.
Official Records of the Union and Confederate Navies in the War of the Rebellion. Washington, DC: Government Printing Office, 1894–1922.
Republic of Liberia. *Liberian Code of Laws of 1956 Adopted by the Legislature of the Republic of Liberia, March 22, 1956.* Ithaca, NY, 1957.
Rossiter, Clinton, ed. *The Federalist Papers*. New York: New American Library, 1961.
    U.S. Congress Reports

Secondary Literature

Ademuni-Odeke. *Bareboat Charter Registration*. Alphen aan den Rijn, The Netherlands: Kluwer Law International, 1997.
Adkins, Roy, and Lesley Adkins. *The War for All the Oceans*. New York: Viking, 2007.
Albion, Robert Greenhalgh, and Jennie Barnes Pope. *Sea Lanes in Wartime: The American Experience*. New York: Norton, 1942.

Alexander, Archibald. *Colonization on the West African Coast*. Philadelphia: William S. Martien, 1846. Reprint, New York: Negro Universities Press, 1969.

Bailey, R. W. *Records of Oman 1867–1947*. Vol. 2, *Historical Affairs, 1871–1913*. Buckinghamshire, UK: Archive Editions, 1988.

Bakka, Dag. *Hoegh: Shipping through Cycles*. Oslo: Leif Hoegh, 1997.

Barrett, Roby C. "Oman: The Present in the Context of a Fractured Past." *Joint Special Operations University Report* 11, no. 5 (2011).

Baughman, James P. *Charles Morgan and the Development of Southern Transportation*. Nashville: Vanderbilt University Press, 1968.

———. *The Mallorys of Mystic: Six Generations in American Maritime Enterprise*. Mystic, CT: Marine Historical Association, 1972.

Beesly, Patrick. *Room 40: British Naval Intelligence*. London: Hamish Hamilton, 1982.

Boczek, Boleslaw Adam. *Flags of Convenience: An International Legal Study*. Cambridge, MA: Harvard University Press, 1969.

Bradford, Richard H. *The* Virginius *Affair*. Boulder: Colorado Associated University Press, 1980.

Brentano, Lujo. *What Germany Has Paid under the Treaty of Versailles*. Berlin: Walter de Gruyter, 1923.

Brown, Roger H. *The Republic in Peril: 1812*. New York: Columbia University Press, 1964.

Brown-Humes, Christopher. "Special Report on World Ship Registers: Striking a Balance on Quality and Cost—Christopher Brown-Humes Looks on the Progress of 'Second Registers.'" *Lloyd's List*, April 1, 1992.

Canney, Donald L. *Africa Squadron: The U.S. Navy and the Slave Trade, 1842–1861*. Washington, DC: Potomac Books, 2006.

Carlisle, Rodney. "The 'American Century' Implemented: Stettinius and the Liberian Flag of Convenience." *Business History Review* 54, no. 2 (1980): 175–91.

———. "The Attacks on U.S. Shipping That Precipitated American Entry into World War I." *Northern Mariner* 17, no. 3 (2007): 41–66.

———. "Danzig: The Missing Link in the History of Flags of Convenience." *Northern Mariner* 23, no. 2 (2013): 135–50.

———. *Effective United States Control—Risks and Opportunities*. Report #N00033-83-M-4574. Washington, DC: U.S. Military Sealift Command, April 4, 1983.

———. "Flagging-Out in the American Civil War." *Northern Mariner* 22, no. 1 (2012): 53–65.

———. "The Flag Insulted: U.S. Merchant Marine Incidents, 1865–1895." *Northern Mariner* 20, no. 3 (2010): 267–82.

———. "Liberia's Flag of Convenience: Rough Water Ahead." *Orbis* 24, no. 4 (1981): 881–92.

———. "The Muscat Dhows Case in Historical Perspective." *Northern Mariner* 24, no. 1/2 (2014): 23–40.

———. *The Roots of Black Nationalism*. Port Washington, NY: Kennikat, 1975.

———. "Second Registers: Maritime Nations Respond to Flags of Convenience, 1984–1998." *Northern Mariner* 19, no. 3 (2009): 319–40.

———. *Sovereignty at Sea: U.S. Merchant Ships and American Entry into World War I*. Gainesville: University Press of Florida, 2009.

———. *Sovereignty for Sale: The Origins and Evolution of the Panamanian and Liberian Flags of Convenience*. Annapolis, MD: Naval Institute Press, 1981.

———. *World War One: An Eyewitness History*. New York: Facts on File, 2007.

Carroll, Francis. "The Passionate Canadians: The Historical Debate about the Eastern Canadian-American Boundary." *New England Quarterly* 70 (March 1997): 83–101.

Chamberlain, Ryan. *Pistols, Politics and the Press: Dueling in 19th Century American Journalism*. Jefferson, NC: McFarland, 2008.

Chandler, Alfred Dupont. *Strategy and Structure: Chapters in the History of the American Industrial Enterprise*. Cambridge: Massachusetts Institute of Technology Press, 1969.

Clark, Michael. "Shipping: An Overview." In *Oxford Encyclopedia of Maritime History*, edited by John Hattendorf, vol. 3. New York: Oxford University Press, 2007.

Cook, A. *The* Alabama *Claims*. Ithaca, NY: Cornell University Press, 1975.

Cowan, Edward. *Oil and Water: The* Torrey Canyon *Disaster*. New York: Lippincott, 1968.

Cristol, A. J. *The* Liberty *Incident: The 1967 Israeli Attack on the U.S. Navy Spy Ship*. Washington, DC: Brassey's, 2002.

Cunningham, Sarah. "Competitive Spirit Vital for Italian Shipping's Survival." *Lloyd's List*, April 7, 1995.

———. "Italy May Start Second International Ship Register." *Lloyd's List*, December 16, 1994.

Dalzell, George W. *The Flight from the Flag: The Continuing Effect of the Civil War upon the American Carrying Trade*. Chapel Hill: University of North Carolina Press, 1940.

Daniels, Josephus. *The Cabinet Diaries of Josephus Daniels, 1913–1917*. Edited by E. David Cronon. Lincoln: University of Nebraska Press, 1963.

———. *The Wilson Era: Years of Peace, 1910–1917*. Chapel Hill: University of North Carolina Press, 1946.

de la Pedraja, René. *The Rise and Decline of U.S. Merchant Shipping in the Twentieth Century*. New York: Twayne, 1992.

DeSombre, Elizabeth. *Flagging Standards: Globalization and Environmental, Safety, and Labor Regulations at Sea*. Cambridge: Massachusetts Institute of Technology, 2006.

Devos, Greta, and Guy Elewaut. *CMB 100: A Century of Commitment to Shipping, 1895–1995*. Tielt, Belgium: Lannoo, 1995.

Drake, Frederick C. *Empire of the Seas: A Biography of Rear Admiral Robert Wilson Shufeldt, USN*. Honolulu: University of Hawaii Press, 1984.

DuBois, W. E. B. *The Suppression of the African Slave Trade to the United States of America, 1638–1870*. New York: Longmans, Green, 1896.

Dudley, William S., ed. *The Naval War of 1812: A Documentary History*. Washington, DC: Naval Historical Center, 1992.

Dunlop, Anthony. "Long Haul to Stem the Exodus from Gaul." *Lloyd's List*, April 4, 1994.

Economist Intelligence Unit. *Open Registry Shipping: Some Economic Considerations*. London: Economist, 1979.

Elliott, Jonathan, ed. *The Debates in the Several State Conventions on the Adoption of the Federal Constitution*. 5 vols. Philadelphia: Lippincott, 1861.

Fettweis, Christopher J. *The Pathologies of Power: Fear, Honor, Glory, and Hubris in U.S. Foreign Policy*. New York: Cambridge University Press, 2013.

Fischer, David Hackett. *Albion's Seed: Four British Folkways in America*. New York: Oxford University Press, 1989.

Fraser, Nicholas. *Aristotle Onassis*. Philadelphia: Lippincott, 1977.

Freeman, Joanne. *Affairs of Honor: National Politics in the New Republic*. New Haven, CT: Yale University Press, 2001.

Fromme, Herbert. "Special Report on Spanish Maritime Industries: Owners Welcome State Plans for Second Register." *Lloyd's List*, May 7, 1992.

Galbraith, John Kenneth. *American Capitalism: The Concept of Countervailing Power*. Boston: Houghton Mifflin, 1952.

Gibson, Andrew, and Arthur Donovan. *The Abandoned Ocean: A History of United States Maritime Policy*. Columbia: University of South Carolina Press, 2001.

Gibson, Fiona. "Special Report on the Canary Islands: Second Register May Be Too Little, Too Late." *Lloyd's List*, December 2, 1992.

Gilje, Paul. *Free Trade and Sailors' Rights in the War of 1812*. New York: Cambridge University Press, 2013.

Goldberg, Mark H. *Going Bananas: One Hundred Years of American Fruit Ships in the Caribbean*. Kings Point, NY: North American Maritime Books, 1992.

Goldie, L. F. E. Review of *Flags of Convenience: An International Legal Study*, by Boleslaw Adam Boczek. *International Law and Comparative Law Quarterly* 12 (1963): 989–1004.

González Echegaray, Rafael. *50 Años de Vapores Santanderinos*. Santander, Spain: Editorial Cantabria, 1951.

Gray, Tony. "Special Report on Netherlands Antilles: Registry Set for Growth as Marketing Moves Take Off." *Lloyd's List*, September 1, 1993.

Greenberg, Kenneth S. *Honor and Slavery*. Princeton, NJ: Princeton University Press, 1996.

Grose, Peter. *Gentleman Spy*. New York: Houghton Mifflin, 1991.

Grotius, Hugo. *The Free Sea*. Edited by David Armitage. Indianapolis: Liberty Fund, 2004.

Guest, Andrew. "Canaries Register Blacklisted." *Lloyd's List*, February 11, 1993.

———. "ITF Blacks GIS-Flag Vessels: German Owners Face Union Boycotts." *Lloyd's List*, March 13, 1995.

———. "U.S. Furor over Talk of Second Register." *Lloyd's List*, September 13, 1991.

Hacker, Louis M. "Western Land Hunger and the War of 1812: A Conjecture." *Mississippi Valley Historical Review* 10, no. 4 (March 1924): 365–95.

Hagan, Kenneth. *American Gunboat Diplomacy and the Old Navy, 1877–1889*. Westport, CT: Greenwood, 1972.

Hall, Henry. *American Navigation, with Some Account of the Cause of Its Former Prosperity and Present Decline*. New York: D. Appleton, 1878.

Hearn, Chester G. *Gray Raiders of the Sea: How Eight Confederate Warships Destroyed the Union's High Seas Commerce*. Camden, ME: International Marine Publishing, 1992.

Heinrichs, Waldo. *Threshold of War: Franklin D. Roosevelt and American Entry into World War II*. New York: Oxford University Press, 1988.

Henderson, J. Welles, and Rodney Carlisle. *Jack Tar: A Sailor's Life, 1750–1910*. Woodbridge, UK: Antique Collector's Press, 1999.

Hervey, Maurice H. *Dark Days in Chile*. New York: Macmillan, 1892.

Hill, Hamilton Andrews. *American Shipping: Its Decline and the Remedies, 1827–1895*. Boston: J. H. Eastburn, 1869.

Hobsbawm, Eric. *The Age of Capital 1848–1875*. New York: Scribner, 1975.

Horsman, Reginald. *The Causes of the War of 1812*. Philadelphia: University of Pennsylvania Press, 1962.

Hughes, David. "Row over Who Should Run Liberian Register Rages On." *Informore*, January 11, 1999.

Hull, Cordell, and Andrew Thomas Hull Berding. *The Memoirs of Cordell Hull*. New York: Macmillan, 1948.

Isenberg, Nancy. *Fallen Founder: The Life of Aaron Burr*. London: Penguin, 2007.

Johnson, Emory Richard, et al. *History of Domestic and Foreign Commerce of the United States*. Washington, DC: Carnegie Institution, 1915.

Johnson, Walter. "Edward R. Stettinius, Jr." In *An Uncertain Tradition: American Secretaries of State in the Twentieth Century*, edited by Norman Graebner, 210–22. New York: McGraw-Hill, 1961.

Jones, Howard. *To the Webster-Ashburton Treaty: A Study in Anglo-American Relations, 1783–1843*. Chapel Hill: University of North Carolina Press, 1977.

Jordan, Roger W. *The World's Merchant Fleets, 1939: The Particulars and Wartime Fates of 6,000 Ships*. Annapolis, MD: Naval Institute Press, 2006.

Kahn, David. *The Codebreakers*. New York: Signet, New American Library, 1973.

Kemble, John H. *The Panama Route, 1849–1869*. Berkeley: University of California Press, 1943.

Kinealy, Christine. "The Liberator: Daniel O'Connell and Anti-Slavery." *History Today* 57, no. 12 (2007): 51–57.

Kinghorn, Jonathan. *The Atlantic Transport Line, 1881–1931: A History with Details on All Ships*. Jefferson, NC: McFarland, 2012.

Kinzer, Stephen. *Overthrow: America's Century of Regime Change from Hawaii to Iraq*. New York: Henry Holt, 2006. Reprint, New York: Times Books, 2007.

Kluger, William Carl. *Lewis Cass and the Politics of Moderation*. Kent, OH: Kent State University Press, 1996.

LaFeber, Walter. *The New Empire: An Interpretation of American Expansion, 1860–1898*. Ithaca, NY: Cornell University Press, 1998.

———. *The Panama Canal: The Crisis in Historical Perspective*. New York: Oxford University Press, 1978.

Langer, William, and S. Everett Gleason. *The Challenge to Isolation*. New York: Harper, 1952.

Langley, Harold. *So Proudly We Hail: The History of the United States Flag*. Washington, DC: Smithsonian Institution Press, 1981.

Lansing, Robert. *War Memoirs of Robert Lansing*. Indianapolis: Bobbs-Merrill, 1935.

Larson, Eric. *The Devil in the White City*. New York: Vintage, 2004.

Larson, Henrietta M., Evelyn H. Knowlton, and Charles S. Popple. *History of Standard Oil Company (New Jersey): New Horizons, 1927–1950*. New York: Harper & Row, 1974.

Lawrence, William Beach. *Visitation and Search; or, An Historical Sketch of the British Claim to Exercise a Maritime Police over the Vessels of All Nations*. Boston: Little, Brown, 1858.

Leepson, Marc. *Flag: An American Biography*. New York: St. Martin's Griffin Press, 2005.

Lerner, Mitchell B. *The* Pueblo *Incident: A Spy Ship and the Failure of American Foreign Policy*. Lawrence: University Press of Kansas, 2002.

Levine, Herbert S. *Hitler's Free City: A History of the Nazi Party in Danzig, 1925–1930*. Chicago: University of Chicago Press, 1973.

Levinson, Jeffrey L. *Missile Inbound: The Attack on the* Stark *in the Persian Gulf*. Annapolis, MD: Naval Institute Press, 1997.

Lovell, Julia. *The Opium War: Drugs, Dreams and the Making of China*. London: Picador, 2011.

Lynch, John. *Causes of the Reduction of American Tonnage and the Decline of Navigation Interests*. Washington, DC: Government Printing Office, 1870.

MacLaughlin, John. "Special Report on Dutch Caribbean: Netherlands Antilles Edges Closer to Ship Registry Structure." *Lloyd's List*, September 22, 1998.

Maclay, Edgar Stanton. *A History of the United States Navy from 1775 to 1883*. New York: D. Appleton, 1898.

Mahon, John K. *The War of 1812*. Cambridge, MA: Da Capo Press, 1991.

Mahoney, Robert J. *The Mayaguez Incident: Testing America's Resolve in the Post-Vietnam Era*. Lubbock: Texas Tech University Press, 2011.

Marolda, Edward J. *The United States Navy and the Vietnam Conflict*. Vol. 2, *From Military Assistance to Combat 1959–1965*. Washington, DC: Naval Historical Center, 1986.

Marshall, Charles H. *The Decline of American Shipping, and the True Methods for Its Restoration*. n.p., 1878.

Martis, Kenneth C. *Historical Atlas of United States Congressional Districts: Seventeen Hundred and Eighty-Nine thru Nineteen Hundred and Eighty-Three*. New York: Simon & Schuster, 1994.

Marvin, Carolyn, and David Ingle. *Blood Sacrifice and the Nation: Totem Rituals and the American Flag*. New York: Cambridge University Press, 1999.

Mason, John Brown. *The Danzig Dilemma: A Study of Peacemaking by Compromise*. Palo Alto, CA: Stanford University Press, 1946.

Matthew, Colin. *The Nineteenth Century: The British Isles, 1815–1900*. New York: Oxford University Press, 2000.

McMichael, Bruce. "Special Report on Ship Registers: Newcomers Seek Share of the Spoils." *Lloyd's List*, September 8, 1998.

McWhiney, Grady. *Cracker Culture: Celtic Ways in the Old South*. Tuscaloosa: University of Alabama Press, 1988.

Mellander, Gustavo A. *The United States in Panamanian Politics: The Intriguing Formative Years*. Danville, IL: Interstate Publishers, 1971.

Millington, Herbert. *American Diplomacy and the War of the Pacific*. New York: Columbia University Press, 1948.

Millis, Walter. *The Road to War, 1914–1917*. New York: Houghton-Mifflin, 1935.

Miner, Ralph. "Panama, the Canal Zone, and Titular Sovereignty." *Western Political Quarterly* 14 (1961): 544–54.

Moore, John Bassett. "The Late Chilean Controversy." *Political Science Quarterly* 8 (1893): 467–94.

Naess, Erling D. *Autobiography of a Shipping Man*. Colchester, UK: Seatrade Publications, 1977.

———. The Great PanLibHon Controversy. Epping, UK: Gower Press, 1972.

Nevins, Allan. *Hamilton Fish: The Inner History of the Grant Administration*. New York: Dodd, Mead, 1936.

O'Brian, Patrick. *Master and Commander*. New York: Lippincott, 1969.

"OECD Study of Flags of Convenience." *Journal of Maritime Law and Commerce* 4 (January 1973): 231–54.

Oudet, L. *In the Wake of the* Torrey Canyon. London: Royal Institute of Navigation, 1972.

Paci, Giovanni. "Costa Crociere Re-flags to Italian Second Register." *Lloyd's List*, December 28, 1999.

Pardoe, Blaine. *The Cruise of the* Sea Eagle*: The Amazing True Story of Germany's Gentleman Pirate*. Guilford, CT: Lyons Press, 2005.

Parks, E. Taylor. *Colombia and the United States, 1765–1934*. Durham, NC: Duke University Press, 1935.

Paullin, Charles Oscar. *Dueling in the Old Navy*. Annapolis, MD: Naval Institute Press, 1909.

Peabody, Henry W. *Some Facts in Regard to the American Merchant Marine and Pending Legislation for Its Re-creation: A Reprint of Four Letters Published by the* Boston Herald *and the* New York Journal of Commerce and Commercial Bulletin. Boston: Press of Samuel Usher, 1901.

Pedrozo, Raul. "Close Encounters at Sea: The USNS Impeccable Incident." *U.S. Naval War College Review* 63, no. 3 (Summer 2009): 101–11.

Perez, Louis A., Jr. *Cuba under the Platt Amendment, 1902–1934*. Pittsburgh: University of Pittsburgh Press, 1991.

Perkins, Bradford. *Prologue to War*. Berkeley: University of California Press, 1961.

Petrow, Richard. *In the Wake of the* Torrey Canyon. New York: McKay, 1968.

Pozo, José del. "Relations between Chile and Canada during the Second World War: The First Experiences of Chilean Diplomats." *Historia* 1 (2006).

Preble, George Henry. *History of the Flag of the United States of America*. Boston: A Williams, 1880.

Quick, E. Robert. *An Affair of Honor: Woodrow Wilson and the Occupation of Veracruz*. New York: W. W. Norton, 1962.

Reckner, James R. *Teddy Roosevelt's Great White Fleet: The World Cruise of the American Battlefleet, 1907–1909*. Annapolis, MD: Naval Institute Press, 2001.

Reminick, Gerald. *An Act of Piracy: The Seizure of the American-Flag Merchant Ship* Mayaguez *in 1975*. Palo Alto, CA: Glencannon Press, 2009.

Republic of Liberia. *Liberia—25 Years as a Maritime Nation*. Monrovia: International Trust Company of Liberia, 1975.

Rolo, P. J. V. Entente Cordiale: *The Origins and Negotiation of the Anglo-French Agreements of 8 April 1904*. New York: Macmillan, 1969.

Roorda, Eric Paul. *Cuba, America and the Sea: The Story of the Immigrant Boat* Analuisa *and 500 Years of History between Cuba and America*. Mystic, CT: Mystic Seaport Museum, 2005.

Rouleau, Brian. *With Sails Whitening Every Sea: Mariners and the Making of an American Empire*. Ithaca, NY: Cornell University Press, 2014.

Sater, William. *Chile and the United States: Empires in Conflict*. Athens: University of Georgia Press, 1990.

Schroeder, John. *Shaping a Maritime Empire: The Commercial and Diplomatic Role of the American Navy, 1829–1861*. Westport, CT: Greenwood Press, 1985.

Scott, James Brown. *The Hague Court Reports*. New York: Oxford University Press, 1916.

Seager, Robert. *Alfred Thayer Mahan: The Man and His Letters*. Annapolis, MD: Naval Institute Press, 1977.

Shaughnessy, Tina, and Ellen Tobin. "Flags of Inconvenience: Freedom and Insecurity on the High Seas." *Journal of International Law and Policy* 5 (2006–2007). https://www.law.upenn.edu/journals/jil/jilp/articles/1-1_Shaughnessy_Tina.pdf. Accessed June 2, 2014.

Shulman, Mark Russell. *Navalism and the Emergence of American Sea Power, 1882–1893*. Annapolis, MD: Naval Institute Press, 1995.

Simon, Edelgard. "EC Court to Rule on German Register." *Lloyd's List*, October 20, 1990.

Skaggs, Jimmy M. *The Great Guano Rush: Entrepreneurs and American Overseas Expansion*. New York: Palgrave/Macmillan, 1994.

Smelser, Marshall. *The Congress Founds the Navy, 1787–1798*. Notre Dame, IN: University of Notre Dame Press, 1959.

Smith, William L. G. *Fifty Years of Public Life: The Life and Times of Lewis Cass*. New York: Derby and Jackson, 1856.

Spurrier, Andrew. "French Seamen in Register Warning: Union Says State Proposal Must Not Threaten Jobs." *Lloyd's List*, January 27, 1999.

Standard Oil Company of New Jersey. *Ships of the Esso Fleet in World War II*. Wilmington, DE, 1946.

Stevens, William Oliver. *Pistols at Ten Paces: The Story of the Code of Honor in America*. Boston: Houghton Mifflin, 1940.

Stevenson, Burton, ed. *The Home Book of Quotations*. 10th ed. New York: Dodd, Mead, 1967.

Stewart, Frank Henderson. *Honor*. Chicago: University of Chicago Press, 1994.

Stopford, Martin. *Maritime Economics*. New York: Routledge, 2007.

Sulivan, George Lydiard. *Dhow Chasing in Zanzibar Waters and on the Eastern Coast of Africa: Narrative of Five Years' Experiences in the Suppression of the Slave Trade*. London: S. Low, Marston, Low & Searle, 1873.

Symonds, Craig. *Navalists and AntiNavalists: The Naval Policy Debate 1785–1827*. Newark: University Press of Delaware, 1980.

Szczesniak, Boleslaw. "Letters of Homer Crane Blake Concerning His Naval Expedition to China, Japan, and Korea, 1869–1872." *Monumenta Nipponica* 13 (1957): 313–28.

Tavner, John. "Special Report on Spanish Maritime: Size of Fleet Faces Critical Decline." *Lloyd's List*, May 11, 1994.

Temperly, Howard. "The O'Connell-Stevenson Contretemps: A Reflection on the Anglo-American Slavery Issue." *Journal of Negro History* 47 (1962): 217–33.

Tuchman, Barbara. *The Zimmermann Telegram*. New York: Macmillan, 1958.

Tucker, Spencer C. *Raphael Semmes and the* Alabama. Fort Worth, TX: Ryan Place Publishers, 1996.

United Nations Conference on Trade and Development (UNCTAD). *Review of Maritime Transport*. New York: United Nations, 1997–2015.

U.S. Congress. *Biographical Directory of the American Congress, 1774–1961*. Washington, DC: Government Printing Office, 1961.

Ward, Robert. "Special Report on World Ship Registers: Distinctions Becoming More Blurred." *Lloyd's List*, February 11, 1997.

Ward, Robert, and Julian Bray. "Manx Register Claims Success." *Lloyd's List*, June 20, 1996.

Welch, Richard E., Jr. *The Presidencies of Grover Cleveland*. Lawrence: University Press of Kansas, 1988.

Whigham, H. J. *The Persian Problem: An Examination of the Rival Positions of Russia and Great Britain in Persia with Some Account of the Persian Gulf.* London: Isbistor, 1903.

Wilkerson, Marcus. *Public Opinion and the Spanish-American War: A Study in War Propaganda.* New York: Russell & Russell, 1932. Reprint, 1967.

Willmott, H. P. *The Last Century of Sea Power.* Vol. 1, *From Port Arthur to Chanak, 1894–1922.* Bloomington: Indiana University Press, 2009.

Wilson, Howard Hazen. "Some Principal Aspects of the British Efforts to Crush the African Slave Trade, 1808–1929." *American Journal of International Law* 44, no. 3 (1950): 505–26.

Wimmel, Kenneth. *Theodore Roosevelt and the Great White Fleet: American Sea Power Comes of Age.* London: Brassey's Ltd., 1998.

Wyatt-Brown, Bertram. *Honor and Violence in the Old South.* New York: Oxford University Press, 1986.

———. *Southern Honor: Ethics and Behavior in the Old South.* New York: Oxford University Press, 1982.

———. *A Warring Nation: Honor, Race, and Humiliation in America and Abroad.* Charlottesville: University of Virginia Press, 2014.

Young, David. "Marshall Islands Proves Quality Attracts Quantity." *Shipping and Trade News,* April 19, 2001.

Zuehlke, Mark. *For Honour's Sake: The War of 1812 and the Brokering of an Uneasy Peace.* New York: Random House, 2007.

Index

Adams, Charles Francis, 45
Admiral Orient Line, 117, 120, 237n1. *See also* Pacific Freighters
Africa, 75, 158, 234n17, 242n5. *See also* Barbary States/North Africa; Liberia; West Africa slave trade
Alabama and claims against for U.S. shipping losses, 39, 43, 45, 48, 50, 51–52, 227n24, 227–28n38, 232n26
Alaska, 60, 72, 74, 75
Alert (Great Britain), 20, 220n9
Algonquin, 100–101
Allianca incident, 69–70, 73
American Century concept, 158, 242n5
American Colonization Society, 29, 72, 184
American Committee of Flags of Necessity (ACFN), 175, 178, 181, 245n10
American Overseas Tanker Corporation (AOTC), 158–59, 167, 242n7
amity, commerce, and navigation (ACN) treaties, 10–11, 220n17
Amphion, 22
Anderson, Robert, 53
Andorra, 42–43
Antarctic exploration, 35, 38
Arctic exploration, 35, 38, 56
Argentina, 26, 125
Argus, 21–22
Arias, Arnulfo, 151–52, 155, 160
Army, U.S., 64, 156–57
Aroostook War, 29, 223n21
Astral, 149–50, 241–42n41

Bahamas, 129, 182, 191, 192, 194, 209, 247n21, 250nn41–42
Baker, Newton D., 88, 102
balancing-of-contacts principle, 173–75, 178
Baltic-American Petroleum Import Company (Bapico): Danzig-flagged ships, 108–10, 111, 112–15, 124,

126, 127, 128, 235n3; fleet size, 109; naming of ships, 109–10, 114, 235nn7–8; Panama-flagged ships, 109, 110, 111, 113–14, 124, 126–27, 128, 129, 236n12, 238n24; Waried management of fleet, 109, 111, 236n12
Barbary States/North Africa, 9, 11, 13–14, 18, 214
Belen Quezada (Canada), 116, 121, 122
Belgium, 147, 193, 194, 200, 211, 248n1
Belize, 190, 191, 192, 249–50n27
Bellamy, Francis, 55
Berle, Adolph, 138, 143–44, 145–46, 148
Bermuda, 42–43, 129, 182, 190, 191, 192, 194, 208
Blaine, James G., 66
blue-water imperialism, 55, 72–75, 228n7
Bolivia, 66–67, 190, 191, 192
Brazil, 20, 27, 31, 147, 224n36, 248nn1–2
Brussels Act, 79, 84, 231n14, 232n16
Bryan, William Jennings, 88, 92, 93
Buchanan, James, 35, 36–37
Burr, Aaron, 13

Canada: border with U.S., 220n16; conquering of by U.S., 17, 31, 32, 222n1; costs of building new ships in, 48, 50; Esso ships flagged in, use of during World War II, 137; Maine–New Brunswick border, 28, 29, 31–32, 220n16, 223n21; Panamanian registration of ships from, 116, 126; population of, 32, 224n29; reflagging ships under U.S. flag, 100–101; smuggling and rum-running from, 116; U.S. ships treatment by, 67–68, 71
Canary Islands, 138, 194, 196, 204, 207, 211
Cargo Preference Act, 216, 218
Caribbean Sea, 61–62, 72

with countries to allow, 30, 31, 34; ship-on-ship duels, 7, 220nn9–10; slave ships, right to search, 27–31, 35–38, 78–80, 85, 214, 224nn23–24, 225n46, 225n54, 232n17; steam-powered warships of, 36

Rufus Soule, 37–38, 225n54

rum-running and smuggling, 111–12, 116, 121–23, 128–29, 237n10, 238–39nn24–25

Russia, 31, 60, 67–68, 89

Sagadahoc, 149–50, 241–42n41

Samoa, 72, 74

Santo Domingo, 27, 60, 72

Savannah Line, 77, 86, 102

second registries: competition among, 198–200, 208–10, 250nn40; development and purpose of, 193–95, 248nn1–2; distinction between open registers and, 208–10, 250n40; impact of, 211–13; port-state control systems, 195–96, 212–13; success and failure of, 198–207, 211–13; success of, 198

Semmes, Raphael, 40, 51–52, 227–28n38

separate but equal concept and racial segregation, 85–86

Seward, William, 48, 60, 72

Shannon (Great Britain), 220n9

Shenandoah, 39, 45

Sherman (*Generalissimo Conquistador*), 66

Ship Requisition Act, 147–48

Ship Sales Law, 159, 242–43n8

ships: belligerent ships, prohibition of travel on, 106, 130, 135, 137; challenges, refusal of, 8; costs of building new ships, 48, 49; courage on board when fired upon, 8, 9, 22, 220n12; decline in shipbuilding, 49–50; duels between enemy ships, 7–10, 220nn9–10, 220n12, 220nn14–15; equivalence of ships for duels, 7–10, 20–22, 51–52, 220n10, 227–28n38; identification of by flag and predictability of encounters between, 9–10;

inferior/lower status, engagement in duels with, 8–9, 220n14; lower orders on, 8; procedures for duels, 7; ritualized courtesies between ships, 8, 11; searching during war, 30, 62, 69–70; searching in peacetime, 28–29, 31, 33, 36–37, 62, 69–70; unequal contests, 7–10, 20–21, 51–52, 227–28n38

Shufeldt, Robert W., 60

Sierra Leone, 29–30, 36, 188–89

Singapore, 182, 186, 192, 194, 210, 248n2

slaves and slave trade: British right to search slave ships, 27–31, 35–38, 78–80, 85, 214, 224nn23–24, 225n46, 225n54, 232n17; conference and convention to suppress slave trade, 79, 231n14, 232n16; congressional balance between slave and nonslave states, 24; empty slave ships, search and seizure of, 29–30, 34; false use of U.S. flag by slave ships, 27, 30, 34, 36–38, 225n54; French flagging of slave-trading dhows, 3, 78–80, 83–85, 86, 107, 232n20, 232n34; inspection of papers to ensure legitimacy of flag, 36–38, 225n54; Navy antislavery squadrons, 29, 34, 37, 224n36, 225n44, 225n46; number of slaves imported to U.S., 225n45; outlawing of importation of slaves, 29; repeal of ban on slave trade, 36; ships for, increase in, 36; slave prices and resurgence of slave transportation, 36, 225n44

Smith, Josh, 229n16

smuggling and rum-running, 111–12, 116, 121–23, 128–29, 237n10, 238–39nn24–25

South America, 75

Spain: *Allianca* incident, 69–70, 73; Basque ships transfer to Panamanian registry, 124, 126–27, 237n14, 238n24; British treaty with on right to search, 30, 31, 34; Civil War in, U.S. neutrality position toward, 131;

About the Author

Rodney Carlisle earned an AB in history at Harvard College and a PhD in history at the University of California, Berkeley, and taught history at Rutgers University from 1966 to 2000. He is the author or co-author of more than thirty books of history. His interest in flags of convenience has led to a prior work with the Naval Institute Press as well as a series of articles in *The Northern Mariner*.

The Naval Institute Press is the book-publishing arm of the U.S. Naval Institute, a private, nonprofit, membership society for sea service professionals and others who share an interest in naval and maritime affairs. Established in 1873 at the U.S. Naval Academy in Annapolis, Maryland, where its offices remain today, the Naval Institute has members worldwide.

Members of the Naval Institute support the education programs of the society and receive the influential monthly magazine *Proceedings* or the colorful bimonthly magazine *Naval History* and discounts on fine nautical prints and on ship and aircraft photos. They also have access to the transcripts of the Institute's Oral History Program and get discounted admission to any of the Institute-sponsored seminars offered around the country.

The Naval Institute's book-publishing program, begun in 1898 with basic guides to naval practices, has broadened its scope to include books of more general interest. Now the Naval Institute Press publishes about seventy titles each year, ranging from how-to books on boating and navigation to battle histories, biographies, ship and aircraft guides, and novels. Institute members receive significant discounts on the Press' more than eight hundred books in print.

Full-time students are eligible for special half-price membership rates. Life memberships are also available.

For a free catalog describing Naval Institute Press books currently available, and for further information about joining the U.S. Naval Institute, please write to:

Member Services
U.S. Naval Institute
291 Wood Road
Annapolis, MD 21402-5034
Telephone: (800) 233-8764
Fax: (410) 571-1703
Web address: www.usni.org